KNOW POWER, KNOW RESPONSIBILITY

How to unleash the potential of every child in America

KEVIN MILLER

KNOW POWER, KNOW RESPONSIBILITY © copyright 2019 by Kevin Miller. All rights reserved. No part of this book may be reproduced in any form whatsoever, by photography or xerography or by any other means, by broadcast or transmission, by translation into any kind of language, nor by recording electronically or otherwise, without permission in writing from the author, except by a reviewer, who may quote brief passages in critical articles or reviews.

ISBN 978-1-63489-278-0
Library of Congress Catalog Number 2019938502

Cover design by Emily Mahon
Interior design by Kim Morehead

Printed in the United States of America
First Printing: 2019

23 22 21 20 19   5 4 3 2 1

Wise Ink Creative Publishing
807 Broadway St. NE, Suite 46
Minneapolis, MN 55413
www.wiseink.com

*For J.J. and all the other children
who left this world never
being able to pursue their potential*

CONTENTS

Note to Parents of School-Aged Children	i
Note to Teachers, School Administrators, and Other School Staff	iii
Introduction	1
Prologue Part 1: Critical Thinking	6
Prologue Part 2: The Committee of Ten and the Factory Model for Schools	8
Prologue Part 3: What Makes You So Smart?	12
Prologue Part 4: *Calvin and Hobbes*	17
PART 1—THE CASE FOR REINVENTING PUBLIC EDUCATION	**19**
Chapter 0: Unsustainable	21
Chapter 1: Achievement and Opportunity Gaps	22
Chapter 2: Premised on Teaching, Not on Learning	30
Chapter 3: Standards Based on Averages	39
Chapter 4: Focus on Compliance	45
Chapter 5: The Vast Diversity in Life Experiences of Students	55
Chapter 6: The Need for Flexibility in an Ever-Changing World	59
Chapter 7: Normalizing Compliance, Discouraging Critical Thinking, and Devaluing Moral Courage	63
Chapter 8: Preserving Our Democracy	69
Chapter 9: Students with Disabilities	73
Chapter 10: Freeing Teachers to Pursue Their Potential	76
Chapter 11: The Cost of College and Student Loan Debt	79
Chapter 12: Technology and Instant Access to Nearly Unlimited Information	83
Chapter 13: How People Learn and Are Motivated	87
Chapter 14: Collaboration between Families and Schools	92
Chapter 15: A Dozen More Reasons	95

PART 2—WHAT MIGHT THE REINVENTED SYSTEM LOOK LIKE? — 113

Chapter 16: The Summitville Learning Community — 117

Chapter 17: Translating the SLC to Other Communities — 144

PART 3—HOW TO REPLACE A CENTURY-OLD INSTITUTION — 147

Chapter 18: The Risks for Our Children Individually — 149

Chapter 19: The Risks for Our Children Collectively — 160

Chapter 20: The Financial Cost of Reinvention — 165

Chapter 21: Education Laws and Rules — 173

Chapter 22: Inertia and Momentum — 178

Chapter 23: Frequently Asked Questions — 181

PART 4—BUILDING A CHAMPIONSHIP CHANGE TEAM — 189

Chapter 24: Finding the Will and Battling Self-Doubt with and through Integrity — 192

Chapter 25: The People — 200

Chapter 26: Critical Role of Children — 213

Chapter 27: Building a Base of Knowledge about Learning, Growth, and Development — 216

Chapter 28: Building Commitment and Establishing a Vision — 226

PART 5—REINVENTING PUBLIC EDUCATION IN YOUR COMMUNITY — 235

Chapter 29: Self-Awareness: Figuring Out Who You Are — 240

Chapter 30: Self-Awareness: Figuring Out Where You Are — 243

Chapter 31: Exploration: Figuring Out Where You Want to Go — 250

Chapter 32: Planning — 257

Chapter 33: Ready, Set, Go — 275

Chapter 34: Other Crucial Considerations — 277

Chapter 35: The Last Chapter — 294

Acknowledgments — 295

References — 298

Index — 303

About the Author — 310

NOTE TO PARENTS OF SCHOOL-AGE CHILDREN

Dear parents,

It is you—parents with school-age children, whom you love and care about and whose future you worry about—that have the most at stake with everything covered in this book. Consequently, you may find its contents a bit frightening, though that is certainly not the intent.

If you're like most parents, you have imagined your child going to school and having experiences similar to or better than your own. We all want our children's lives to be better than ours, no matter how good our lives have been. You may find comfort in the warmth of familiar sights, sounds, and smells at your child's school.

So to consider drastically changing your child's school is scary. How do you know the changes will be for the better? Why can't changes wait until your children are done and have moved on? Why should your child be the guinea pig?

These are great questions. I find comfort in the familiarity of my children's experiences, similar to visiting old neighborhoods and places from my youth. But I must counter that comfort with reality and thoughtfulness, and I ask you to do the same.

The world is vastly different than when I was a child, and, in retrospect, my *academic* experiences in school did little to prepare me for the world in which I live today. In fact, they set me up for a lot of challenges. I know I've benefited from working through these challenges, but I wonder how much more I could have accomplished—how much more I could have contributed to this world—had my K–12 experiences been tailored to me rather than the average of all the kids in my grade.

For most children, change is exciting until they are taught otherwise. As parents, we strive to balance protecting our children with the excitement of change and learning. They can't learn to talk until we stop to listen. They can't learn to walk, ride a bike, skate, dance, jump, tumble, or so many other things that bring them joy until we let go.

Your children are the heart and soul of the changes advocated in this book. They will not be guinea pigs; rather, they will be leaders of those changes and will drive their success. They cannot do it on their own, of course, but our children are the only ones who can fully and truly know what they need in order to learn, grow, and reach their potential. Once freed from their constraints, children will shock us with their abilities and potential.

I challenge you to avoid getting stuck in the comfort of your own memories or believing the school you attended is what's best for your child. Instead, try to remember your curiosity and excitement about learning before it became a structured activity driven by others. Then imagine what your child could accomplish if the world of learning contained no limitations.

It can happen. We can create an educational system that makes this a reality. It will be scary for us adults, but we need to flip that fear into excitement and share it with our children. Continue reading to see how we can change our school systems so our children can change the world!

—Kevin

NOTE TO TEACHERS, SCHOOL ADMINISTRATORS, AND OTHER SCHOOL STAFF

Dear school staff,

I expect many of you will take some offense at this book. You may think I'm bashing public schools and teachers or blaming them for problems in our world. I am not. In fact, I commend teachers, administrators, and all other educators for the fantastic work they do. Rather, I am showing how the *institution* of public schools is at the heart of many challenges in our world and responsible for holding back the potential of generations of students. What you have accomplished is amazing given the shortcomings of the system.

At the same time, I understand why my criticism of the system seems like an indictment of those who are part of that system. It is natural to take offense and come to the defense of an institution with which one is strongly associated. As a former teacher, administrator, and strong advocate for public schools, the decision to take aim at the institution has been difficult. However, our current system is not meeting the needs of our children, and it is our duty to change that.

You have a crucial role in building an educational system that allows all students to approach their potential so they are truly prepared to thrive in the twenty-first century and beyond. That means you must be willing to acknowledge the shortcomings of our current model. I hope this book helps you see these flaws and realize that we can—and must—develop a superior system.

I have spent my career in public education trying to figure out how to improve learning for every student. I finally realized the current system is maxed out; we've tapped its potential. It needs to be replaced with one that significantly exceeds the current system's capacity. That also means you—teachers, administrators, and other school staff—will be freed from its limitations and discover incredible opportunities you never imagined.

I truly hope you see this book as it's intended—a catalyst for schools to exceed even the most optimistic expectations of today. I further hope you will become the leaders of this transformation. Thanks for at least giving this your consideration and keeping an open mind.

—Kevin

INTRODUCTION

How to read this book

Prior to publication, some of this book's reviewers recommended shortening it so it would appeal to a broader audience. I seriously considered doing so. At the same time, I wanted the book to be comprehensive. I wanted to address, to the greatest degree possible, all those "What about . . . ?" queries that such a book is likely to prompt. So, at the risk of scaring away some readers, I have erred on the side of being comprehensive.

I expect, therefore, that many will not want to read the book in its entirety, and that is fine. While I believe there is value throughout and benefits from reading it cover to cover, some may want to focus on certain sections. The book is not an end in itself meant to draw in readers and deeply engage them with its prose. Rather, it is a tool and a resource for understanding the shortcomings of the current model and seeing how to replace that model in a community. For anyone who does become involved in education reform and reinvention in their community, I hope it becomes a go-to reference and a catalyst for change.

The purpose of this book

If you could roll the calendar back to 1893 and live at that time, would you? Are there things about the late nineteenth century that might make your life more enjoyable and bring you greater contentment and happiness?

Would you rather travel by horse, carriage, or steam train than by car, bus, or plane?

Would you prefer coal and wood stoves to heat your house rather than radiators or forced air? Would you like to rely on oil lamps instead of LEDs that reliably come on at the flick of a switch or even through the programming of an app on your smartphone?

Speaking of phones, how would you like to receive and share information? You could use a telegraph to send personalized messages, or, if you don't mind it taking a few days or weeks, send a letter. You could get your news, possibly a bit delayed for non-local news, strictly from a newspaper. Or do you prefer the ability to send texts and to receive news—even international news—within minutes of an event?

Of course, similar questions could be asked about health care, housing, recreation, entertainment, and a great deal more. We often look back at the past through rose-colored glasses. A slower pace of life and an existence that's less accessible to others can sound nice, but the truth is, little about our world in 1893 seems more appealing than our world in 2019. Yet we have carried forward a vestige of that world for the last 126 years with virtually no significant changes: public education.

In the late nineteenth century, our society strove to make everything more efficient—food production, product production, transportation, and, yes, education. During the early industrial age, government and business leaders realized the workforce—and citizens in general—needed a higher and more consistent level of education. The National Education Association convened the Committee of Ten to develop a model for delivering instruction to all children in America. Many aspects of this effort were progressive for that time, including that all students would receive essentially the same instruction regardless of their demographics. In fact, they made a point that basic instruction should not differ regardless of the path a student was expected to take after high school.

The Committee of Ten's recommendations became the foundation for public education throughout our country, with most private schools also adopting the structure and basic curriculum. Of course, in practice, it wasn't as equitable as may have been intended—and, in many cases, the delivery of instruction was often very inequitable—but the bottom line is that these recommendations were the foundation of our public education system. This is the foundation on which nearly all K–12 schools continue to operate today.

Our schools have changed but have remained consistent with the basic structure that was put forth in 1893. The Committee of Ten called for twelve school grades divided generally into eight years of elementary and four years of high school. They recommended that all high school students receive instruction each year in English, math, and history or civics and that chemistry and physics would be taught in that order.

The ensuing century-plus has created an institution entrenched like no other in our society. It has become a given that children will start formal education at or about age five and progress with their similar-aged classmates through to high school graduation. They will have summer breaks. They will take almost all the same classes in the same order until they reach high school. In many high schools, at least through ninth and tenth grade, students will continue to have most of the same classes before finally being presented with a small set of options from which to choose. They will be expected to achieve the same level of performance in each subject at the same time as their classmates. They will have their grades determined by how they do against an age- and time-based standard.

The world around us has changed in ways nineteenth-century citizens couldn't even imagine. In other aspects of our world and society, we replace outdated models and structures when they limit our ability to advance and improve. But our public (and most private) schools have not changed in any truly meaningful way. Rather than leverage the potential of technological and other advancements by adapting, our educational institutions attempt to fit the advancements into the old model. It's like trying to adapt the technology from a Tesla to fit a horse and buggy.

Given that our educational system is so deeply entrenched in the current model, calling for a complete overhaul seems more quixotic than tilting at windmills. However, I have faith in both adults and children.

Our most significant accomplishments have come from ideas and processes that flew in the face of convention. They didn't happen overnight, nor without resistance. I believe almost everyone can open their minds and hearts to new and different things; they just need to recognize and acknowledge their emotional ties to the status quo.

I also have faith in the potential of our children. I believe the current model of education has created an almost universal underestimation of the capabilities of our children. I believe with all my heart that our children could surpass every current expectation if only we created the circumstances that would allow it. Here again, the current model of schools inherently restricts these circumstances so almost no children achieve their true potential while they are in school.

This book lays out the case for why we must change our educational structure now and quickly; it provides an example of how this might look; it explains how this can be done without risking the growth and development of current students (in fact, current students will benefit from being part of the change); and, finally, it shows how this can be done in nearly any community in our country.

There are three purposes of this book, and they are straightforward:
- To convince every reader that we cannot continue to advance as a society without fundamentally reinventing our public education system;
- To further convince every reader it is possible to make this change without an influx of money or legislation and that it is best achieved beginning at the local level; and
- To encourage every reader to become an advocate or even champion of making this change occur and seek out ways to help accelerate that change.

The title of this book

There is a line commonly attributed to Spider-Man's Uncle Ben but which has roots back at least as far as the Bible: "With great power comes great responsibility." The reverse of that idea is the underlying reason our current educational model must be replaced—with no power comes no responsibility. The title reflects that when students "know power"—when adults truly cede real power and control to students—they will then "know responsibility" and will take charge of their own learning.

Our current school structure and paradigm gives students almost no power. While many schools claim to give students options, few give students any real power over anything substantial or important to the students themselves. Consequently, they have no reason to adopt a sense of responsibility toward their learning. Even schools and staff who would like to give students more real power are hemmed in by the structure itself. That is why the structure must be replaced.

Maybe more distressing is that our current educational model creates a mindset that carries over into adulthood. We tend to feel powerless about those things that are most important in our world, so we feel much less (or no) responsibility toward these things.

The idea of ceding power to our students is woven throughout this book. That is because the only way students will be able to achieve—or even consider pursuing—their personal potential is to take responsibility for doing so. But they will not—they really cannot—take on this responsibility unless they are actually given the power to do so. This book will illustrate why our current system won't allow this and how to create a system that can.

PROLOGUE PART 1

CRITICAL THINKING

The most important skill readers can bring to this book is critical thinking—being aware of, acknowledging, and accounting for our biases when approaching a thought task. To think critically is to recognize when an initial reaction to an idea, opinion, or information is being influenced by one's personal biases. This is not easy, especially in an age when critical thinking seems to largely be discouraged.

Critical thinking doesn't mean eliminating one's biases—an impossible task, since biases are typically developed and strengthened over time, much like habits, and are based on one's experiences. Critical thinking also doesn't mean ignoring or violating one's values, morals, or belief systems. However, critical thinking does require striving to find the truth behind an idea, opinion, or bit of information, and getting at that truth or fact requires accounting for one's biases.

This is not an easy skill to develop and use regularly. This is especially true in situations that are emotional, have years or even decades of familiarity, or are related to an important personal value or belief. Yet all rational human beings are capable of doing this, often unconsciously. For example, we may reach out to help or support someone who is in great need despite that person representing something that is distasteful to us. In such cases, the immediate circumstances push our biases behind our instinct to help a fellow human being.

This book will challenge ideas, beliefs, and biases that are based on our own experiences attending schools and on our educational institutions being so deeply embedded in our culture and society. Those who work in education may feel significant changes are an attack on their work, a threat to their future employment, or both, and those with school-age children may be concerned about how new and different approaches will impact those children and their education. I had to face all these concerns as I came to write this book.

These are all legitimate concerns and biases, and the book attempts to acknowledge and address them. However, it is also imperative that the reader acknowledge how his or her biases are affecting consideration of the ideas being expressed. Think critically while reading this book, and don't feel you should take anything in it at face value. Rather, apply your own knowledge, experience, and research to determine whether this book contains ideas that we should consider for future generations of our country.

PROLOGUE PART 2

THE COMMITTEE OF TEN AND THE FACTORY MODEL FOR SCHOOLS

As noted in the introduction, at the behest of government and business leaders, the National Education Association convened the Committee of Ten in 1892 to develop a model for delivering instruction to all children in America. The committee considered various approaches to this model for public education, including systems that would focus on critical thinking, rote learning, or sorting students based on their likely future paths as well as race and ethnicity.

In the end, the Committee of Ten and its supporting "conferences"[1] advocated that all children should have an equal opportunity to the same foundational education regardless of who they were, where they lived, or the path they were expected to take after completing their childhood education. The result was a set of expectations for the nature and amount of instruction students should receive in each subject area. The conference reports provided specifics on what should be taught in each subject.

While the Committee of Ten framed their recommendations as the amount of instruction that students should receive, they did not advocate that education should be centered around lectures. In fact, the conferences strongly advocated that lecture be a minority aspect of education.

---

1 The Committee of Ten created nine separate "conferences" to provide recommendations for the subjects in each content area. Each conference was made up of ten or so experts on their respective subjects and developed recommendations based on questions provided by the overall Committee of Ten. The conference reports then informed the final overall recommendations (National Education Association, 2017).

They felt it was critical for students to experience subjects through hands-on methods whenever possible. They also strongly recommended that, within a given subject, students begin to create their own "demonstrations" reflecting their ability to apply the knowledge they were learning to new situations and to express what they knew through these demonstrations (National Education Association, 2017, p. 25).

For example, the History, Civil Government, and Political Economy Conference reiterated multiple times that history must be taught in such a way as to foster critical thinking by students (though they did not use the term "critical thinking"). They summarized this by noting that the chief object of historical study "is the training of the judgment, in selecting the grounds of an opinion, in accumulating materials for an opinion, in putting things together, in generalizing upon facts, in estimating character, in applying the lessons of history to current events, and in accustoming children to state their conclusions in their own words" (National Education Association, 2017, p. 170).

Similarly, the Committee of Ten and the conferences did not advocate for various subjects to be taught in isolation by teachers who focused only on one subject in which they were expert. Rather, they expressed that the various subjects must be intertwined for greatest effectiveness and that the teachers of each subject must "feel responsible for the advancement of pupils in all subjects, and should distinctly contribute to this advancement" (National Education Association, 2017, p. 16). The Committee of Ten even provided examples of places where subjects should be intertwined, such as the study of arithmetic being connected to instruction in elementary physics.

In reading the full Committee of Ten report, it seems clear that the overall committee and the individual conferences understood that school needed to be much more than just delivery of instruction. Unfortunately, the final school design did not include the Committee's delivery recommendations. Instead, the public-school design only used the recommendations for the amount of instruction students should receive each year and the elements of each subject that should occur in each grade or at each age.

The intent at the time was to provide an education for all children in the US. To achieve that, compromises were needed. So the recommendations would not be implemented as envisioned by the Committee and its conferences. Those building the system of public education had to make it manageable and affordable. Therefore, they applied lessons learned about efficiencies from industry and business. They broke down the overall process into its components so experts could ensure efficient delivery of the same instruction to all students. The result was the factory model of schools.

The Committee of Ten and the individual conferences recommended what students should be taught at roughly each age or grade. They also advocated for teachers with sufficient expertise in the given subjects, at least at the high school level. To make this cost-effective, groups of students would be collectively taught by subject matter experts. Thus, groups of same-age students would move from teacher to teacher being taught the respective subjects. At the elementary grades, generalist teachers could teach multiple subjects, but most subjects were still taught individually rather than being integrated.

Like a factory, students enter kindergarten (or, before the universalization of kindergarten, first grade) with a group of students their same age. They move through the subjects from year to year with each teacher providing their assigned instruction. When a student struggles to keep pace, the schools make adjustments to try to keep the student on track with their classmates. If things get bad enough, the school may move the student back to another group that's a bit younger. If a student seems to be outpacing other students his or her age in enough subjects, the student may be moved ahead or given other opportunities that may be more challenging.

Eventually, when a student has gone through all the required subjects satisfactorily, he or she is moved out of the school and is deemed ready for whatever might come next. That, in a nutshell, is the factory model of schools. It takes advantage of economies of scale by teaching large groups of students the same things concurrently by experts in those subjects. It has the added benefit of teaching students compliance, which employers sought in the majority of their employees throughout much of the twentieth century. As with cars, there may be some variations (colors, trim packages, options), but the vast majority of the process is the same for each student.

In practice, the factory model isn't as cold and impersonal as this makes it sound. To their immense credit, schoolteachers make most schools and classrooms warm, caring, and welcoming places for students. They do a tremendous job teaching students and, by doing so, contribute to advancements in technology, medicine, art, science, and all other aspects of society. However, they have tapped out nearly all room for improvement and growth within the current structure, while our children have potential that remains hidden and untapped.

The recommendations of the Committee of Ten led to our current educational model, but if the committee and conference members were around today, they would certainly demand that we reinvent public education. In fact, I have little doubt that many of them would be appalled at how their recommendations were put into practice and how little has changed in our public education systems over the ensuing century and a quarter.

We owe it to the Committee of Ten and all the conferences to reinvent public education in a way that reflects our current world, continually adapts as the world changes, and leverages existing and emerging technologies.

PROLOGUE PART 3

WHAT MAKES YOU SO SMART?

You may wonder what qualifies me to write a book calling for the complete reform of public education. What makes me so smart?

I actually don't think anyone, including me, is smart enough to come up with an adequate structure or design that will effectively educate all children. In fact, I don't believe there is one. That's really what this entire book is about, as you will soon see.

Here, then, I will share how I came to write this book. In many respects, it has been in the works for over forty years. I was aware back in middle school that the structure of school was ineffective and inefficient. While I couldn't articulate it at the time, seeds were being planted for revelations that emerged only recently.

I graduated high school with honors but didn't want to go to college. I spent four years in the workforce before heading off to the University of Wisconsin–Stout, where I majored in technology education and minored in English. While at Stout, I joined the Wisconsin Army National Guard for the education benefits. I graduated from Stout in 1990.

I taught automotive technology and graphic communications at Oregon High School in Wisconsin, where I enjoyed teaching but also found a lot of frustrations. I was teaching elective courses, so my students had chosen to take my classes, but often they were not engaged—and certainly not enthusiastic.

I rarely had conduct issues, but it was clear that students were not effectively engaged, and much of the time they were clearly not learning. I sought to implement more relevant classes, joined the School Improvement Team, and worked to make my classes more engaging. But the limitations of the school structure itself severely limited available options.

One of my mentors encouraged me to accept a position at the Wisconsin Department of Public Instruction (DPI) as a technology education consultant. This was an opportunity to affect education at a higher and more influential level. Over the next seven years, I worked on state-level career and technical education initiatives and served as the state director of Wisconsin SkillsUSA (called VICA then), an organization for students preparing for careers in trade, technical, and skilled service areas.

During this same time, I fulfilled my military service obligation and could have left the National Guard. As with teaching, my service had rewards but also many frustrations. I saw a need for better leadership and was encouraged to stay in and attend Officer Candidate School. I did so and was commissioned as an officer in the United States Army in 1995.

I continued trying to figure out how to substantially improve education for all students. I spent time with others striving for more innovation. We discussed the need to reinvent education while several state and national efforts emerged toward this end, but they had little to no impact. I thought being a school administrator might provide the answers I was seeking, so I left DPI. My experiences over the next fifteen years brought clarity to the shortcomings of our current school model and its focus on student compliance.

During that time, I taught eighth-grade English (while attending grad school), interned in a large urban high school, served as a suburban middle school associate principal (where I had primary responsibility for student conduct and discipline), served as the director of career and technical education in an urban school district, and returned to DPI as the dual-enrollment consultant. I led the opening of two charter high schools and the development of numerous innovative programs. Yet, time after time, the factory school model limited any chance of fulfilling students' potentials.

One DPI initiative, however, showed how a different approach to implementing innovation could pave the way for significant change and improvement. The Wisconsin Academic and Career Planning initiative and its statewide implementation were innovative in many ways. They affirmed my evolving belief in and understanding of how much better our public education system could be if it ensured students took true ownership of their learning, with teachers serving as mentors and facilitators.

Throughout this time, I was diving more fully into personalized learning and innovative practices. I presented at national conferences, had in-depth dialogues with leaders in these areas, and visited schools implementing these practices, where I spoke with many students and staff members. I was the lead writer for a document published by DPI called "Fostering Innovation in Wisconsin Schools" (Wisconsin Department of Public Instruction, 2017). Its purpose is to help schools find flexibilities in Wisconsin laws and rules so they can implement innovative practices. (For more information on this, see the sidebar on page 175 in chapter 21.)

Concurrently, my military journey continued. I was commissioned an engineer officer and served as an engineer platoon leader, engineer company commander, and a battalion-level engineer officer. I served several years as a TAC (train, advise, and counsel) officer in the Officer Candidate School—including as the senior TAC officer—and as an instructor for the Command and General Staff Officer Course (CGSOC). In 2017 I was selected as the 80th Training Command Officer Instructor of the Year. As I write this, I am the Director of Instruction for a CGSOC battalion.

In 2008–09 I was deployed to Afghanistan in support of Operation Enduring Freedom. There, I commanded a Provincial Police Mentor team in Kunar Province. While this seems barely relevant to the subject of this book, it was a critical piece of the puzzle. I was trained in counterinsurgency, and my team trained Afghan police leaders in a variety of organizational-level skills. Concurrently, we were helping them overcome centuries of a paradigm that corruption and violence would always be a part of their world. We were truly trying to foster changes within systems that were deeply entrenched and institutionalized. What could possibly provide better experiences preparing me to foster change in our 126-year-old educational system?

Supplementing these experiences has been a voracious appetite for reading and studying professional literature and other media on learning, brain development, human development, motivation, innovation, organizational development and change, human culture, spirituality, educational practices, quantum physics, evolution, and more. I've read numerous biographies and autobiographies of diverse individuals, each providing clues about how life experiences affect one's future and expanding insights on significantly improving our educational system.

In addition to my professional and military journeys, I have been on a more personal journey. I married my beautiful wife Katherine in 1995, and we have had two sons, Samuel in 2000 and Matthew in 2003. As I write this, Samuel is in his first year of college and Matthew is a high school freshman. Watching and experiencing their journeys through a traditional public-school system has been truly enlightening.

I have, of course, been doing this in partnership with my wife. Katherine entered this child-rearing partnership with what I would call a "traditional paradigm," in which parents are in charge and children listen and behave. All of us have evolved as a family over the past nineteen years, and this too has substantially contributed to my understanding of why we must change our educational system and how we can do so.

I believe in a sort of destiny—that each of us is called to somehow contribute to the greater good of our world and society if only we will pay attention and answer when called. I have been searching for my "calling" most of my life.

In 2016, my calling became clear. My education, training, and experiences were coalescing to create a vision of what our American educational system *could* be. I realized I was not the first to see this; many before have provided such a vision and called for change. The diversity of my experiences, however, has provided a unique perspective and understanding of both why and how we can achieve this change.

I decided to leave my DPI consultant position in February 2017 to pursue this calling full time. When I left, I wasn't sure how it would play out. I planned to offer my services to schools and districts who were ready for change. One of the leaders in the field of school innovation and personalized learning, Dr. Richard Halverson from the University of Wisconsin–Madison, recommended I write a book laying all this out. I initially resisted, but as I worked on school innovation and talked with people about my vision, I realized the only forum for laying out the entire vision was in a book.

That is how I ended up here. Does all this make me qualified to write a book on designing a new model of school in and for the twenty-first century? I guess that remains to be seen. Fortunately, that's also irrelevant. I don't believe anyone should jump aboard this reform/reinvention train because they trust in my opinions and statements or because they think I have the necessary expertise.

Instead, I want you to reflect on your own experiences and observations, confront your own biases and fears, and then consider whether you believe our current educational system is the best we can do for our children and all future generations. If after reading this book you still believe our current system is adequate, then hopefully you got the book at a discount or from the library so little was lost. On the other hand, if you realize we can do better, then I hope you join with others in reinventing education in your community. If this book helps you do that, then all the better.

PROLOGUE PART 4

CALVIN AND HOBBES

I have been a huge *Calvin and Hobbes* fan since I first read it. I believe it is popular because it plays out thoughts and feelings most of us have experienced but didn't feel at liberty to express. This seems especially true with Calvin's experiences in school that illustrate shortcomings of our educational system. Like most of the best humor, they are rooted in truth.

I planned to include a variety of the strips throughout this book to help illustrate many of the points being made, but I decided the book was already too long and only used a couple. I truly appreciate the genius of Bill Watterson, *Calvin and Hobbes*'s creator, and maybe I'll write a version of this book entirely built around *Calvin and Hobbes*. I'd like to think Bill and Calvin would endorse my arguments. This one four-panel strip sums up numerous points that are made in this book:

CALVIN AND HOBBES © 1993 Watterson. Reprinted with permission of ANDREWS MCMEEL SYNDICATION. All rights reserved.

PART 1
THE CASE FOR REINVENTING PUBLIC EDUCATION

PART 1

THE CASE FOR REINVENTING PUBLIC EDUCATION

As noted in the introduction, the basic structure of our public education system celebrates its 126th birthday in 2019. That is not, in and of itself, sufficient reason to make significant changes. Some things stand the test of time and require only minor modifications, not wholesale reinvention. Public education has not stood this test of time.

While I do believe the population of the United States is currently the best educated it has ever been, I also believe this level of education is not sufficient for the world in which we live—and certainly not for the world for which we are heading. This first part of the book will lay out the reasons I believe our current public education system is not adequate for the demands of our current world, let alone those of the future, and why the current model does not have the capacity to get us where we need to be.

CHAPTER 0

UNSUSTAINABLE

Yes, a chapter 0 is odd, and it's hardly long enough to justify being called a chapter. The title comes from a book by Tim McDonald that lays out the reasons our current educational model cannot last much longer. McDonald argues we have tapped every ounce of productivity from the current model. Any gains now will come at great financial cost or losses elsewhere. Immense efforts have been made to improve student performance and close achievement gaps, but the result has been only small improvements because the capacity of the current system has been reached.

Our options, then, are to either pump more and more resources into the system in an attempt to spur additional improvements or to replace the current model with one that has the capacity needed to make large improvements in learning and eliminate achievement gaps. Rather than reproduce all his excellent work here, I will encourage you to seek out *Unsustainable: A Strategy for Making Public Schooling More Productive, Effective, and Affordable* and take a look at McDonald's research and arguments. The bottom line is that our current system is not sustainable. So, let's begin to design a replacement system that has the flexibility to adapt and endure well into the twenty-second century (McDonald, 2011).

CHAPTER 1

ACHIEVEMENT AND OPPORTUNITY GAPS

Many people believe the "American Dream" is available to anyone willing to work hard enough to attain it, regardless of a person's starting point. Within our educational system, there is a related belief that every child begins with comparable levels of potential and maintains that equal potential regardless of the benefits or challenges they face early in life.

Unfortunately, our current educational model is unable to allow every student to begin approaching his or her potential. Instead, it perpetuates inequity by allowing children's early advantages or challenges to multiply and build upon each other. The result is achievement and opportunity gaps that grow as students move from grade to grade.

There are two forms of achievement and opportunity gaps. The first is gaps between groups based on race, ethnicity, gender, socioeconomic status, and other factors; the second is the gap between the knowledge and skills students receive from our current system and what will be needed for them to thrive in the world to come. Neither of these gaps can be closed in our current educational system.

Gaps between demographic groups

When we talk about the first form of these gaps—the gaps in achievement and opportunities between various demographic groups—we tend to generalize. We then strive to close the gaps by applying strategies to the students within those groups based on race, ethnicity, socioeconomic status, etc. But these gaps don't result from one or a select few factors. The ability of a student to learn is influenced by countless factors that are unique to each student, and these are lost when we address gaps using groups. While some students within a given group may share some factors that affect learning, it is these *combined with a variety of individual factors* that determine each student's ability to learn.

That doesn't mean the gaps aren't real or that we can or should ignore them. It's just that generalizing can actually interfere with our ability to honestly identify the causes of the gaps. This generalization then interferes with implementing effective strategies to close them. We must dig deeper and look beyond the generalizations, because it is not demographic factors alone that affect a student's academic performance or the opportunities available to that student.

This is not a new revelation. Most people realize that group factors simply compound other factors. The argument, however, is that addressing group factors should improve the outcomes for the entire group. On the surface, this seems like a valid argument and a more efficient approach than directing limited resources at students' individual challenges. However, it's not that simple.

Factors that are more prevalent in certain demographic groups still affect each individual differently based on a host of other factors. Consequently, trying to address them collectively will have mixed results for the individuals within that group; for some students, the effects of some intervention might actually be negative. Unfortunately, we often fall into a trap when the collective results show an improvement—we then consider the effort successful, though some students might actually have regressed. We might then replicate or expand the effort at the expense of those for whom the efforts will make things worse.

> ### MYTH: MORE TIME OR NEW PROGRAMS WILL LEAD TO IMPROVED TEST SCORES
>
> My sons' middle school decided to double the amount of time students spend in English Language Arts (ELA) classes based on evidence that more time in ELA results in improved literacy scores on state standardized tests. However, for my youngest son—a voracious reader who in middle school could read and have deep discussions about complex books such as *The Hobbit* and *The Hidden Reality*—the extra time and work were frustrating and caused a serious dislike of ELA. It also reduced time available for other classes that he enjoyed and that challenged him. While the extra ELA time may improve the school's collective performance, it actually reduced my son's enjoyment of reading and language arts while not notably increasing his individual knowledge and skills.
>
> I worked with numerous students in charter and alternative high schools who had been required to take additional literacy or math classes due to poor performance in these subjects. The extra classes didn't help and came at the expense of classes they enjoyed. The students fell further behind while also losing interest in school and either dropping out or not earning enough credits to graduate. Only when they got into a school that personalized their program to address their specific needs were these students able to begin learning and meeting the performance expectations.
>
> Similar scenarios play out in most schools and districts. A new curriculum, a new program, or additional time is added to address an identified collective shortcoming. The changes will almost always bring improvements for some students, while being immediately worse for other students. Over time, when no longer a focus of the school, they may end up worse for many or most students.

In using our limited resources for programs aimed at students' shared challenges, we leave none to address unique student needs and challenges (unless required by law, such as for an Individual Education Program). Concurrently, the emphasis on group challenges can allow students to ignore individual challenges over which they may have some control.

In the short term, due to focusing on some specific area, collective performance is likely to improve. Some students will suffer due to the changes, and, in many cases, performance in other areas will also suffer—until they, in turn, become the area of emphasis, just like a game of whack-a-mole. In the meantime, individual students' unique needs and challenges are not addressed, thus limiting their ability to pursue their potential.

This is why there is so little significant progress closing gaps. The reasons for each student's poor performance are unique to that student, but our current structure requires that nearly every intervention be implemented at a larger scale. The biggest drawback to interventions, whether collective or individual, is that they come *after* students struggle and are based on what people other than the student (that is, the adults) think the student needs.

Instead, we need to account for individual factors right from the start. This is impossible under the current model due to its calendar, schedule, budget, and structure, among other factors. A model that can accommodate each student's individual needs could be designed, and it could be implemented at a lower cost than the existing model; this is explored extensively in part 3 of this book.

> ## A RISING TIDE RAISES ALL SHIPS, EXCEPT . . .
>
> This common phrase "a rising tide raises all ships" is often used to justify devoting resources to something that benefits everyone rather than targeting resources to those who are struggling. An example is when schools implement policies or initiatives for all students while some students face significantly more struggles. The argument is that these students will benefit along with all others.
>
> The analogy itself, however, reveals the shortcoming of this approach for educational challenges. Consider ships that are not currently seaworthy—ships that are resting on the bottom of the bay. When the tide rises, they end up further underwater. This is not to say that all collective initiatives will be harmful to students who are already behind in some way. But it is meant as a cautionary thought. Some initiatives will, in fact, just put struggling students even further behind.
>
> The point of this book is not to keep the seaworthy ships—the students doing well—from getting additional opportunities. In fact, the point is to give them opportunities in line with their potential. That cannot happen through initiatives that "raise the tide." Rather, it's by designing new systems and enhancements aligned to the unique needs of each ship—giving each student what they need to learn, grow, and develop to their potential based on their unique needs and circumstances.
>
> Even if my boat is seaworthy, I may not want the tide to continue rising and the water below me to get deeper; rather, I may want a calmer and more appropriate place to sail. Let's make sure our efforts to float students higher don't end up drowning some.

Gaps between student preparation and needs

The second achievement and opportunity gap is almost entirely related to a single factor—the limitations of our current educational model. Our current model cannot support the level of preparation students will need to survive and thrive in an incredibly dynamic and uncertain world. This stems primarily from our current model being premised on teaching, not learning. (This is covered in detail in chapter 2.) The current model is designed to deliver a specific curriculum to all students as cost-effectively as possible. It can't accommodate every student achieving her or his individual potential.

When individual students are unable to meet their potential, the collective potential is also severely restricted. Multiply this across all the schools in our country. What is the cost of such lost potential—of the gap between student preparation and their real capabilities?

The technological developments of the last hundred years have demonstrated incredible possibilities. Some have played out in our general standard of living. The percentage of people with cars, televisions, computers, internet access, and cell phones is certainly at its highest point ever in the United States and much of the rest of the world. In the US, we take this for granted. Our ability to produce nutritious food is also exceptional, and breakthroughs in health care have increased life expectancy and reduced infant mortality rates. Yet there is still immense poverty both in the US and around the world. We continue to lose hundreds of thousands of lives every year to preventable causes.

Why does our world continue to face so many avoidable crises and challenges given all our advancements? I believe it's because relatively few people achieve their individual potential and contribute to technological—as well as cultural—advances. Most of us are content to do what we can but don't realize just how much potential we possess. Interestingly, those who are changing the world through innovation were often the very students who refused to comply and settle in school.

> ## OUTLIERS
>
> There are numerous stories of students who overcame horrible early life situations to become great scholars, breaking free from the perpetuation of their early disadvantages. These are still, however, the rare exceptions. In his book *Outliers*, Malcolm Gladwell explores the reasons behind exceptional situations and reveals that almost every exceptional performer, rather than simply being born exceptional, was the result of a series of events and much hard work and practice (Gladwell, 2008).
>
> This is great news for those of us striving to provide every student with equitable opportunities to approach and grow their potential—while also revealing the futility of trying to do so within our current educational structure. Essentially, Gladwell found that advantages perpetuate, so that a system that treats everyone pretty much the same will increase gaps between those with and without advantages. However, this also shows how a model that treats students and their situations individually can counter disadvantages from the beginning and provide advantages that can be perpetuated for each student according to their needs and circumstances.

As Eric Barker discusses in his book *Barking Up the Wrong Tree*, longitudinal research of high school valedictorians and salutatorians shows that these high-performing students do not become world-changers. They do well compared to other students, but they generally end up "fitting in" and not pushing themselves to the highest levels and most notable achievements. That is because, during their K–12 career, they were adept at and rewarded for fitting in—for complying. (Barker, 2017)

Faced with the mindset that compliance is necessary to get ahead, few students consider reaching for their true potential while in school. The result is a gap between what students demonstrate in school and their potential. Additionally, potential is not static. The human ability to grow and develop means that even as we begin approaching our current potential, that potential increases. We can go even further, should we choose to put in the necessary effort.

The two gaps addressed in this chapter differ significantly, but they are hindered in the same way. Our current educational system does not allow personalizing educational opportunities to meet the true needs of any students. Those who start out with challenges, who enter with capabilities below their grade level, or who do not learn in ways easily compatible with the existing system will not catch up to others—and certainly will not achieve their true potential. And those who start with minimal challenges, who enter the system at or above grade level, and who learn in ways directly aligned with the system will not achieve their full potential because the system can't sufficiently facilitate their needs in order to continuously grow.

We need to reinvent the system so that all students move toward their true potential. Our job is to design a system that contributes to all students growing and flourishing toward their individual potential.

CHAPTER 2

PREMISED ON TEACHING, NOT ON LEARNING

Just because someone is "teaching" us doesn't mean we will learn. Even when students appear to be engaged and on task, there is no certainty they are learning the most important or intended knowledge and skills from a given lesson. Learning assessments rarely assess long-term retention and deep conceptual understanding. Over the past few decades, increased attention has been paid to whether or not students are learning—that is the point of standardized testing—yet the entire current structure is premised on and built for delivery of instruction. A new system is needed that is premised on and built for learning.

As noted in the prologue, the Committee of Ten made instructional recommendations. Their report supports and advocates for teaching that goes beyond an instructor lecturing and students retaining what was taught. Unfortunately, their recommendations were viewed and implemented in the context of teaching rather than learning.

This is an important distinction, though probably not one that was given much consideration 126 years ago. Even today, few discussions about improving schools and education seem to give deep thought or credence to the difference between teaching and learning. And when we do have these conversations, we run into the seemingly immovable object of our institutionalized, factory model of education, so the effort is compromised, thus limiting any gains that may result.

The compromise is rarely conscious. The structure and its limitations are so ingrained that when ideas arise which everyone agrees have incredible potential but that would be impossible within the existing model, they are filtered out or quickly dismissed. Occasionally, an innovative, paradigm-shifting idea is proposed and may even lead to a small-scale or temporary pilot, such as a charter school. But in the end, ideas requiring real, systemic change are passed over or compromised in ways that severely limit their effect and keep them from fulfilling their potential.

Despite genuine good intentions, trying to improve all students' learning in a system designed to deliver instruction can actually lead to unintended negative outcomes for many students. Consider how efforts to create equity in education have played out over the past few decades.

Equal student readiness

Educators strive to ensure all students are at a similar state of readiness for a given course. A course taught by one teacher to a group of equally ready students should mean they all have an equal opportunity to learn the material. This leads to a slippery slope.

For all students to start a course (or school grade) equally prepared, logic dictates they must leave the previous course at an equal readiness level. This means they must have entered that previous course or grade at an equal readiness level. And so on.

This has led to growing calls for universal preschool and four-year-old kindergarten. The theory is that if we can get all students to a comparable readiness level when they enter formal education in kindergarten or first grade, it will be more easily maintained through high school. And the reverse argument is made that, if students begin formal schooling behind their peers, they may never catch up.

If students are not showing necessary levels of progress in a course or subject, an intervention is used. This is done to try to maintain all students at an equal state of readiness at all times. Once again, this is premised on the educational model that says all students must be receiving the same instruction at the same time and generally in the same way.

This rationale is used in larger school districts to offer essentially the same timeline, courses, course outcomes, and curriculum in every elementary, middle, and high school, with the potential exception of some elective courses for upperclassmen.

This entire readiness progression is necessitated by the instruction-centric school model, and, as noted, it leads to a number of negative outcomes while delivering the limited benefit of instruction being efficiently delivered to all students. Unfortunately, the actual amount being learned is only a fraction of what is being taught.

The worst outcome of the focus on instruction is probably the reinforcement of the paradigm that each person has control over what he or she learns and that everyone is capable of learning a given concept or skill at the same chronological age. Students and their parents receive the message that it is their fault, in some way, when students are not learning or performing at the expected level for their age cohort. They may be led to believe that the student is not smart enough, is not working hard enough, has a learning disability, or is not being provided sufficient parental support or a conducive home environment.

All these create negative self-images that can hinder future learning and create a vicious cycle. Further, we force students and families to adapt to this situation rather than strive to accommodate them where they are because every student must be ready to receive the instruction when the school has decided it must be delivered.

Most students and parents also tend to accept that students can only learn as much and perform as well as the instruction allows. While some parents will take advantage of gifted and talented programs, the vast majority of students will settle for what is being offered and will be praised if they get top grades and scores—even if they are capable of significantly more.

A century ago—and maybe even fifty years ago—this approach made sense based on the workforce's needs, the available technology, and the world in which we lived. In 2019, it no longer makes sense. If our real goal is for students to learn, then it makes a lot more sense to figure out how we can ensure each and every student is able to learn to the greatest possible extent.

Of course, that would mean adapting the schools to the students rather than adapting the students to the schools. Many would argue that the current model teaches students how to be adaptable. I would counter that students need to learn how to adapt themselves as well as how to adapt the world around them.

THE STUDENT'S JOB IS SCHOOL

It's often said the student's responsibility is to learn—it is his or her job—and that schools and teachers should not be catering to the vagaries of students. While that seems reasonable and fair to us who had to endure such an approach in our childhoods, it has serious flaws, especially if we want all children to have an equitable opportunity to pursue their personal potential.

Throughout much of the twentieth century, work was viewed as just that—work. It was a means of earning a living and not meant to be rewarding beyond a paycheck and, hopefully, some benefits. In such a job market, there was a need to know the importance of showing up on time, complying with the rules, and not challenging authority. Schools taught knowledge needed for many jobs, but this was less important than simply teaching students to tolerate work.

As technology advanced and workplace needs changed, shortcomings in students' readiness began to emerge. Numerous reports such as *A Nation at Risk* (National Commission on Excellence in Education, 2018) and the SCANS Report (The Secretary's Commission on Achieving Necessary Skills, 2018) identified knowledge and skills future generations would need for our country to remain an international economic power. That trend continues as states and countless organizations try to define what constitutes "college and career ready."

Unfortunately, our school structure was built to mimic the preparation needed for jobs of the nineteenth and twentieth centuries. If a new, twenty-first century business tried to use the structure and approaches of a nineteenth or twentieth-century business, it would almost certainly fail in our free market economy. The same is true of arguing that schools can prepare students for twenty-first century jobs by telling them their current "job" is to learn in nineteenth-century schools. Would we as adults accept nineteenth-century working conditions in our job? We shouldn't expect our children to thrive in an out-of-date school structure. That they haven't revolted en masse against this model is a testament to how effectively we have convinced them to be compliant. Unfortunately, that will not prepare future generations for the world that is coming.

Who should adapt, the student or the school?

Consider the grade-based timeline that drives education from kindergarten through high school graduation. Even if all students were ready for learning a given concept at the same chronological age, there would still be challenges because student ages regularly vary by two years or more at a given grade based on choices made by the parents and educators in the local school district.

One reason for this large range is that students demonstrate different levels of readiness for school when they are three to five years old. While a four-year-old may be assessed as ready to start kindergarten on the early side, another child at age five might be kept out for an additional year. This is, of course, an attempt to start all students at a comparable readiness level. Unfortunately, this readiness does not progress in a linear fashion. Within years or even months, the student who started early may be struggling while the older student is not being challenged.

Neither of these has anything to do with the student's ability to adapt. They have to do with brain development and other factors not under the control of the child or anyone else. From a strictly biological standpoint, no two students are at the same learning readiness at the same chronological age. Even five-year-olds born on the same day will be at different cognitive, social, and developmental levels. Readiness to learn and understand various concepts, as well as coordination and ability to develop certain skills, varies with each person the same way physical growth does; some students will grow tall early and then not grow much at all, while others will not gain much height until later in life. For neither of these can we expect students to adapt on demand.

> ## DIFFERENTIATION
>
> The concept of differentiation is to adapt instruction and activities to account for varying student abilities, readiness levels, and learning styles. While largely driven by efforts to meet the needs of students with disabilities, the concept is valid in trying to meet the unique needs of all students. However, in a traditional classroom—one teacher with a large group of students—the ability to meet all students' needs via differentiation is nearly impossible. So this concept is typically employed to address those students furthest from the expected level of skill and knowledge development.
>
> Done effectively, differentiation will help students meet a given course, subject, or grade-level expectation, but it cannot help every student achieve or even approach his or her potential. The limiting factor is not the teachers or the desire of administrators to meet all their students' needs; the limiting factor is the factory model of schools.

Beyond this biological element of readiness, there are thousands of external variables that affect a student's readiness to learn. In some communities, the population may be rather homogeneous, with most students having similar life experiences (chapter 5 explores this in greater depth). In other communities, there is vast diversity in the life experiences of students. Regardless, the range of student readiness and the experiences they bring to school are incredibly varied. Is it reasonable, then, to expect each student to adapt to the educational system and then to expect those students to all perform to a comparable standard on the same timeline?

Further, schools only have direct influence over students a portion of each day (up to a third, typically, or about half of a child's waking hours) and only about 180 days each year. Schools may make heroic efforts to get and maintain all students at comparable levels of readiness, but there are thousands of factors outside of their control during the majority of each student's waking hours. Most of these factors are in some way affecting the school's efforts for good and bad.

In addition, students are exposed to multiple teachers, many of whom are out of sync with one another. The students may see as few as two to four teachers in a day (in elementary school and in high schools on a block schedule) or as many as seven or eight; and of course, they are also exposed to multiple subjects, each with its own learning readiness expectations.

As it is, every student must adapt in dozens—maybe hundreds—of ways every day in order to learn. It's an incredible testament to our students' adaptability and capability that they learn as much as they do. The real question is, are they learning anywhere near as much as they could? I argue they are not learning even close to their potential.

> **GIFTED STUDENTS**
>
> For nearly all the reasons discussed in this chapter, the focus on instruction limits high-achieving students. The current model typically uses an "intervention" approach for gifted students just as it does for students who are struggling. That is, schools offer talented and gifted programs that provide additional opportunities for select students.
>
> While these are helpful, many students must still do their regular classes and fulfill all those requirements, even if they are not challenging or benefitting the students. When higher-level courses are available, they tend to be in limited subject areas (typically only math through middle school), and then the students must make a choice between the regular course and the advanced option, though they may be at a readiness level somewhere between the two or even beyond both.
>
> These limitations stem from the focus on teaching. Within this model, fully meeting the needs of gifted students is cost prohibitive, so compromises must be made. Adopting a model built on ensuring each student approaches his or her full potential—in all subjects and on each student's unique timeline—will ensure the needs of gifted students are met, as well as the needs of all other students.

Teacher preparation

Another systemic challenge coming from the focus on teaching rather than learning is that teacher preparation programs are based on what the teachers-to-be will *need to teach*. These programs essentially fall into one of two tracks: preparing generalist elementary teachers or specialized secondary teachers. In both cases, the programs are predominantly built around what the future teachers will be expected to teach.

While they may include research on learning and discuss this in various classes, at their core they are focused on what the program graduates will be teaching, along with courses on classroom management, administration, and data collection, among other topics. A new school model could prompt teacher preparation programs to focus more on future teachers' ability to help students learn.

Our current model and structure of schools is built specifically for the delivery of instruction. No matter how much we talk about student learning, the factory model of schools will limit how much we can accomplish. The focus—and the principal purpose—of our schools and teachers must be on all students learning to their potential. Once that overrides other considerations, then we begin to fully see the limitations of the factory model and can begin to work toward replacing it with a model and structure that will actually enhance student learning.

CHAPTER 3

STANDARDS BASED ON AVERAGES

"'The tendency to think in terms of the 'average man' is a pitfall into which many persons blunder,' Daniels wrote in 1952. 'It is virtually impossible to find an average airman not because of any unique traits in this group but because of the great variability of bodily dimensions which is characteristic of all men.' Rather than suggesting that people should strive harder to conform to an artificial ideal of normality, Daniel's analysis led him to a counterintuitive conclusion that serves as the cornerstone of this book: Any system designed around the average person is doomed to fail.

"Daniels published his findings in a 1952 Air Force Technical Note entitled The 'Average Man?' *In it, he contended that if the military wanted to improve the performance of its soldiers, including its pilots, it needed to change the design of any environments in which those soldiers were expected to perform. The recommended change was radical: the environments needed to fit the individual rather than the average."*
—The End of Average *by Todd Rose (Rose, 2015, p. 8)*

As noted in chapters 1 and 2, once students start school, they are expected to keep pace with their age-based cohort in all subjects and classes for the next thirteen years. That "pace" and corresponding measures are based on standards, which are built, for the most part, around averages.

Here's how that works. Student outcomes are determined based on data showing an average reasonable expected outcome for a particular age of student in a given subject. This seems like a logical approach, since there are decades of student data available from standardized tests and other measures. Unfortunately, this approach is actually harmful because there is no such thing as an average student.

The quote at the beginning of this chapter refers to research conducted by Lieutenant Gilbert S. Daniels in response to a rash of plane crashes by US Air Force pilots following World War II. Prior to Daniel's study, Air Force planes had cockpits designed based on average dimensions, and pilots were recruited specifically to fit within those dimensions.

However, Daniel's research found that on ten dimensions used for designing cockpits, less than 3.5 percent of Air Force pilots met even three of the dimensions. In other words, a pilot for whom the pedals were at the correct distance might have one other control at the correct distance, but rarely would three controls be at the correct distance. Consequently, for over 96 percent of the pilots, at least eight controls were not within proper reach, and their ability to fly safely was then compromised. This only became a serious problem after World War II when the complexity and performance of planes increased.

In his book *The End of Average*, Dr. Todd Rose, a professor at Harvard University, shares this story along with substantial other research demonstrating that there are no average people. He goes on to explain why any system—including our educational system—that is based on averages is actually detrimental to those who are supposed to be served by it. This chapter will not attempt to capture all the important points from Dr. Rose's book, but it will explain how the use of averages is another element of the problems with the factory model of schools (Rose, 2015).

In our society, we have made countless decisions around averages, including how we design facilities, create businesses, develop movies, and build marketing campaigns. In many cases, this is not a problem, especially when the averages are applied in a narrow scope or the stakes are low. The problems arise when applying averages more broadly or in complex, high-stakes situations. I strongly encourage you to read Dr. Rose's book or watch his presentations available online to see his outstanding examples. In the realm of education, here is how it plays out.

The problem of using averages in education

Let's consider reading in third grade. Data from numerous sources can tell us that a certain level of reading is the average for all third-grade students. Reading experts then factor in other research and knowledge about reading abilities at given ages and the progression of reading abilities needed to achieve a certain level by high school graduation. All these factors are used to set a benchmark for proficiency at the end of third grade for all students.

We then develop other benchmarks throughout third grade that, if achieved, should result in a student meeting the end-of-third-grade benchmark. Throughout the school year, students are regularly assessed to determine if they are on pace. These assessments are often teacher observations and class assignments. Students lagging behind are given additional instruction or other interventions to get back on pace.

Within any narrow subject, this approach may be effective. But once all subjects start to be considered, it gets messy. Since no student is likely to be average in more than a couple subjects, almost all students need some sort of intervention (if they are behind the benchmark) or supplemental work (if they are ahead) in most subjects. Since providing this level of personalization in the current structure is not realistic, students must instead accept that they will always be either ahead or behind to some degree. As long as they are close enough and don't become disruptive, they'll get through. This dynamic leads to bigger challenges because small early gaps often grow year after year.

Developmental readiness

One factor in whether a student is at or near a benchmark is whether they are developmentally ready for that subject. In this example, a student whose brain is just not developmentally ready for reading at the expected level will struggle regardless of any interventions, while a student who is advanced may become bored and frustrated. One solution is moving the advanced student ahead a grade and keeping the struggling student behind a grade.

However, as Dr. Rose illustrates in *The End of Average*, almost no one falls near the average on more than two or three distinct measurements. So moving a student up or down a grade can only go so far in meeting that student's needs. Once moved, the student may fall closer to the average in some subjects but may have moved further from the average in others.

The use of averages—and the corresponding academic benchmarks that are based on these averages—provides data that seems to validate our educational structure. Since most students (and, in some schools, almost all students) are meeting or exceeding the benchmarks, we consider the schools to be doing a good job. We even provide special recognition to schools with high percentages of students exceeding the benchmarks. This validation is fine if our goal is to have all students meet or exceed a set of benchmarks based on averages. However, if our ultimate goal is to help all students approach their personal potential, this is a false validation.

We also use average-based benchmarks to identify students we consider in need of interventions, when they may just not be developmentally ready. We may require students to get additional instruction, take a summer course, or repeat a course. When the student eventually reaches the benchmark, we may falsely believe it was because of the interventions, when in fact it may just have been the student having now reached developmental readiness. Our current model of education does not provide any way of knowing what eventually allowed this student to achieve the benchmark.

> **MIDDLE AND HIGH SCHOOL START TIMES**
>
> Averages also get applied to nonacademic school elements that can significantly affect learning. Starting middle and high school classes later in the morning is a practice gaining significant traction in schools throughout the country. There is substantial research that later school start times lead to academic gains, improved student mental health, improved attendance, fewer discipline referrals, and even reductions in student traffic accidents. There are also scientific and medical rationales that explain why this occurs and that strongly support these efforts. Consequently, many schools and districts have adjusted or are considering adjusting their schedules accordingly (Whalstrom, 2018).
>
> What these efforts fail to acknowledge is that while many students benefit from a later start time, other students thrive early in the morning. They go to sleep early, get up early, and are ready to be deeply engaged in learning early. These students may wane in the afternoon and have difficulty staying alert and engaged later in the day. By moving the schedule back, these students will suffer, but because they are the exceptions, they'll just have to deal with it.

Fitting the school to each student rather than the average

As long as students are grouped with dozens of other students and subjected to a time-based curriculum and a set of benchmarks, they will be outside the average significantly more often than they will be on track with the average. Our entire model is built on averages, yet there are no average students.

For every student to approach his or her potential, we need an educational structure that can adapt to each student and their unique circumstances. We need a model that meets each student where they are in terms of developmental readiness and current levels of ability within each subject area. As Lt. Daniels noted in his Air Force report in 1952, "Any system designed around the average person is doomed to fail." The solution, as Daniels recommended to the Air Force, is for environments to be designed to fit the individual, rather than the average (Rose, 2015). While our educational system built on averages has not failed entirely, it's time to replace this model with one designed to ensure every student has the true opportunity to approach their potential.

CHAPTER 4

FOCUS ON COMPLIANCE

As long as schools retain a significant focus on compliance, student achievement will be limited—not just for those who tend not to comply but for all students. Schools could instead be designed to maintain and foster students' innate curiosity and build a commitment to learning. They could adapt to meet each student's developmental readiness and current ability levels. Compliance would then cease to be a concern. Compliance—and enforcement of behaviors associated with compliance—is unnecessary where there is sufficient commitment.

There have always been expectations about children's behavior, but the context and our response to misbehavior have changed. Up to and throughout the nineteenth century, children were expected to learn how to treat others and how to act in various settings, like church and school, from their families and from older children and adults. There was no formal instruction. Rather, the instruction occurred as needed. Children learned behavior much the way they learned to walk and talk—through experimentation and experience. They learned from observing others and from the reaction of others to their behaviors. And they learned by being corrected or directed by those around them—especially parents. Children still learn to behave this way.

Why, then, is it necessary for almost all schools to provide some form of instruction on conduct and behavior? Why do schools need conduct policies and extensive lists of acceptable and unacceptable behaviors along with related rewards and punishments? And why aren't these necessary in most other settings that children frequent? It's because factory model schools are unable to foster children's sense of commitment.

Compliance vs. commitment

When someone is personally committed to something, their actions, decisions, and behavior will all correspond in ways that contribute to that commitment. The greater the level of commitment, the more significantly the actions, decisions, and behavior will support it. On the other hand, when there is a lack of commitment, there is no compulsion to act in a certain way. A reward or punishment becomes the only means of getting a desired behavior from someone who is not committed.

The best example of this is the realm of work. Most of us need to be employed. If the work is not something we truly enjoy and is not working toward a cause we're committed to, then the pay must be sufficient to motivate us. We need a reward—sufficient pay—to comply with the expectations of our employer. Our employer may also need numerous rules and policies that drive our conduct at that job.

On the other hand, many of us are involved in activities that require work (effort) but for which we receive no pay. We may volunteer, serve on the board of a nonprofit, or coach a youth sports team. While there may be some form of reward for many of these things, that is not what drives us. We do these things because they contribute to a goal we believe in and to which we are committed.

The difference in these situations is compliance versus commitment. Where there is a commitment—such as to a cause or to pursuing something we truly enjoy—there is no need for a system that encourages or enforces compliance. However, when people are forced to do something to which they are not committed, a compliance system is needed.

The reason schools have instituted instruction in behavior and extensive systems for compliance is that few children are committed to school or to learning in school. Most don't begin with a lack of commitment. In fact, many children are excited about the prospect of school and learning. Unfortunately, they discover that the methods and timeline of instruction in school do not match their readiness and the way they enjoy learning. Their commitment disappears, and it becomes necessary to enforce a system of compliance.

Of course, the compliance system itself perpetuates the need for a compliance system. Since most students are willingly compliant, those who are not become the argument for needing the system. In addition, the compliance system is defended for bringing objectivity to how students are treated, because the system dictates the expectations and the consequences and many leave little or no room for differing or extenuating circumstances.

Systems of compliance create stress which interferes with learning

These systems are all about asserting control. They are meant to direct the conduct of those within their purview, meaning people in these systems must, in turn, relinquish their control. When humans lose their sense of control, they are subject to stress; when stress grows beyond a certain point, effective learning cannot occur. In their book *The Self-Driven Child*, authors William Stixrud and Ned Johnson provide an in-depth look at the numerous ways stress occurs for children and the detrimental impacts of stress on learning (Johnson, 2018). One of their key points is this:

> It is frustrating and stressful to feel powerless, and many kids feel that way all the time. As grown-ups, we sometimes tell our kids that they're in charge of their own lives, but then we proceed to micromanage their homework, their afterschool activities, and their friendships. Or perhaps we tell them that actually they're not in charge—we are (page 11).

Stixrud and Johnson go on to note the impact this stress has on learning:

Stress disorganizes the brain. It reduces brain wave coherence, the desire to explore new ideas and to solve problems creatively. It kicks our prefrontal cortex out of the driver's seat and limits the flexibility with which we can pull ourselves together to learn (page 18).

This is why compliance systems are so harmful to students who are not likely to cause behavior problems. The students who have learned how to be compliant—who have internalized the system and want to avoid related punishments and earn related rewards—are the ones who stress about remaining compliant. They know they have given up control and are concerned about doing anything that appears inappropriate. When they, inadvertently or in a weak moment, break a rule, the impact of the consequences will be even more stressful.

On the other hand, students with regular behavior problems don't care about the compliance system or its consequences. (See the sidebar "The Token Economy Student Conduct System" on page 54.) Rather, their stress and challenges with school performance stem more from a negative self-image.

> ## "TEACHING" RESPONSIBILITY
>
> A focus on compliance is often rationalized by claiming students must be taught to be responsible. Thus, students earn a grade for turning in work on time, being present at school, and behaving in class.
>
> In truth, directed consequences do not teach or reinforce responsibility. Rather, they are a check on students' priorities relative to the corresponding rewards and punishments. Most students are perfectly capable of meeting the expectations (being compliant) if the directed outcome is of sufficient value to them. If the related reward or punishment is meaningful enough to the student, the student will comply. Those who don't comply are either unable to do so or don't find the reward or punishment sufficient motivation.
>
> Students will only develop and strengthen their sense of responsibility through things over which they have power, and it will come from the natural consequences of their actions. Schools and teachers still have a role to play by helping students learn the norms and values that are important in our society, in their community, and in the workforce. However, imposing these on students and tying them to rewards and punishments robs students of the opportunity to develop a sense of responsibility.
>
> See also "Fostering cooperation, collaboration, and respect for differing ideas and beliefs" on page 99 in chapter 15.

Systems of compliance stifle children

Another consequence of a compliance system is the muting of children's inherent energy, curiosity, and creativity. Humans are born with a need to learn. Despite most early learning coming through failures—some of which, like falling while learning to walk, can be painful—humans persevere. Our early learning comes through observations, experience, and experimentation. It does not come in a structured, controlled environment.

Then children enter preschool or kindergarten and are directed what, when, and how they are supposed to learn. Compliance systems are enforced to maintain order so that instruction can be delivered according to the school's schedule. Is it any wonder that students begin to sense a disconnect when they encounter formalized learning situations? And does this explain why formal learning situations are often chaotic until sufficient compliance measures are in place?

It is a testament to our children's adaptability that we get compliance from so many so quickly, but this compliance comes at the expense of learning. Although instruction is being delivered, it doesn't necessarily result in students learning the intended content or the intended scope of the content. Even worse, things known to be conducive to learning—such as control over what, when, and how—must be repressed in the interest of compliance and in order to keep instructional delivery on schedule.

Students who choose to be compliant see what happens to students who are not, and this reinforces their choice to be compliant. Even when children sense something isn't right about the system or the instruction, their sense of self-preservation typically keeps them quiet. This learned compliance can carry over so students do not speak up when they are struggling with the instruction.

When the pace of instruction or the learning expectations don't match a student's readiness to learn or current developmental level—whether it is too fast or too slow—that student may be afraid to raise concerns. They know what happens when students challenge the rules or expectations, so they may choose to stay quiet and make do with the situation. While most students still do well enough to continue, they learn significantly less than they would if their learning needs were being met or if the pace matched their levels of readiness.

Compliance vs. engagement

As noted, when students become committed to learning, their conduct aligns with whatever activities contribute to the learning. That is, they become deeply engaged in learning activities so that they are both learning deeply and displaying appropriate conduct. Compliance systems become irrelevant.

Know Power, Know Responsibility

On the other hand, when students are not committed to learning—when they don't have a fully internalized reason for learning—their levels of engagement will be lower. Besides implementing systems to gain compliance, schools (along with individual teachers as well as parents) implement systems to elevate students' levels of engagement.

Grades and academic recognitions are tools meant to incentivize student engagement. Teachers may offer prizes or recognitions toward the same end, parents may offer cash or rewards for good grades, and students may earn scholarships—all of which may prompt better engagement. Sometimes the opposite approach is used, with penalties for low academic performance. At a certain point, the compliance and academic systems may become intertwined if the engagement level also becomes a conduct concern.

Building on the work of Robert Merton (Merton, 1968), Phil Schlecty developed a model of levels of engagement that helps illustrate what we regularly see in schools (Schlechty Center, 2018). These are the levels of engagement Schlecty has identified:

- Engagement—The highest level, reflecting that a student has found personal meaning and value in an activity.
- Strategic Compliance—The extrinsic value of the activity is not embraced by a student, but the student substitutes his or her own value (e.g., a good grade, parent approval, college admission) as being sufficient to engage in the activity.
- Ritual Compliance—Activity has no personal value to the student and there are no meaningful substitutes; the student complies to avoid confrontation or some consequence.
- Retreatism—Student is disengaged, withdraws from activity, does not participate, and sees no point in doing so.
- Rebellion—Student is disengaged from directed activity and engaged in some other agenda; often viewed as acting out and encouraging others to rebel.

Anyone who has spent time in a classroom can remember students who fit into each of these levels. Unfortunately, it is rare to see students achieving the highest level of actual engagement. This is because students do not design their own education based on their own passions, needs, goals, and desires. Many students will engage at the "strategic compliance" level, but this doesn't lead to deep learning. Far too many students are at "ritual compliance," and those at the lowest two levels challenge teachers and other staff while detracting from the rest of the students.

Of course, only students at the highest levels of engagement even have a chance of learning at their full potential. The lesson for compliance, however, is that aiming for a model that engages students at the highest levels will also move children away from the disruptive levels of engagement.

Don't some children still need a system of compliance?

Some would argue that certain children are so out of control that they need a compliance system. I would counter that it is impossible to design a compliance system that would be effective for every child; the evidence is present in nearly every school. If compliance systems worked effectively, there would be no conduct problems in schools. Even the highest-performing schools I've encountered still have conduct problems—except where compliance systems have been all but eliminated.

In many cases, the out-of-control behavior is a product of the compliance system and the instructional approach and expectations in the school. Other factors—such as learning disabilities, which can significantly increase student stress levels—may compound this. I have seen countless examples of out-of-control students who are in complete control in other environments.

In *The Self-Driven Child*, William Stixrud shares the story of a student with whom he worked who "struggled with math and had significant trouble regulating his emotions." The student's challenges were actually compounded by promises of rewards, which amped up his stress because he wanted to earn the rewards—but which then made it even harder to control his emotions.

With some exploration, Dr. Stixrud helped the student discover the heart of what was happening with his mind and emotions. They then developed a plan that put the student in control of the situation such that he was able to readily—and almost happily—work through the same math problems that previously caused uncontrolled outbursts (Johnson, 2018, p. 243).

My own observations completely confirm this. Nearly every child I have ever encountered has demonstrated an understanding of proper conduct and an ability to demonstrate this conduct in certain settings—typically where there was no compliance system in place.

Some children, however, feel greater anxiety than normal when their sense of control is threatened. This can be for any number of reasons, but the bottom line is that the very compliance system meant to create order becomes the source of anxiety and literally represses some children's ability to exert self-control. Their rational, thoughtful mind—the mind that could process the rewards and punishments at stake—is overwhelmed by their emotional mind. Increasing the rewards and punishments in an attempt to bring such children into compliance will actually have the opposite effect.

I would argue that there is no child for whom a system of compliance is beneficial. Rather, the means of helping students maintain self-control—which could include extrinsic incentives—must be personalized for each student. Equal is not equitable in human systems because everyone is unique. Consequently, a school model that fosters children's commitment to learning would also allow development of personalized systems that ensure necessary conduct. This would not be done in a vacuum but, rather, with adult mentorship and guidance helping students learn appropriate conduct in varying settings and situations.

THE TOKEN ECONOMY STUDENT CONDUCT SYSTEM

I experienced a "token economy" system as a middle school associate principal. The system assigned negative points to unacceptable conduct and awarded positive points for positive acts. When a teacher issued a referral for unacceptable conduct, the student lost the preassigned number of points. When a student did a positive act, she or he earned points that were deducted or banked.

Various point totals equated to preassigned consequences, such as detentions and suspensions. Students with negative points would also be ineligible for quarterly "reward days." Once a consequence had been served, the points were reduced or eliminated. Students with banked points who received a referral would need to serve the corresponding consequence but would salvage reward day.

The system seemed great when I first arrived. I just assigned points when a referral came in and assigned the student the appropriate consequence. Easy peasy. Boy, was I wrong.

First, relationships and individual circumstances were removed from the equation. The system was designed for every staff member to treat every incident and student the same. Of course, no two students or staff members are the same, and neither are any two incidents. There were several inherent wild cards for every referral, but the system couldn't function properly unless every situation was treated the same. Thus, the system had no integrity. Also, trying to build relationships with students and consider their unique selves complicated using the system, and the system sabotaged attempts to build relationships.

In addition, the system was conducive to manipulation. Once students knew the system, they could decide whether or not the conduct they were considering would be worth the corresponding cost within the token economy. Often, our students decided it was. They were well aware the consequences made work for staff members and that the cost to them as a student was reasonable for the pleasure of disrupting a class and inconveniencing staff members.

On the other hand, the generally well-behaved students who had an occasional slipup or outburst could get caught in the system in a disproportionate way. The system was essentially rewarding those who were of greatest concern and punishing those who were not of great concern, all in the name of trying to force compliance.

CHAPTER 5

THE VAST DIVERSITY IN LIFE EXPERIENCES OF STUDENTS

When the current education model was instituted at the turn of the twentieth century, our individual schools were relatively homogenous, so addressing diversity was of little concern at the time. In fact, there may have been some desire to increase homogeneity through the common schools. Even so, from the standpoint of learning effectiveness, those schools could have benefited from leveraging the diversity of student experiences, family structures, and standards of living. If our students are to be prepared for both an increasingly diverse country and an increasingly interconnected world, our schools must be structured to take these into account.

The previous chapters looked largely at the shortcomings of the current model and structure of education itself. This chapter looks more at how external factors require a different model and approach.

The United States is regularly referred to in terms that reflect the mix of peoples that make up our country. The diversity of ethnicities, races, and cultures is compounded by diverse experiences, standards of living, belief systems, family structures, and more. This diversity extends to the students in our schools, though the level of diversity varies across the country and within school districts.

These points are valid for any school or district, even those in less ethnically or culturally diverse communities. First, migration patterns and destinations for groups of new immigrants are constantly shifting. Communities that were homogeneous a decade ago are suddenly much more diverse. Dan Keating and Laris Karklis explore and quantify this in a *Washington Post* article from November 2016, "The increasingly diverse United States of America" (Karklis, 2017). Almost any community and its schools could rapidly become diverse.

Further, even within more homogeneous communities, the experiences, standards of living, family structure, and much else will be varied among the students. These differences bring many of the same challenges found where there is greater ethnic, racial, and cultural diversity. The current approach cannot adequately account for or leverage this diversity, thus limiting student ability to reach their potential.

As noted previously, our current model of education strives for efficiency by delivering instruction collectively to groups of students in classrooms. Several chapters explain the many challenges already inherent in this approach. Because all students have different backgrounds, experiences, abilities, and home lives, this "efficiency" becomes an additional burden and a significant obstacle to effective student learning.

Our schools have tried countless tactics to account for student diversity, but the school structure limits the ability to do so effectively. Some schools with highly diverse student populations perform well compared to other schools, but the inability to personalize and account for or leverage student diversity will always keep students from achieving their potential. The factory model can't tap into each student's unique gifts and contributions.

In the current educational model, schools try to address and honor student diversity in all areas—race, ethnicity, socioeconomic status, English language ability, life experiences, family structure, physical abilities, emotional circumstances, and on and on—but they must do so collectively. The model doesn't have the capacity to address and honor individual diversity because it must adhere to the instructional delivery timeline. Instead, schools strive to be equal in their treatment of diversity while being unable to leverage that diversity for the good of the group or the individuals.

There is also diversity of student developmental levels and readiness to learn in various content areas. As noted previously, the reasons for being behind or ahead are unique to each student, but as long as the driving factor of the model is time rather than mastery—and everyone has to arrive at each benchmark at or about the same time—the model cannot fully account for this aspect of student diversity.

Add in each student reaching levels of developmental and learning readiness at different times for different subjects, concepts, and skills, and the ability to help each student meet his or her potential becomes nearly impossible in our current model of education.

Given the limitations of the factory model, many schools should be commended for their work with diverse populations. These schools are not, however, getting these students anywhere near their potential. Even students who are outperforming most others on our common measures—such as grades, honors, and standardized tests—are not achieving anywhere near their potential. The school structure simply cannot accommodate their unique and diverse characteristics and circumstances.

CULTURALLY RESPONSIVE TEACHING

Many schools and districts have implemented "culturally responsive teaching." The idea is to consider the diverse backgrounds, experiences, and beliefs that stem from each student's culture and strive to ensure instruction and activities are sensitive to those cultures. This, in turn, is meant to create a classroom environment that enhances learning for all students.

While creating such classrooms is laudable, it is still largely premised on the idea that all students coming from a given background or culture are more the same than different. This may be the best we can expect within our current school model.

What if a new model allowed complete or nearly complete personalization? Wouldn't it be better to offer individually responsive teaching? Or, better yet, individually responsive learning facilitation? Creating a school built on this recognition and leveraging it for more effective learning would be much more effective than our current approach, even when we strive to be culturally responsive.

CHAPTER 6

THE NEED FOR FLEXIBILITY IN AN EVER-CHANGING WORLD

The cost to our society of not fostering critical thinking and entrepreneurial skills for all students is immense; in the more complex and dynamic world of the future, it will be devastatingly high. To date, the cost has been limiting advances in our society. In the future, it might be survival itself. It's time to implement an educational model that ensures future generations are not being hampered by the limited vision and imagination of prior generations.

Driven largely by advances in technology, our lives are vastly different from those of earlier generations, and the rate of change will likely accelerate. The big question is, how are our schools doing at preparing students for the nature and rate of change we are experiencing and might expect? Unfortunately, I believe our current school model hinders our ability to change and adapt to change.

CALVIN AND HOBBES © 1989 Watterson. Reprinted with permission of ANDREWS MCMEEL SYNDICATION. All rights reserved.

In the accompanying comic, Calvin laments how disappointing change has been. None of the futuristic things imagined midway through the twentieth century had yet come to pass. Even though the comic is nearly thirty years old, the technologies Calvin mentions still have yet to enter our lives. While change seems to be a constant and some aspects of change seem to be accelerating, other elements seem to be stagnant. I contend our 126-year-old educational structure has contributed to reducing the rate and nature of change in our world. In addition, that structure has kept us from guiding and leveraging change toward the long-term best interest of our world and society.

Previous chapters illustrate how we have limited our children's ability to achieve their individual or collective potential. In addition, children adopt the almost universal acceptance of what school should be and carry this into adulthood. Even as people recognize that their school experience could probably have been better and more effective, they won't challenge the status quo.

This acceptance of the status quo shows up in other aspects of life and society. As adults, we often recognize when policies, practices, and events don't seem to be in the best interest of ourselves, our community, the world, society, or our children's future, but we believe there's nothing we can do about them. Similarly, many people have not learned to think critically, so they are at the mercy of others' opinions, information, and influences.

In a slowly changing world, this would not be a serious concern. In a rapidly changing world—one where some changes have the potential for both positive and negative large-scale impacts—this is an existential threat. Consequently, future generations must be prepared to do all of the following:

- Contribute to technological advancements
- Guide and influence implementation of technologies
- Guide and influence policies and laws that affect technologies and their implementation

- Address negative outcomes of the use of technologies
- Leverage the opportunities that new and advancing technologies present

Of course, current and past generations should have been prepared for all this. Ideally, our society would have been able to influence change and technological development to better our country and world while avoiding detrimental outcomes. Unfortunately, many changes and developments also brought devastating outcomes. Sometimes these outcomes were unforeseen, while other times there were unheeded warnings. In either case, a population better prepared for change and advancements could likely have avoided some and maybe most.

Today, ideologies, opinions, and those who stand to profit are increasingly driving decisions about technologies and their capabilities. Critical thinking, research, science, and cooperation are often ignored or twisted to support one ideology or opinion. Insufficient numbers of citizens are willing and able to present a challenge even when there is public consensus.

Policies are developed and implemented based on who has the political and economic power and influence at a given time, sometimes with little or no consideration for available research and science. When the power and influence shift, the new "leaders" may discard current practices and disregard science, regardless of their effectiveness, if they impede their desired outcomes.

Some people align themselves with powerful and influential groups and refuse to challenge the information, ideas, or opinions they provide. These same people will not challenge the policies and practices the groups endorse (chapters 7 and 8 look at this in greater depth). Without any thought, many will automatically reject and even denigrate ideas, policies, and practices supported by opposing groups. They will not apply critical thinking but rather fall into step.

Unfortunately, those not affiliated with ideological groups often sit out the debates and process, even when proposals arise with which they disagree and that lack scientific rationale, research support, or even common sense. While often in the majority, they will remain uninvolved because they feel they have no power.

In a similar vein, some people *are* able to leverage opportunities that arise through technological innovations and advancements. This includes entrepreneurs who can think critically and creatively and are willing to take risks to see what they can create and accomplish. Often, these people didn't fit in or try to comply when in school and never adopted the mindset of accepting the decisions and actions of those with the power and influence.

Unfortunately, there are also selfish people who crave power or wealth and who will take advantage of opportunities that arise. These are people who might have learned in school how to play the system to their own advantage even at the expense of others. While change and technological advances can provide great opportunities, there are those who will use them in ways that most would consider unethical, if not illegal.

The vast majority of people, however, will only benefit from advances and changes if they trickle down. Here again, our current school structure largely encourages being part of the pack and not standing out. It rarely rewards risk-taking except in contrived situations. Rather, the factory system typically discourages and may even punish students who take risks on issues that are truly important to them. The usual rationale is that this is necessary to maintain order, structure, and control for the benefit of all the students. While some educators might want to encourage independence, the current structure significantly limits this.

As noted at the beginning of this chapter, the cost to our society of not fostering critical thinking and entrepreneurial skills for all students is already too high, and that cost will grow in the more complex and dynamic world of the future. It's time to implement an educational model that will ensure future generations are ready to drive and guide change rather than become subservient to it.

CHAPTER 7

NORMALIZING COMPLIANCE, DISCOURAGING CRITICAL THINKING, AND DEVALUING MORAL COURAGE

Students should graduate from high school ready, willing, and able to stand up to those who would strive to manipulate and take advantage of them. That, however, requires students to develop and practice critical thinking skills, develop the confidence to use these skills regularly, and develop the will to actively protect themselves and others from those who would abuse their power and influence.

Normalizing compliance

Chapter 4 describes how our focus on compliance interferes with student learning. This approach of normalizing compliance also contributes to significant societal challenges.

Children become accustomed to compliance. They learn to function as well as possible in an environment of rewards and punishments. They also learn that those with power and influence dictate the rules, limitations, freedoms, and consequences. Those same people determine what will be learned, when, and how, and that there are negative consequences for noncompliance. Essentially, compliance becomes normalized and considered necessary.

When students move on to college, compliance continues to influence most aspects of their lives with countless rules, rewards, and consequences, including those for academic performance. After college, this continues to be accepted as the best way for society to function.

When people join a group, they often gain a sense of power from that group, even if that was not why they originally joined. The leaders of some groups leverage this sense of power to gain additional influence. Whether or not by design, schools do this when they strive to build school spirit and then use that to influence student conduct and actions. As adults, people may find their only sense of power comes from aligning with an individual or group they see as powerful.

Unfortunately, those who crave real power but lack a moral foundation can leverage the compliance mindset to gain support and allegiance. In the absence of critical thinking from their followers, they use calls for loyalty and trust to maintain support.

I believe this is a root cause of our current levels of divisiveness and political dysfunction. A small number of wealthy and powerful individuals and groups wield incredible influence over political parties, ideological organizations, media outlets, elected officials, and various other aspects of society. They leverage the compliance mentality and their members' need for a sense of allegiance and power to support actions and decisions that many would never consider otherwise.

Unfortunately, even people and groups with a moral foundation are prone to acting in similar ways because they don't see any options. Many people default to compliance and are unaccustomed to critical thinking, so they continue to follow "their" groups and leaders. Thus, even ethical groups may adopt manipulative, uncompromising practices.

Discouraging critical thinking

Which leads to the next outcome—discouraging critical thinking. Critical thinking requires one to view a problem or situation objectively. It requires consideration of various points of view and delineating facts from assumptions, opinions, and false information. To think critically, one needs to have an open mind and be willing to accept sometimes being wrong and having flawed opinions.

Equally important is having an outlet for critical thinking. If people think critically but their ideas and conclusions are ignored or lead to a negative consequence, then they learn to avoid thinking critically. In our current compliance-centric model, students do not learn to question, validate, and challenge sources of information or what they are being taught. Instead, they learn that doing these things will often have negative results.

Probably worse, students aren't learning to challenge their own opinions and thinking. In the absence of critical thinking, discord, and disagreement about things important to them, students can't learn how to reflect on their own thoughts and ideas, which are essential to critical thinking. Even schools that include instruction in critical thinking often lack integrity because they won't accept students doing so in the areas that really matter to the students.

Further, students learn it is best to stick with their decisions. Whether choosing a specific answer, choosing courses, or joining a group of friends or a club or sports team, there are often rewards for sticking with one's decision, while changing one's mind can bring complications, discomfort, and sometimes harassment from others.

This continues into adulthood. People are honored for being a member of an organization for years or decades. Others are honored for sticking to their "principles" even when these are actually opinions and biases rather than commonly shared values. People put great importance on loyalty and stick-to-itiveness, but those qualities have a downside.

> ## THE PARADOX OF THE
> ## SECOND AMENDMENT
>
> Some people have a strong law-and-order bias while also being vocal about supporting the Second Amendment and opposing firearm restrictions. On its surface, this seems reasonable. However, a little deep reflection and critical thinking reveals a paradox.
>
> The argument for the Second Amendment is the ability to defend one's freedom against potential government infringement. This presumes the possibility that the government cannot be fully trusted and that individuals must be willing to question government decisions and actions and be ready to take up arms to support one's rights.
>
> Support for law and order stems from a belief that everyone must obey the law and those who don't must suffer the consequences. When someone believes a law is wrong or that rights are being violated, they must work within the system to change the law and not act illegally in protest.
>
> Thus, the paradox. An advocate for law and order shouldn't be able to entertain the possibility of taking up arms against the government, while a supporter of the second amendment must allow the possibility that some laws may need to be broken. It is possible to reasonably hold both these views, but only by thinking critically about each and considering the many nuances that come into play.
>
> Critical thinking on hot-button issues from all parties involved would allow those with opposing perspectives to discover common ground and seek collaborative solutions to societal challenges.

Many people find ways to rationalize their continued allegiance to an organization even in the face of immoral or illegal acts. The need to be part of a group can outweigh our own awareness and personal values. In defending our allegiance, we further cement our bond, making it even harder to break away. When the group or its leaders move further from our base beliefs and values, we continue to accept it and retain our "loyalty." This can occur slowly over time such that we find ourselves supporting actions and individuals that, at one time, we would have condemned.

Devaluing moral courage

Compounding these outcomes is the devaluation of moral courage. Most people believe courage is a virtue—but determining a person's act as courageous often depends on one's ideological leanings. People will praise a student who stands up to a bully but condemn a student who stands up to a teacher or the administration, even on issues of student rights. Students quickly learn that demonstrating moral courage may not be worth the price.

This follows into adulthood. Tragic events such as school shootings and natural disasters become politicized; actions and decisions get twisted to align with an ideology. People who speak out and take a stand come under attack from those who feel that stand threatens their power and influence. Those in power then leverage their aligned groups to pursue the attacks and undermine the person or ideas being expressed.

Some may argue this stems from differing values among people. However, values are much more consistent than most realize. The differences that emerge during discussions and debates—and much more quickly and viciously on social media—often stem from refusing to apply critical thinking and objectivity. Instead, people filter events and actions through their biases and the influence of the groups with which they're aligned. The actual values and moral courage get lost among ideologies and the self-interest of the various parties.

Rushworth Kidder explores this in depth in his book *Moral Courage*. Kidder dissects this concept, illustrates with dozens of examples, and provides significant evidence of values that are almost universally shared and considered most important across cultures, countries, and generations of people as well as within professional organizations and businesses (Kidder, 2005).

It is not differing values at the heart of our divisiveness and political dysfunction; it is the ability of a small number of people and groups to maintain their power and influence by leveraging our compliance mentality, our unwillingness to think critically, and our fear of demonstrating moral courage.

We need a school model that requires students to think critically about things that are important to them and then guides them through the process until it becomes second nature. That means students need real power over their own education. Such a model would also lead students to value their own opinion and power and to strengthen their resolve to use these when necessary; that is, to demonstrate moral courage.

> **HOW'S YOUR CRITICAL THINKING?**
>
> Think about groups or individuals you oppose politically, ideologically, or otherwise. After reading this chapter, do you think they are manipulative? If so, then do a little reflecting. Ask yourself honestly and thoughtfully whether or not those you *support* are guilty of this.
>
> It is not critical thinking to simply confirm a bias or opinion. Anytime you reject or embrace an idea, suggestion, opinion, or news story based on the source or how it aligns with your current opinions and beliefs, you are not thinking critically. Critical thinking requires reflecting deeply about the subject—and that means considering peripheral factors, indirect impacts, second- and third-order effects, etc.
>
> Want to know how you're doing at critical thinking? Try this: Select something about which you feel very strongly. Now, consider opposing points of view. Can you do this? Is the opposing viewpoint upsetting to you? Can you get past that and look at it objectively? Can you contrast your and the opposing viewpoints to see good and bad about both? Can you recognize why someone might support that opposing viewpoint? Can you recognize where your viewpoint might be wrong or at least unattractive to others? Can you think deeply about opposing points of view, ideas, or stories? Then you are capable of critical thinking. Now practice that as you continue to read.

CHAPTER 8

PRESERVING OUR DEMOCRACY

I don't believe our schools contribute to a compliant populace by design or that there is some conspiracy at play, but I do believe our democracy is at risk if we don't change our educational system.

Our country was founded on the ideal that all men are created equal, largely in response to abuses under the rule of a monarchy. Colonists believed that all citizens (though only property-owning men fell under that label at that time) should have a voice and influence over the laws of a country and the running of its government. Our democratic republic, of course, is the result of the revolution fueled by this belief.

Our founding fathers understood that, for the democracy to work, the population must be educated. That is, the people selecting our government leaders must be able to understand pressing issues, sort facts from bluster and opinion, and choose the person who will best serve their interests. Essentially, for our democracy to work as intended, voters must be able to think critically. In addition, they must be willing and able to stand up to those who would try to manipulate them into acting against their values, beliefs, or best interests.

I believe our democracy is threatened. A fairly small number of influential people and groups have amassed an inordinate amount of power to influence our nation's politics. These people and groups claim vast vocal support, at least in part, due to people supporting anything they do or say. Many supporters refuse to take a step back and consider whether the people and groups they are following are acting morally, appropriately, or in their best interests. They have aligned themselves and now feel obligated to stand with them for reasons explained in chapter 7.

Others, who may not be aligned with manipulative individuals and groups, have largely chosen to steer clear of the fray because they feel they have no power or influence. They accept what those in power say and do as mostly inevitable. Even when our "leaders" make decisions with which most disagree or find disturbing, they will not take any significant action. Years of compliance-centric schooling are likely a contributing factor to this willingness to acquiesce.

GERRYMANDERING

Gerrymandering demonstrates how a compliance mindset and a lack of critical thinking threaten our democracy. For reasons cited in chapters 7 and 8, many people align themselves with one or the other major political party and rarely deviate from voting with that party. Sophisticated computer programs allow the party in power to draw legislative and congressional district boundaries that consolidate as many voters of the opposition party as possible into the smallest number of districts. This dilutes the power of the opposing party's voters and can lock in the majority's control for a decade or more, even if the majority of voters in the state support the opposing party and oppose gerrymandering.

Some states where citizens can force binding referendums have adopted an independent process for establishing these boundaries so the parties are unable to influence them. These states consistently have more competitive elections that require candidates to be responsive to the voters. States that allow gerrymandering have less competitive elections, and the candidates are more responsive to those with power and influence rather than to voters themselves.

When something inarguably horrific happens, there may be shared outrage and mourning. However, even then it can quickly turn into partisan attacks used to maintain or increase the divisiveness among groups.

Occasionally, someone will have the courage to protest or even condemn an act or statement from their group, but others in the group then attack that messenger and continue toeing the group's line.

As noted previously, the underlying values among most Americans are not all that different, regardless of their ideologies or the groups with which they align themselves. In numerous circumstances, when ideologies and politics are out of mind, people get along, work together, support many of the same causes, and generally have good relationships. However, on high-profile issues, they may find themselves treating each other like lifelong enemies. Too often, this animosity is fueled by those who seek to benefit from the divisiveness or whose power and influence would be threatened by thoughtful dialogues, objective thinking, and setting aside of partisan biases.

However, that's what the vast majority of us should want—for individuals to be well-informed, think objectively, and set aside (at least temporarily) partisan biases to have thoughtful dialogues with others, including those with whom we disagree. That is what the founders of our country seemed to have intended. A plutocracy—government by the wealthy—can be just as bad as a monarchy. If those who are ruling are selfish and self-serving, we are right back where we were prior to the Revolutionary War.

To strengthen our democracy, we need a school structure that ensures students learn to think critically and to recognize and counter those who would manipulate them. It needs to encourage thoughtful dialogues and dissension and foster collaboration for developing mutually agreeable solutions to challenges. The structure must model effective democracy by treating students as the critical heart of the school, just as citizens are the heart of our democracy. None of this can simply be taught; it must be modeled and practiced so it becomes ingrained in the very essence of our students, much as our current structure ingrains compliance.

ARE COOPERATION AND COMPROMISE DIRTY WORDS?

As noted previously, an absence of personal power or control often leads people to align themselves with groups that wield power. Some such groups have narrow agendas primarily benefitting the group leaders, though they'll claim their agenda is what's best for everyone in the group. The leaders leverage the absence of critical thinking and moral courage to manipulate members into believing that compromise is a sign of weakness. They demonize anyone who calls for compromise and anyone showing the moral courage to challenge the group leaders.

While some will leave a group when they realize what's happening, those remaining often become stronger in their refusal to compromise on the group's agenda even as they compromise their personal values. They may state their distaste for things being said or done or the way the agenda is being carried out, but they maintain their support as long as they believe those in power are acting in their best interest, though they won't think critically about it. Like kings of old, the leaders have us, their followers, waging their battles while they grow in wealth and power.

Our collective willingness to compromise our personal values to support "our" group's agenda and the subsequent divisiveness have fueled congressional dysfunction. Congress feels no compulsion to work in a bipartisan manner and seek collaborative solutions despite record low approval ratings from US citizens. In fact, rather than answer to those who want a cooperative and effective Congress, the elected officials move further and further toward extreme partisanship due to the threat of facing an intraparty primary opponent who is even more extreme. Some who have tried to act in a cooperative, bipartisan manner have lost primary elections to more extreme candidates.

We must ensure future generations are able to think critically and develop the self-confidence to demonstrate moral courage, or the dysfunction of our government will only get worse. The fate of our democracy may hang in the balance.

CHAPTER 9

STUDENTS WITH DISABILITIES

While this is a stand-alone chapter, every reason noted in the other chapters for why we must replace the current models of schools applies to students with disabilities.

One of the greatest changes in public schools over the past century is the inclusion of students with disabilities in all aspects of the educational process. Although the system is not completely equitable for students with disabilities and there are still schools that are failing to meet their obligations, tremendous strides have been made. That being said, like nearly every other aspect of our current schools, there is no means of achieving additional significant improvement within the current structure.

Under the current school model, a student with disabilities has a case manager who works with the student, parents, teachers, other school staff, and occasionally non-school staff to develop a plan—the Individualized Education Program (IEP). The IEP includes goals, interventions, and services designed to ensure the student has all the necessary opportunities to remain on track with his or her age cohort. The people involved and the scope of the plan will vary based on the nature and extent of disabilities. All of a student's teachers must accommodate the student's plan for the classes in which the student is enrolled.

Compared to earlier times in our schools—when students with disabilities were excluded from many or all regular school activities or sent to completely different schools—this approach is a vast improvement. Unfortunately, the current approach and the ability of schools to meet the needs of students with disabilities suffer from all the same limitations noted in previous chapters, and some of these issues are compounded for students with disabilities.

Because our current model is built around teaching instead of learning, plans for students with disabilities are often focused on ensuring the student can receive the instruction and participate in related activities, regardless of whether that is the best way for the student to learn the desired knowledge and skills. This is one more place our current school model is driving decisions rather than what would be most effective and maybe even most cost-effective. The added costs of students with certain disabilities participating in the same activities—especially when they may not even foster learning for most students—add to the argument that there must be a more sustainable approach.

A new school model could be created that would develop educational activities specific to the needs of *every* individual student. Students with disabilities would then receive the same opportunities as every other student and have them tailored toward their learning objectives, not receipt of instruction. The model could also be designed to meet these needs in cost-effective ways for every student. In some cases, these costs might still be higher for a student with disabilities, but it would almost certainly be less costly than having to accommodate disabilities within a structure not designed to be flexible.

Everything about closing achievement and opportunity gaps (chapter 1) and basing most instruction and assessments on averages (chapter 3) applies to students with disabilities. Beginning with averages—or even setting a "higher bar" that exceeds averages to push students—simply cannot allow any students to approach their individual potential. A student's disabilities are only one aspect of that student, all of which need to be considered in developing a plan for the student to achieve his or her learning goals and reach his or her potential. If this is done for all students, then it will just be routine for students with disabilities.

Students with disabilities are often unique in more obvious ways than other students, but we must keep in mind that *all* students are unique and all bring a diversity of experiences to their learning. As a new school model emerges that takes into account and leverages the diversity of student experiences, everyone will come to see that the experiences of students with disabilities enhance the school community and everyone's learning. Similarly, students with disabilities may have experiences that better prepare them to thrive in an ever-changing world.

Students with disabilities must be ready and able to vocally and forcefully advocate for themselves to be treated equitably and have fair opportunities. They must be ready to defend themselves against those who would try to manipulate, cheat, or take advantage of them. Essentially, they must develop the same skills needed to ensure our democracy stays strong and is not compromised by those who would abuse the power they have acquired.

Students with disabilities will benefit immensely if schools are designed to personalize the educational experiences of all students in order that every student can approach his or her personal potential. Currently, students with disabilities are the exception with a personalized plan—but its execution is only as effective as the structure and staff will allow.

On the other hand, if the school were designed to accommodate a unique plan for every student with the intent of bringing each near his or her potential, then executing the plan of a student with disabilities, as noted above, would be routine. Consequently, the plan could be much more effective and more likely to achieve the stated goals and outcomes, which would be set significantly higher because they would not be limited by the curriculum and standards being used today.

CHAPTER 10

FREEING TEACHERS TO PURSUE THEIR POTENTIAL

Our current school model does not allow teachers to perform anywhere near their full potential. A new educational system needs to be adopted that will fully leverage the passions and expertise of teachers to allow every student to approach his or her full potential.

People have many reasons to become teachers, but nearly all have a true desire—a calling—to positively influence future generations. People want to be teachers to help prepare children to be successful as adults and to contribute to making the world a better place. However, most teachers find that only a portion of their time and effort goes into actually influencing their students, at least in a direct manner, and that they are only having truly meaningful influence over a small number of students at any given time. The best teachers provide meaningful influence more regularly and to more students, but even they are rarely able to provide the level of influence of which they are capable.

This is rooted, again, in the emphasis on delivering instruction (as opposed to an emphasis on learning) combined with the need to "manage" the classroom and fulfill the other expectations stemming from our current educational model. As long as teachers are expected to "deliver" a set curriculum to all their assigned students within the current schedule and calendar, they will be unable to meet the actual learning needs of each of their students. The most significant concern of most schools and districts is that most students achieve the expected performance benchmarks on whatever standards are in place. Little or no consideration is typically given to whether students are actually pursuing their individual potential, because this is impossible under our current system and the corresponding paradigms.

In addition, teachers must ensure their classrooms are in compliance with conduct and behavior expectations. Few students are enthusiastic about the instruction they are receiving or the educational activities occurring. Rather, they attend school because it is required. They make the best of school by enjoying the social aspects (their friends must also be there) or finding ways to entertain themselves as best as possible—which includes finding creative ways to make school more interesting.

This means teachers must find ways to attain compliance from a group of students who would, for the most part, rather be elsewhere. Imagine what these teachers could accomplish if the students were deeply engaged by their own volition and the teacher could focus fully on student learning. What if the students really wanted to be engaging with and learning from the teachers?

Most teachers are incredibly dedicated to helping educate children. That they continue in this career field despite the many challenges is a testament to their devotion. And there are thousands of others who would love to be teachers but who opt for other careers because they know they would have to take on many nonteaching burdens in addition to teaching. Some teachers become "burned out" from these extra tasks and are largely just going through the motions.

The current model hamstrings teachers

Nearly everything limiting teachers' ability to devote their time and effort exclusively to their calling—to prepare children for successful futures—is tied to our educational model. It is like taking a recently graduated, MIT-trained engineer and telling her she has to apply her skills in a nineteenth-century factory with nineteenth-century technology—and be responsible for worker morale and performance. While she may be able to do more with that technology than a lesser-trained engineer, she will never be able to work to her potential.

Reinventing our educational system can take into consideration how to best use the skills of our teachers. They would not be teaching as we understand it now. Rather, they would be responsible for facilitating their students' learning instead of just delivering instruction. Many teachers have moved in this direction already, going from being a "sage-on-the-stage" to a "guide-on-the-side." However, teachers must still teach essentially the same content to all the students, so they are unable to unleash their full ability to serve as that learning facilitator.

In the reinvented school, rather than deliver a predetermined curriculum, teachers would be working to ensure students achieve certain learning outcomes, which would vary for individual students. The timeline for achieving those outcomes, as well as the means of achieving and demonstrating them, would also be flexible.

These changes would free teachers to focus their passion, talents, and energy on helping students prepare to be successful now and in the future. It would also allow teachers to help every student pursue his or her full potential. For the sake of both students and teachers, we need to reinvent our educational system with this as an underlying goal.

TEACHER-PREPARATION PROGRAMS

Altering the system would require changes to teacher-preparation programs and would be an incredible opportunity for them to focus on their core purpose. The teacher-preparation programs could eliminate or minimize instruction in classroom management and administration and refocus on helping students learn. These programs could increase instruction on brain development, motivation, and other content underlying the learning process. Where appropriate, they could add to the content knowledge of the program so the graduates are better prepared for students who begin to move beyond the traditional limitations of a given course curriculum—which will end up being nearly all students.

CHAPTER 11

THE COST OF COLLEGE AND STUDENT LOAN DEBT

College costs are only too high if there is an inadequate return on that cost. We need school models that prepare students to do planning and make choices through which they receive the highest possible return on their education and training investment—in other words, to apply critical thinking. If all students approached their future with this mindset, educational institutions would need to adapt their cost structures and operations accordingly. Critically thinking high school graduates could largely alleviate concerns about untenable student debt.

There is a growing cry for middle and high schools to teach financial literacy, largely driven by significant increases in the cost of college and the corresponding increase in student loan debt. Some schools have added personal financial literacy to their curriculum as a course, while others have integrated it into their existing courses.

The intent of these efforts is great, but the outcomes fall short of what is needed and possible. As with any subject taught in a traditional setting, the effectiveness of the learning for any given student is varied and unpredictable. Some students will see the relevance and may retain some of the desired knowledge and skills, but others will forget these lessons immediately after completing an assignment or class.

In theory, college costs, student loans, and the impact of student debt seem relevant to high school students nearing entrance to college. It turns out, however, there are numerous factors at play when students consider taking out student loans, including cultural considerations, the influence of family and friends, and the prevalence of college experience in one's family. In addition, recent research shows that adolescent brains are very poor at distinguishing between high- and low-stake decisions; many students are no more concerned about college expenses and student loan debt than they are about what clothes they should wear on a date (Hamzelou, 2017).

It turns out being knowledgeable about college financing and the risks of debt is not enough; emotions and outside influences can render knowledge and common sense powerless. That is why students must have opportunities to apply related skills throughout all aspects of their lives and education. Effectively managing one's finances is simply applying critical thinking skills to personal economics, and the economic aspects are not really that complicated. However, emotions add to the complexity.

The brain's frontal lobes—the logical thinking part of the brain—is one of the last parts to fully develop. The amygdala—the part of our brain tied to emotions—develops earlier and so has a greater influence on thoughts, decisions, and actions during adolescence (Sweeney, 2009, p. 86) (Feinstein, 2009, pp. 82, 128). Consequently, emotions can overpower logic and effectively render the development of personal financial literacy meaningless during adolescence, which lasts into the midtwenties.

The way to counter this—and to accelerate the development of the frontal cortex—is to place students in situations that require them to analyze and think past their emotions. The more often students practice this critical thinking, the better they will become at doing so. Like a muscle, the more it's exercised, the stronger it grows.

Return on investment of postsecondary education

The cost of college and the challenges of student loan debt have become significant political issues. However, if all children developed strong critical thinking skills and applied them to planning for the future, market forces could address many of these challenges. The proof is in those college students and graduates who have found ways to get the education and training they need without overwhelming debt and without having outside sources of wealth such as families or trust funds.

Compounding the cost and the debt are students who enroll in programs that won't lead to living-wage jobs, programs that are not aligned with the student's interests or strengths, or programs that don't provide value for the student. These choices are almost always made on emotion or through outside pressures and often lead to or exacerbate the cost and student loan issues. Further, colleges and universities target student emotions through marketing campaigns meant to attract the greatest number of applicants. Some even do this with no purpose other than to turn a profit.

Many people with overwhelming student debt say they saw warning signs but felt they had no choices. Many students will slowly work their way into untenable financial situations before they realize how bad things are getting. Lessons in personal financial literacy alone will not overcome these, but well-honed critical thinking skills can.

Applying critical thinking to college costs and loan debt

In a new system of schooling, students would practice and improve their critical thinking skills prior to reaching the age when college costs and debt are a major concern. At some point, they would develop a vision for their future, set goals, and plan for achieving those goals. Key within this process would be considering the fiscal and opportunity costs of various paths the student might take. Students would consider all the factors including variables and unknowns. Through the application of critical thinking, students would do their own research and calculations to lay out a plan for developing needed knowledge and skills and paying for it.

By taking ownership of and being invested in this process, students will develop a plan and prepare for when that plan must somehow be changed or even abandoned. Students who are deeply invested will be able to adapt their plan when the landscape changes, overcome challenges that arise, and leverage opportunities that unexpectedly present themselves.

Reduce need for government interventions

Adopting a school model that fosters critical thinking will reduce the need for government interventions. Rather than Congress and state legislatures imposing laws and rules to help students avoid unnecessary college loan debt or poor decisions, students would seek out the information needed to make good choices. If they can think critically, they will know to avoid options that don't have adequate information and will not be unduly influenced by fancy marketing campaigns.

The cost of college or other means of developing knowledge and skills is only too high if there is not an adequate return on the cost. We need a school model that will ensure every student can make the necessary choices and plans to receive the highest possible return on their education and training investment. This, in turn, will force educational institutions to adapt their cost structures and operations to be more cost-effective—without the government requiring them to do so. Institutions who deliver no or poor training just to make a profit for the owners would be put out of business. Critically thinking high school graduates will make concerns about untenable student debt a thing of the past.

CHAPTER 12

TECHNOLOGY AND INSTANT ACCESS TO NEARLY UNLIMITED INFORMATION

Technology, and the instant access to information it provides, is both a reason that students must have opportunities to practice critical thinking skills and a means of providing that practice. We need a school model that fosters critical thinking through and due to the abundance of information.

According to a September 30, 2015, article on the Forbes website, more data had been created in the previous two years than in the previous history of the human race (Marr, 2018). The amount of data that exists in information systems around the world and the data shared among people and systems is now discussed in exabytes (one billion gigabytes) and zettabytes (one trillion gigabytes). According to YouTube, one billion hours of videos are watched every day (YouTube, 2018).

There is an inconceivable amount of information available to most American citizens pretty much instantly. Unfortunately, this doesn't seem to mean much for schools in terms of making more effective use of available time for student engagement.

Many schools and teachers make use of the internet to supplement lessons, and some have moved away from traditional textbooks in favor of web-based materials. Some teachers try to leverage web-based information to tap into things they hope will make lessons more engaging for students. They are, however, missing opportunities to use this access to personalize instruction for each student or to challenge students to think and drive their own learning.

Once again, to their credit, our students demonstrate their patience and ability to comply by agreeing to learn facts and figures while knowing that finding the capital of Vermont is only ever an Alexa, Google, or Siri request away. While there is value in having certain knowledge committed to memory, which knowledge deserves memorization is highly debatable. Further, the vast majority of people will not retain most of the facts and figures they learn while in school. Rather, they will retain those that have personal meaning or have some ongoing value. As quoted in Philipp Frank's biography, Albert Einstein said, "The value of an education . . . is not the learning of many facts but the training of the mind to think something that cannot be learned from textbooks."

History as more than dates and places

As noted in the prologue, even the Committee of Ten conference on history, civil government, and political economy didn't believe memorizing facts was the chief object of historical study. Rather, they said it was, "the training of the judgment, in selecting the grounds of an opinion, in accumulating materials for an opinion, in putting things together, in generalizing upon facts, in estimating character, in applying the lessons of history to current events, and in accustoming children to state their conclusions in their own words" (National Education Association, 2017, p. 170). The other conferences made similar points about developing valuable skills rather than just being taught information.

In effect, they wanted students to learn how to think critically using lessons from history. Doing this, however, requires personalizing the activities. As noted previously, these skills cannot simply be taught; they must be applied to situations that are meaningful while a trusted adult guides the student through probing questions and various prompts.

Discernment and analysis of information sources

One of the tertiary skills that students must develop is discernment, specifically in the area of information access. Students must learn to analyze sources of information to determine whether they can be trusted to be accurate, objective, and factual. This is a form of critical thinking, and, once again, it is not enough to teach students what a trustworthy website looks like or some checklist for validating information—the Internet and all its sites change too rapidly. Students need to learn and practice the concepts and processes they can use to validate information they access.

Fortunately, the same information access that requires students to develop these skills can be a tool for doing so and personalizing it for each student. Every student is unique, so they do not share universal interests. While we may develop a lesson that will engage many students, it is unlikely we will find something that engages all students, and certainly not one that will engage them all deeply and meaningfully.

Appropriate use of technology

Beyond leveraging available information to personalize educational experiences and make them more effective, we must ensure students develop skills in assessing and using technology appropriately and safely. As with Internet access, students can't simply be taught what constitutes appropriate and safe use of technology or rely on some sort of checklist. Students must understand the principles that determine what is appropriate, and these are not absolute. They must have opportunities to consider these principles, discuss them, and even debate them. Otherwise, students will adhere to dictated rules and principles when necessary and then ignore them when no one is looking.

In addition, when we restrict student access to technology (such as their personal devices) and the wealth of available information, we are being hypocritical. Students know the technology and information are there and readily accessible, and they know schools are supposed to prepare them to live in the world of the twenty-first century. Yet the schools don't trust the students to use technology responsibly. The schools say they want the students to be responsible and that they respect and trust the students, but then they set up rules and consequences to force them to comply or establish filters and walls that limit what the students can access.

Most students determine that, as with other rules and restrictions put in place by schools, the easiest option is to comply. This, of course, contributes to points made in previous chapters about the ways our schools create a compliant generation of adults and the downsides of doing so.

Further, when technology use and information access are limited in school, students will instead access the technology mostly in unsupervised, less restricted settings with no one present to serve as a guide. This is why students must have opportunities to practice critical thinking skills. Students need access to technology and information so they can practice critical thinking under the guiding hand of a trusted teacher and mentor.

As with personal financial literacy, many schools add lessons on using the internet with a focus on safety and differentiating objective, fact-based information from biased and false information; but also as with financial literacy, teaching this has a limited effect. For it to be learned and retained, this critical thinking must be practiced in ways that are meaningful to the students, which requires unique learning opportunities for each student. Consequently, use of technology and the Internet can become both a means and an end for helping students to develop critical thinking skills.

CHAPTER 13

HOW PEOPLE LEARN AND ARE MOTIVATED

We need to redesign schools so students will enthusiastically pursue knowledge and skills for their own intrinsic reasons. That means applying known research and understanding about motivation as well as research and knowledge on brain development and learning.

Carrots and sticks. This pretty well sums up how most people seem to view motivation. It's also how too many institutions and organizations approach motivating people. In addition, most of us were raised within a structure of rewards and punishments and use them in raising our kids. Parents offer rewards for certain behaviors and accomplishments while threatening punishments for unwanted behaviors and failing to meet certain expectations.

Our justice system is built on threats of punishment for breaking the law. Employers offer bonuses or raises for performance that exceeds expectations or for meeting certain goals or measures while threatening to dock pay, withhold bonuses, or fire someone for failing to meet expectations, goals, or measures. Health insurance companies, seeing we aren't sufficiently motivated by better health and longevity to adopt healthy lifestyles, offer rewards—including cash—for participating in activities that will contribute to our good health.

In every conceivable setting, parents use the carrot and the stick to motivate children—prizes, ice cream, and new video games or grounding, extra chores, and docked allowances. Schools are no different. Nearly everything that occurs in schools is based on rewards and punishments. There are extensive codes of conduct ruling nearly every aspect of school with corresponding sets of consequences. There are honors for students who perform well academically and who exhibit especially good behavior. And there are grades hanging over students' heads that will serve as reward, punishment, or both for demonstrations of student performance.

Compliance gained at the cost of learning

All these and more are used under the guise of motivating students to be engaged in a school's instructional practices. And they are very effective at gaining compliance. Unfortunately, rather than contribute to student learning, they detract from it.

When the factory model of school was adopted, there was little understanding about effective learning or motivation. Since that time, immense research has been done on how learning occurs, how the brain develops, and what actually motivates people. The research is clear: rewards and punishments are only effective at controlling behavior, not at prompting learning beyond what is necessary to execute some desired behavior.

We are under the illusion that rewards and punishments motivate learning because we see the evidence in our students. The reality is very different. Think about your own experiences, whether in school or in some other setting. Consider what motivated you to learn. If it was your own curiosity or desire to know something for personal, intrinsic reasons, you were probably enthusiastic about seeking sources of information, teaching, and guidance. You may have sought to learn more than you originally intended, branched out on your learning to new things you discovered during your search, and been able to build upon what you learned.

On the other hand, if you were seeking knowledge or skills to earn a reward or avoid a consequence, you may have learned what you needed, but you were probably not enthusiastic about it. You likely learned only as much as needed to fulfill the expectation, and—unless you were applying the learning with some regularity—you probably didn't retain the learning or seek ways to build upon it.

I want to be clear: some learning and other benefits can occur through the use of rewards and punishments. Some learning can occur through drilling and other memorization methods, and some students can learn very effectively this way. Further, using rewards and punishments may get students to explore things they would not have otherwise. Yet such benefits and learning could be designed into a new model without all the collateral damage.

Rewards and punishments diminish learning

Probably the most devastating consequence of using rewards and punishments to "motivate" learning is that it actually diminishes innate curiosity. Desire to learn is a critical survival tool, but children lose their inborn curiosity when they lose control over their learning. Curiosity is further diminished when students are punished for being distracted or breaking a rule due to being curious about something. They figure out that they should only strive to learn within the structure and direction provided by the teachers.

In his book *Drive*, Daniel Pink taps into research showing what actually does motivate people. There is significant research that people are best motivated not by rewards or punishments but by providing them with autonomy, giving them challenges over which they are capable of mastery, and giving them the opportunity to be part of a bigger purpose beyond themselves (Pink, 2009).

Beyond identifying these elements of motivation, Pink notes the unintended and frightening consequence of trying to motivate people through the use of rewards. The research shows that children's innate interest or enjoyment in a subject or activity will diminish when they are rewarded for it.

In one study, children who enjoyed drawing pictures were left alone in a room. They drew, without being prompted, for their own enjoyment.

Researchers then rewarded some of the children for the drawings they had done. After receiving rewards, those same children would no longer draw for their own enjoyment but instead would only draw when offered a reward. In other words, students who enter formal education with interests, curiosity, and a longing to learn may see all these diminish once they start to be rewarded for them with grades, gold stars, or praise. (Pink, 2009)

The bad news goes further. Other research demonstrates that people promised a reward have diminished creativity and problem-solving abilities. The promise of a reward actually reduced the ability of individuals and groups of people to solve a given problem or come up with creative products or solutions. This is in addition to the ways learning is inhibited by stress as noted by Stixrud and Johnson and discussed in chapter 4 (Johnson, 2018).

Rewards and punishments for algorithmic tasks

The one place Pink found value in rewards and threats of punishment was performance of what he calls "algorithmic" tasks. These are repetitive tasks that can be broken down into repeatable steps. Our schools do a good job preparing workers for jobs with such tasks, which don't require high-level thinking skills, creativity, problem-solving, or much mental effort. They also tend to be boring and undesirable to most people and are the tasks most readily automated. These were common in many well-paid jobs during much of the twentieth century, but many such jobs no longer pay a decent wage (Pink, 2009).

Our society has become good at learning that which is done to meet others' expectations and for which we will receive a reward or avoid a punishment. Those who are unhappy in their jobs yet perform them well have learned what they need to get their paycheck, but they are not usually enthusiastic about learning more than necessary. Instead, people unhappy in their jobs look for things that are personally meaningful and interesting elsewhere. Sometimes, people can turn their personal interests and passions into a job they will pursue with vigor—including learning and applying all they can. That is really how this book came to be.

We must redesign our schools so students will enthusiastically pursue knowledge and skills for their own intrinsic reasons. That means applying Pink's lessons about motivation as well as research and knowledge on brain development and learning. Many great books that should inform educational design (such as *Drive*) were not written for schools and educators because they would be of little value in our current structure. Their insights and recommendations—often directed toward business leaders—require organizational flexibility, dynamic structures, and viewing people as individuals rather than cohorts. Our current school model does not reflect such an organization.

The research and data we have were not available to the Committee of Ten. They didn't know that children would have their innate sense of curiosity and an inherent need to learn diminished through forced instruction in settings that are anathema to effective learning. Today we have such research and data. The question is whether we have the courage to change our educational system to leverage it and move every student toward his or her personal potential.

CHAPTER 14

COLLABORATION BETWEEN FAMILIES AND SCHOOLS

A new educational system and model of schools could be designed to tap the immense potential of students' families. Such a model would have parents deeply invested in their children's school and provide a wealth of new resources for personalizing the educational experiences for all students.

Although some districts and schools are striving to increase parent and family engagement—with some even dedicating staff to this—the current system makes it nearly impossible for parents and families to play any truly meaningful role in a student's school-related learning. Like students, families are unique. Meaningful engagement, therefore, needs to be personalized for each student and family. Doing this in a system that relies on structure and sameness would be disruptive in most current schools.

Instead, schools involve parents and families in ways that are generally controlled and predictable, outside the school day and outside the classroom (at least while instruction is being delivered). Schools often measure success through surveys of parents or attendance at parent-teacher conferences, but such measures don't reflect real collaboration or contributions to student learning.

This is unfortunate because there is incredible potential in engaging families. Collaborative parent and family engagement in the learning process—where parents are committed and invested in that process—would bring validity to the school's instructional activities and the value of each student's learning objectives. The parents, student, and school could collaborate in determining what the student should be learning and why, which would make all three full partners in guiding and mentoring the student toward meeting the learning objectives. The current model designates what will be learned and when, removing both the student and parents from this process.

Most parents would jump at the opportunity to substantially improve the learning, growth, and development of their child. However, they've been convinced it's not their role and that they don't have the necessary expertise, so they are content with a peripheral role in school.

Of course, many parents also face logistical challenges to being part of their child's education. Jobs, health, other children, relatives, and numerous other situations may severely limit a parent's availability. This exposes another shortcoming of our current school model: the inflexible schedule limits the times parents can be involved in school activities. A new model could account for these situations to ensure every parent has the best possible opportunities to be involved. A new model could also account for nonparent caregivers and students in unique situations without readily available caregivers.

A lost wealth of resources

The current school model is also unable to tap the wealth of resources families could bring. Collectively, parents and other family members have an incredible breadth and depth of experiences and expertise. They have knowledge, skills, and wisdom that would contribute in untold ways to the growth and development of students in a school, but they are kept at a distance because they are not educators. This is like knowing how much information is available on the Internet but not having a search engine or map for accessing it. It exists but has little value except when you accidentally stumble across something worthwhile.

Under the current model, the typical approach to tapping the knowledge, skills, and experience of parents is sending them a letter or e-mail asking for volunteers at school; occasionally they'll ask for specific skills or experience, but mostly they are seeking chaperones and people to make treats and perform other tasks that really only require time.

A new educational model could factor in this untapped resource by creating a network that connects the expertise or experiences of family members with those for whom it would have value. Whereas parents should collaborate in the overall learning for their children, they could also channel more specialized knowledge, skills, and experiences to select students who could benefit.

This is also a cost-effective means of personalizing student learning. Currently, we limit what is taught in school in an effort to be efficient. One argument against personalized learning is that schools can't afford to teach every student a different curriculum. That's true. However, teaching students is the old factory model. The new model, which would be built on student learning, could allow students to acquire their learning in nearly any possible way, and that could include being connected with a member of another student's family who has relevant knowledge, skills, and experiences.

Part 2 of this book explores in greater depth what this parent collaboration—both with their own children for overall learning and with other children for specialized learning—might look like and illustrates why it is completely possible in any community.

CHAPTER 15

A DOZEN MORE REASONS

This chapter provides twelve additional reasons the factory model of school needs to be replaced by a model and structure designed in and for the twenty-first century. The explanations are shorter and not explored as deeply, so they don't justify full chapters, but each is compelling and contributes to the overall rationale.

Gender Equity

The importance of gender equity could justify its own chapter, but the explanation is straightforward and pretty brief.

Nearly all other reasons the factory model needs to be replaced contribute to or perpetuate gender inequity. Such inequity was the societal norm in 1893 when the current model was created. Consequently, it is inherent in the design and nearly impossible to address without implementing a new model that specifically ensures equity for all students—which can only occur through a model that respects the unique aspects of each student.

The compliance-centric nature of the current model perpetuates biases and inequity, many of which are based on gender and other traits. Further, the elements that inhibit critical and creative thinking and that discourage students from challenging norms, paradigms, and authority also discourage students from challenging the causes of gender inequity.

There are ongoing efforts to instill female students with a greater sense of self-worth and self-advocacy so they will graduate with the knowledge, skills, and—most importantly in this context—the disposition to become leaders in business, government, and communities. Yet the compliance-centric model and the lack of integrity this model forces upon students has severely limited achieving these goals. A community designing a new model of schools with the specific purpose of moving every child toward her or his potential would, by default, address gender equity—as long as the design and implementation were done with integrity.

The disproportionate impact of the factory system of schooling on female students alone would be sufficient to consider redesigning our schools. Every citizen—and therefore every high school graduate—should be able to help address challenges and advance our culture and technology. All should contribute in ways and to the extent of which they are able. We need to redesign our educational model to ensure all students—of any gender—are able to approach their potential in school and beyond.

Social-emotional learning and developing resiliency

School leaders are increasingly emphasizing social-emotional learning (SEL). These are skills associated with understanding and dealing with emotions, being empathetic, being patient, working with others, and setting and pursuing goals. Such skills allow people to deal with new situations and work through trauma and other challenges.

For over a decade, the US Army has been training units and individual soldiers in resiliency in an attempt to counter challenges such as post-traumatic stress disorder (PTSD), depression, and suicide. Resilient traits and using various resiliency skills allow people to be happier, more content, and better able to survive traumatic events as well as avoid their disabling long-term effects. Essentially, social-emotional learning is a means to developing resiliency.

While we hope students will not be subjected to traumatic events, we know many will be. Groups of students may face traumatic events such as school shootings or natural disasters, while individual students may face traumatic events such as a family member's death, severe illness, injury, abuse, assault, or homelessness. Such events can lead to the same outcomes as those faced by soldiers. Consequently, if students can develop and strengthen resiliency through their school experiences, they will be better prepared when faced with traumatic events.

A key element of resiliency is mental flexibility—being able to deal with results that are counter to our expectations or that challenge our core beliefs and values. Stress is created when reality doesn't match expectations. When that stress reaches a critical level, it can manifest itself in debilitating ways, including PTSD, depression, and suicidal thoughts.

The current school structure purposely limits opportunities for students to use mental flexibility by limiting choices and standardizing nearly everything. Consequently, it is a challenge to foster actual social-emotional learning. Instead, students are often subjected to contrived situations to practice SEL-related skills, which does not lead to deep adoption of these skills. Further, infusing mindfulness and whole-child education (or other SEL skills) in the current model often requires removing or reducing something else.

By replacing our current structure, we can provide real opportunities for social-emotional learning. We can design the model so that most or all educational activities contribute to developing mental flexibility and mindfulness. This, in turn, will contribute to improved responses when faced with traumatic events along with other important benefits as noted throughout other chapters.

Intellectual and emotional well-being of future generations

All humans are born vulnerable. We leave the womb incapable of surviving on our own and depend on others to protect us and provide us with all we need to survive until we are self-sufficient. Yet even as we become able to perform all the physical tasks necessary to survive, we remain vulnerable until we develop the ability to fend off threats to our intellectual and emotional well-being.

In many parts of the world—and for too many people in our country—threats to the basic human needs of food, shelter, clothing, and general safety are the greatest concern. However, for most Americans, the biggest threats fall higher on Maslow's hierarchy. We remain vulnerable to threats to our self-worth, independence, and potential—which can restrict our ability to meet the more basic needs.

Unfortunately, there are people who strive to influence and intimidate those who are vulnerable. This may be for self-serving purposes or because they have been mentally and emotionally abused themselves. They may mistakenly believe their only salvation will come through making others suffer as they have. Essentially, they are bullies.

The best defenses against mental and emotional threats are thoughtfulness and resilience. Like any strength and skill, these can only be developed through meaningful practice. One cannot become fit and healthy just by reading about fitness and health, nor can one build and strengthen thoughtfulness and resilience this way. All require applying related knowledge and skills regularly and in meaningful ways. While teaching and simulations may raise awareness, they will not lead to real skill development and certainly not mastery.

Many children have opportunities to learn and practice these skills, but they don't come through academic school activities. Rather, they come through sports, extracurriculars, and their families and communities. Schools cannot provide these opportunities until they provide meaningful power and authority to their students. That is, they must have students take charge of their own learning and development.

Fostering institutional adaptability and resilience

Like individuals, institutions and organizations need mental flexibility to be resilient. When a natural disaster, such as large-scale flooding or a tornado, makes a school building unusable or shuts down an entire community's educational system, there is usually a scramble to figure out how the students will be able to attend school.

Most schools rely on the structure of a building and the school model to deliver instruction and struggle when these structures are not available. However, many schools discover that fostering student learning outside the usual limiting structures can be liberating. They may be surprised—though they shouldn't be—at how well students can adapt when forced into these unexpected situations. Imagine what they could do if their educational model actually prepared them to thrive when confronted with sudden change.

The current school model is designed to limit surprises and typically becomes dysfunctional when the structure is removed. By discarding the factory model of schools, it's possible to design an educational system that is fully adaptable to any changes, whether those changes are planned or unplanned. In fact, the system can be designed to use such changes to enhance student learning rather than being hindered by them.

Fostering cooperation, collaboration, and respect for differing ideas and beliefs

It seems that if ever there were a time our society needed the ability to cooperate, collaborate, and respect different ideas and beliefs, it's now. We are technologically advanced and have the highest standard of living in history, yet countless challenges continue to afflict our country and world. What could we accomplish and how many challenges could we vanquish if we were better at these skills?

Parents, teachers, employers, and broader society all seem to agree that helping students develop skills in cooperation and collaboration is extremely important. Most also support developing respect for different ideas and beliefs. Toward that end, almost all schools include these in their goals for students, and many include them somewhere in their curriculum. As with most skills discussed in this book, these can't be taught, and our current school model does not allow the experiences necessary for them to be developed. For students to truly develop, strengthen, and build an appreciation for these skills and their related attributes, they must have ongoing opportunities to apply them in ways that are personally meaningful and through which the outcomes are of significant, personal value.

We need a school model through which students (not teachers) create teams based on shared learning goals and purposes, combined with common or synergistic interests. The students would practice effective communication, teamwork, cooperation, collaboration, and responsibility with immediate, relevant, and natural consequences around something of intrinsic value to the students. This could be a regular, ongoing element of the school model so that these attributes become deeply ingrained and practiced.

In addition to learning and practicing cooperation and collaboration, students would learn the value of diversity on their teams—not just racial or ethnic diversity but diversity of all sorts. When the outcomes of their efforts are personally important, students will develop a real appreciation for the value of different perspectives, experiences, opinions, and beliefs. Only in personally meaningful forums will students come to understand how such differences foster growth and progress. They will also, then, discover the shortcomings of relying on their own self-supporting ideas and opinions and how it limits their ability to grow and improve.

Teacher shortages and attrition

Due to fewer people choosing to become teachers and the career's high rate of attrition, there is a growing shortage of well-qualified educators. Numerous reasons have been cited for this (Sutcher, Darling-Hammond, & and Carver-Thomas, 2018), but I would argue that a principal element underlying many of these factors is what it means to be a teacher in our current school model.

Within our current educational model, being a teacher almost always requires adherence to a set schedule and calendar and a prescribed methodology for delivering instruction. Teachers are typically required to use an approved curriculum for all classes, and their classes may be cancelled if they don't achieve a minimum enrollment. The level of student commitment to any of a teacher's courses or school in general will vary greatly. The working conditions in some schools can be extremely challenging. And teachers spend a significant portion of their day doing things other than teaching.

Such a situation is not very attractive to potential teachers even before considering pay and benefits. Those willing to jump into such positions are likely dedicated and doing so for reasons beyond pay; they often see being a teacher as a calling more than just a career choice. However, if the pay and benefits are not sufficient, many potentially high-quality teachers will opt for alternative careers that offer flexibility, provide a better work environment along with better pay and benefits, and fulfill the three elements that fuel human motivation as discussed in chapter 13.

As noted in that chapter, to be motivated and do their best creative work, people need autonomy, the opportunity to master challenging skills, and the opportunity to be part of a bigger purpose. On their surface, schools offer these things, but digging deeper we find that the current structure places severe limits on all of them—especially for the most creative and driven teachers. We need a school structure that actually leverages these elements so they contribute to increasing student opportunities.

Such a system could provide flexibility that allows teachers to foster student learning. Rather than being limited to teaching between eight o'clock and four o'clock, teachers may be able to flex their schedule or offer their expertise in an on-demand model as they pursue other endeavors that will improve their expertise. Rather than requiring teachers to base classes on an approved curriculum, they would constantly be challenged to assist students in achieving individual learning goals through means that are most effective for each student. Rather than focus on "classroom management" and student compliance, teachers could focus their entire effort on facilitating student learning.

The result would be "teaching" positions (that title may need to change due to the implications it holds) that are exceptionally rewarding beyond pay and benefits. The best and brightest would be clamoring to fill these positions the way many now want to work for cutting-edge companies. Many entrepreneurs—especially those creating socially conscious products and businesses—would see the field of education as enticing.

There are plenty of people who would love a job that contributes to a better society by preparing future generations, but many are put off by the current environment and culture of schools. Changing that culture so that students are excited about and committed to being there will create an environment that attracts highly skilled teachers who will stick around for the long term.

Accommodating diverse family situations

The current school structure—in particular the annual, weekly, and daily schedule—is a relatively good fit for families on a schedule that was the norm in the '50s through '80s—that is, where the parents work Monday through Friday, eight o'clock to four o'clock, and can figure out childcare during the summer. Parents who don't work such schedules have always needed to make adjustments to deal with childcare, parent-teacher conferences, school events, a sick child, or any number of other school-related activities.

Many schools try to accommodate parents and families with extraordinary circumstances, but our current structure means such families will almost always be less connected to the schools. That has an impact on their children's school performance. Even families who fit a more traditional schedule may have to compromise when planning vacations and other activities that would take students out of school.

A new model could provide flexibility that benefits all families, including those with limited transportation options, families of military members who may be deployed for extended periods, families that are transient and frequently move within or between school districts, parents facing significant health problems that limit their mobility or ability to attend public events, or any number of other situations. This would also benefit families who are faced with emergencies and unforeseen circumstances that would, under the current model, create numerous challenges and typically compromise a student's learning.

Such a model would also be attractive to a broad range of potential teachers and be better able to leverage volunteers, engagement of parents and other family members, and learning opportunities that are outside the classroom and school building. Designing a school model that accommodates families would accommodate numerous situations that could improve student learning.

Countering societal challenges

Despite incredible advancements in science and technology, our world remains flush with challenges such as poverty, death in vehicle accidents, shooting deaths, violent crime, drug-related crimes and deaths, costly health care, heart disease, cancer, and general divisiveness. I believe a primary reason for the continuation of these tragedies is that we are collectively stuck in a paradigm of limited ways to address most of them. When other options arise, they often cause controversy due to partisanship or misinformation or because they seem to threaten some aspect of our lives.

I am a true believer in humanity and our ability to come up with solutions that can satisfy everyone's actual concerns and fears. This, however, requires looking beyond our strongest biases and being open to thoughtful conversations with others, including those with whom we regularly disagree or even have open disputes. It also means, eventually, being able to trust these same people.

Unfortunately, the current school structure actually models this very challenge. The message to students, parents, and everyone else is that there is one way to do school—one model and structure. This structure requires that all students adhere to the norms and requirements of the school. When someone proposes a different approach, it is often rejected and turns into a contentious issue within a community.

As noted elsewhere, the current structure also fuels the divisiveness that stops us from having thoughtful, productive conversations about these challenges. Concurrently, the almost universal acceptance of this structure reinforces the acceptance of existing paradigms, processes, and expectations while discouraging changing paradigms, innovation, and higher societal expectations.

Instead, we could design a school model based on current research and created through an innovative, collaborative process that uses practices similar to those used in creating cutting-edge organizations. That model could be a learning organization that models flexibility, adaptation, innovation, and risk-taking for its students, staff, and the community. Such a model could ensure students learn and practice the skills that would allow them to flourish in a dynamic, uncertain world. These students would be better prepared to confront new, challenging situations they encounter and to address numerous societal challenges, both as individuals and working collaboratively.

> ## ONE SOCIETAL CHALLENGE: THE OPIOID EPIDEMIC
>
> Consider how a compliance-centric nature might be contributing to our nationwide opioid epidemic. A primary source of this epidemic is patients becoming addicted after being legitimately prescribed painkillers by their doctors for an injury or illness. Many patients misunderstand the risks and alternatives and don't question their physicians, due to a learned deference to those in authority or a lack of confidence.
>
> Some doctors fail to volunteer information about how using such narcotics could lead to dependence on the drug or other opiates, even when asked about side effects. Patients may be unaware that some doctors receive incentives from companies supplying the drugs being prescribed.
>
> Numerous efforts are underway at the local, state, and federal levels to find legislative solutions to address the opioid epidemic. I would argue the long-term solution is to ensure our students learn to think critically, advocate for themselves, and know that there are times it is expected they will question and even challenge authorities. Then, when a doctor recommends a narcotic painkiller, patients will be able to ensure they are fully informed before making any decision.

Increasing and decreasing student enrollments

Districts and schools that have dynamic student enrollment numbers face numerous challenges that are primarily a result of the current school model. Funding sources and formulas are often tied to student enrollment, so when student enrollments decrease, districts may face a funding crisis. However, the costs to the school and district usually don't decrease proportionally. The decreased enrollment is typically spread across several grades and schools, making it difficult to reduce staffing. Consequently, staff costs remain fairly steady while funding drops. The operational costs of the schools don't drop proportionally either, so the gap between costs and funding grows as well.

When student enrollments climb quickly, adequate space must be found that is conducive to instructional activities, and funding needs to be procured for this space and associated costs. Funding sources and formulas may or may not adequately offset these costs, and rarely do existing funding sources cover construction costs. Thus, the districts must often pass a community referendum to build additional facilities. Schools either need to increase class sizes or hire more staff, although they may be unable to find enough teachers to maintain a reasonable student-to-teacher ratio.

The worst situations occur in districts that see a substantial enrollment increase requiring new construction but then see a later enrollment decrease, leaving them with new construction and other costs while facing decreased funding. Similarly, districts may act and budget based on enrollment projections, only to find the projections don't pan out.

Our current educational model leaves very few options for districts facing changing enrollments, and nearly all the options compromise student learning. A new model of education could be designed to account for this volatility without compromising learning. In fact, it might be designed to leverage the volatility in ways that contribute to opportunities for learning. The model could also be designed to reduce or eliminate the cost challenges that typically arise from volatile enrollment numbers.

Creating a true sense of community for all students

Our current educational model is an obstacle to developing a true sense of community among students and staff. For a true sense of community, there must be mutual respect and real trust among the community members. This develops through shared experiences—in particular, experiences that are meaningful, sometimes emotional, and occasionally traumatic—and in an atmosphere of integrity. Although many schools develop such a sense of community, there are almost always some students who end up being excluded.

A primary obstacle to building community stems from our ongoing efforts to improve learning within an outdated system. As educators, we constantly try to convince students (and ourselves) that everything we're doing is necessary and important. We continue to operate in a model that most people, on reflection, would recognize is out-of-date and ineffective. And students can see through all of this.

We implement activities and events meant to build community and strengthen relationships because we know they are important. However, to have integrity, our efforts need to honor student individuality and trust them by ceding power to them. The current school structure simply cannot accommodate this. The students see through it and, rather than creating community, the school's integrity is diminished. While many students recognize the good intentions of the school and staff, they also sense how the school structure is not conducive to community or learning and wonder why this isn't addressed.

Of course, the current model itself creates challenges to meaningful relationships and a sense of community. With its rigid structure and organization, it's difficult to get to know students and allow them to get to know us. At the middle and high school level, this becomes even more challenging, as students in most schools move from classroom to classroom several times each day and change classes each semester or year (sometimes even quarter).

Recognizing this, many schools implement homerooms or advisors to provide opportunities for relationships and community to be built. However, in many cases, this is actually counterproductive because the efforts lack integrity. Students are assigned to a teacher or group rather than selecting one with whom they might better connect. Some students will end up with an advisor or homeroom teacher who is just not up to building relationships and creating a sense of community. Activities are often directed and contrived with no opportunities for organic relationships to bloom and trust to build. No matter how genuine the intention, some students will be worse off from this experience.

It's not for lack of care or effort that schools lack a sense of community or that some students feel disconnected. A new model of school could be designed to foster true community and real trust and do so with integrity.

> ### COMMUNITIES EASE TRANSITIONS— TO AND BETWEEN SCHOOLS
>
> One of the biggest challenges families face is the start of formal schooling. Deciding when a child should begin kindergarten can be overwhelming for some parents, and there is no absolute means of determining the correct age. The change to an entirely new environment—whether from a preschool or in-home care situation—can be traumatic. Later transitions, from elementary to middle and then to high school, can also be challenging and can inhibit learning—especially in larger districts where multiple schools feed into the next level school.
>
> A sense of community among students, staff, and others can significantly ease such transitions. In small districts, where all students know each other and move from grade to grade and school to school together, the transitions are much easier. The size of these districts facilitates a greater sense of community. This can be done in even the largest districts, if the school model is designed to do so. In addition, a new school design can take transitions into account and make them significantly less challenging. Transitions could be part of a process that enhances learning rather than inhibiting it.

Economic vitality and the "skills shortage"

Our country's economic stability and vitality depend largely on having the necessary workforce. We need sufficient workers with the necessary skills and who are willing to work for the offered wages and benefits to fill the available jobs. As businesses grow and need new workers and as entire new industries emerge, workers who have or can develop the necessary skills will be needed. Those workers then become consumers, continuously feeding money into the economy.

Anyone paying attention over the past few years has heard the term "skills gap" or "skills shortage." Even at the height of the recession, when unemployment was high and jobs were in short supply, there were numerous stories about tens of thousands of available jobs for which there weren't people with the necessary skills. This is not, however, a recent problem. This claim and similar terms have been around for decades. There have been reports, task forces, and recommendations created over the years aimed at closing the "skills gap," apparently without much effect.

The current school model and the paradigm about what students should do after high school graduation are primary reasons for this situation. While we expect those who advise students to have their best interests in mind, they are too often trapped by old paradigms about college and careers. Concurrently, those marketing their colleges and programs are often self-serving, as are those industries marketing their career opportunities.

This is another reason students must develop critical thinking skills—so they can see through the hype and marketing and get to the facts. While knowledge of personal financial literacy and labor market information will be crucial to informed choices about employment and careers, it is skills in critical thinking and information analysis that give this knowledge value. Further, students need self-assurance and adaptability. With the rapidly changing job market and economy, students must have the ability and confidence to prepare for and pursue new opportunities.

These skills must be a focus of the new model of education that will replace our current factory model. In addition to developing graduates who are able to leverage skills gaps and adapt to changing job markets and opportunities, these skills will help address another looming challenge—the general shortage of working-age adults.

A low birth rate in the US means we are not creating enough new workers to replace those who are aging out of the workforce, let alone to fill the new jobs being created. Since it is unlikely the birth rate is going to increase, future generations must understand this challenge and its implications and then work collectively to adapt our society. Being part of the solutions to this challenge—or being able to objectively support electoral candidates who will help develop solutions to this challenge—will require critical thinking and analysis skills and the ability to adapt. We need to create schools that can turn out such graduates in order to ensure our future economic vitality.

Strong, effective national security and defense

As a senior military officer, I regularly encounter service members that reflect the shortcomings of our educational system. Chief among these is a struggle or inability to think critically. Some may think the military is an inflexible hierarchy that values compliance and discourages critical thinking. The exact opposite is true. Today's military missions require service members at all levels who can think critically. They must also be intrinsically motivated and have the confidence to express ideas and opinions that could improve our operations and avoid disasters.

The military needs service members who follow orders because their own critical thinking and their experiences with a given leader provide confidence the orders are necessary and right, not service members who follow blindly out of fear of the leader. Military history is filled with examples where blindly following orders has led to disasters. We also need military leaders who inspire this sort of confidence.

Of course, the vast majority of our service members went through the same educational system as everyone else, a system that, for twelve to sixteen years of their lives, rewarded compliance. Consequently, service members of all ranks and positions often fail to think critically, and they readily fall into mind traps. Even worse, our military as an institution has its own serious structural and operations challenges due to an inability to consider large-scale reinvention that could make it much more efficient and effective. The military tries to develop these skills in service members, but it battles institutionalism and inertia similar to what is found in public education.

For strong national security, the general population also must be able to think critically and be willing to challenge things when they don't seem right. Our entire population must be able to discern accurate, objective information from opinions, biased data, and outright lies when they may impact our lives. This is especially true for things that affect national security, such as choosing whom to vote for, what legislation to support, where to spend our money, and balancing liberty with security. We must be able to recognize when someone is trying to manipulate us, especially when this might be foreign governments, criminals, or terrorist organizations.

Nearly every reason stated in this book is relevant to ensuring future generations are able to contribute to our nation's defense and to national security, whether as citizens or as members of the military.

PART 2

WHAT MIGHT THE REINVENTED SYSTEM LOOK LIKE?

PART 2

WHAT MIGHT THE REINVENTED SYSTEM LOOK LIKE?

"The reasonable man adapts himself to the world: the unreasonable one persists in trying to adapt the world to himself. Therefore, all progress depends on the unreasonable man."

—*George Bernard Shaw*

Put your critical thinking caps on; this is going to be a bumpy ride. I expect you will find this section challenging but also appealing. You will, hopefully, think the ideas explored here sound wonderful and the community described would be a place you'd want to raise your children. But you will also probably think it's simply not possible. This section will push against your experiences and your ideas of what school is—ideas that have been formed and solidified for multiple generations.

It's difficult to imagine an educational system that is nothing like the one we have used since the nineteenth century. Each element of a new system will seem impossible if you frame and filter them through paradigms of that 126-year-old model. This section of the book is designed to create an image of what an educational system could look like if it had been allowed to evolve and change like so many other aspects of our society.

At the same time, this section is not meant to dictate what a reinvented educational system should look like. The contention of this book, as noted more substantially in parts 3 and 4, is that the educational system at the local level will look different in every community. That is both the biggest benefit and the greatest challenge of everything spelled out in these pages.

We have come to accept that uniformity is necessary for cost-effectiveness, equity, and continuity. We have become convinced that schools must be very similar to ensure we deliver the same basic instruction and offer the same opportunities to all students. Without uniformity, we believe, equity will break down as those with greater resources and more influence improve the opportunities in their schools and those with fewer resources and less influence languish. This is a legitimate concern that must be considered (and is addressed in parts 3 and 4 of the book), but it is also a huge obstacle to moving our schools toward what should be their true purpose—ensuring every student can approach his or her full potential.

This section of the book will allow you to imagine what is possible and develop a mind-model of what could be. It will allow you to contrast the possible with the current model. Then, when reading the last three sections of the book, you will be able to consider the "what's possible" model as an alternative when encountering ideas that sound promising but impossible.

This section of the book will imagine a community that has implemented an educational system intended to ensure all children in the community are able to strive toward their potential. The example will be built around a midsize community that, in our current model, would have one elementary school, one middle school, and one high school. Chapter 17 explains how this might translate into other sorts of communities, such as those that are different sizes or more diverse.

This section was very challenging to write. Despite my advocacy for the ideas in this book and the evolution of my own thoughts and ideas, I have similar experiences and biases as the rest of our society. Like most educators, I have spent my entire life immersed in the current model and structure. So, as I work to imagine and narrate a model that would not be beholden to anything that came before, I catch myself falling back to paradigms and biases of that old model. That's why I know how difficult it will be for most others to believe we can change in the ways this book insists we must.

Don't hold in your doubts and disbelief; express them to anyone who will listen. But always try to leave at least a glimmer of a possibility. Use what you're reading here and your reactions to it to start dialogues in your community. (Part 5 of the book delves deeply into doing this.) I am convinced that we as a society can do this if we can get past our past—so to speak—and are willing to put faith in ourselves. Our world will be a far better place for our efforts.

Finally, as you read through this section of the book, do your best to set aside thoughts of how we might arrive at the system being described. That is covered in parts 3, 4, and 5. The biggest challenge of reinventing public education is getting past the emotional hold of the current model. That hold will likely manifest in the form of, "Sure, that sounds great, but we could never do it," and will originate from the current paradigms. Every significant accomplishment in our history had to overcome old paradigms and biases. We can do that with education.

CHAPTER 16

THE SUMMITVILLE LEARNING COMMUNITY

Summitville is a fictional city used to illustrate what a new model of school and learning might look like. Following the description of the Summitville Learning Community are three case studies to illustrate examples of student learning activities.

The city and school district

Summitville is a suburban/rural community of approximately six thousand people. It is located about thirty miles from a nearby urban area. The school district draws from the city of Summitville as well as a large area around the city in which most adults work on farms or in farming-related jobs. Most adults living in the city itself work jobs unrelated to farming. Many work in Summitville or similar nearby cities, while a significant number commute to the metro area.

The racial makeup of Summitville is 92 percent white, 5 percent Latinx, 1.5 percent African American, and 1.5 percent from other or two or more races. The school district enrollment has a similar makeup. There is a small but not insignificant migrant population that includes school-age students who, consequently, enter and leave the district with some frequency.

The Summitville Learning Community

Several years ago, the Summitville School District decided to reinvent itself. The district as a whole chose to design an entirely new system of learning for all children within the district boundaries. When this was initially implemented, families could choose to enroll children in a traditional district school or in the new model. Over time, all families chose to enroll their children in the new model, so the traditional school was discontinued. The school district is now called the Summitville Learning Community (SLC).

The SLC is not just composed of educators, administrators, and staff like in a traditional school district. Parents and families are considered integral members of the SLC. It also includes most of the local churches and service organizations, along with the chamber of commerce, local businesses, and numerous individual community members. Rather than being peripheral partners, all are integral members who see the importance of helping every child achieve his or her potential and contribute in numerous ways toward that end.

This community approach is reflected in the vision established during the early design stages of the SLC, which became an important tool for maintaining the integrity of the process. The vision has changed in small ways from the beginning to remain relevant and continues to serve as a compass and an occasional litmus test for the community. Here is the vision statement:

> *The Summitville Learning Community meets the learning, growth, and development needs of all children to ensure every child approaches and continuously expands their potential so that each is prepared for the paths they pursue in the future. Individually and collectively, they contribute to making our world a better place to live.*

Supporting and reinforcing this vision are several principles of the SLC. Here is a sample:

- The SLC will commit every available resource to meet the needs of every child in the community so they will have the full opportunity to approach and expand their personal potential.
- The SLC will never turn its back on a child who resides in the community.

In addition, at the heart of the SLC are several important beliefs:

- The outlook of our community is dependent on the quality of the education provided to its children; the better the education, the better the outlook for the community.
- Readiness to learn a given concept or skill occurs at different times for different children.
- Maintaining a love for learning and learning to learn are the two most important outcomes for every child.
- Everyone in the community has a role to play in helping everyone else learn.
- Learning and the need to learn never stop; every one of every age in the community will model the importance of learning by continuing to learn.
- Children cannot approach and grow their potential unless they have real, substantial power and control over their own learning.

Prenatal involvement

One of the most significant differences between the SLC and traditional school districts is that children do not start a formal education program at some date set by a law, policy, or calendar. Rather, each child transitions from a family-centered learning environment to a community-centered learning environment when it makes the most sense for that child. Most families that live in the school district boundaries choose to start the transition before a child is even born.

In many respects, this is similar to prenatal programs offered formally through hospitals and community organizations and informally through extended families and social networks. The SLC involvement is meant to ensure parents receive prenatal guidance and assistance that will contribute to a healthy child and help parents better prepare for the challenges of raising a newborn. The difference—compared to prenatal programs found elsewhere—is that this allows the SLC to build early connections and relationships with the family and the child. These will continue as the child gets older and begins transitioning toward the community-centered learning environment—the SLC.

Early childhood

As in all communities, there is a wide spectrum of needs and desires for early childhood care. While everyone knows that children are learning from the time they are born, the SLC embraces and acts on this. The SLC realizes the learning environment during early childhood substantially affects a child's readiness to learn at later ages. Consequently, the SLC wants to ensure that every child has a nurturing, positive learning environment available from birth. Toward that end, they strive to provide anything a family would need to create such an environment.

Many families are willing and able to provide such an environment themselves. For these families, the SLC continues to nurture a relationship and seeks to create connections and interactions that will help smooth later transitions. These families are welcome to access SLC resources and services at any time. If families have different needs for different children or if their care and learning circumstances change, the SLC will be ready to assist.

Other families need or choose to use an SLC community-centered learning environment. This is similar to childcare centers and preschools, though there are some important differences. At traditional childcare centers, hours and days are limited; the SLC, however, figures out how to provide the care each child needs when it is needed. This is possible because the SLC encompasses such a significant portion of the city and surrounding area along with the corresponding breadth and depth of resources, both human and structural. Using this vast collaborative network, the SLC is able to meet every child's and family's needs.

Providing care to every child when needed ensures the SLC treats every family and child equitably. Families with exceptional circumstances have their needs fully met while not being made to feel different because they need something beyond the norm. This approach recognizes that all family situations are different and honors this diversity through complete flexibility. Connecting and collaborating with all families through early childhood maintains strong relationships with and among families and truly fosters a sense of community.

Another important difference from traditional day care centers and preschools is how children are grouped. While children may be in a care setting any time of any day, there are times when larger numbers of children are together at the same time. When this occurs, children are grouped based on multiple factors, with all decisions based on what will best help each child thrive. The child groupings are dynamic and may change at any time. The environment adapts to meet the child's needs rather than forcing the child to adapt to the environment.

Because a child's care situation is regularly adapted to meet the child's needs, children experience and are guided through numerous transitions. These are great learning opportunities, and children become self-assured and self-sufficient. When unexpected changes or situations occur for a child, he or she is well prepared to deal with them so that they don't become traumatic events. Transitions are no longer a deterrent to learning, as they often are for children in traditional settings.

Student support teams

As noted previously, one critical belief of the SLC is that readiness to learn a given concept or skill occurs at different times for different children. The SLC, therefore, begins the learning process with every child—

from the youngest to the oldest—based on where they are in terms of prior learning, current developmental level, and current readiness to learn. The intent is to help every child approach her or his current potential and then push that potential constantly higher. To help facilitate this, every child gets a support team.

The support team's purpose is to guide, mentor, and assist the child along her or his journey to adulthood. The makeup of these teams is not predesignated but is formed based on the needs and circumstances of the child. Typically, the support teams include the child's parents and one or more other SLC children, along with at least one person trained in child development. The support teams might change as a child's needs and circumstances change as well as when support team members become unavailable.

Having SLC children serve on support teams benefits everyone involved. The children being supported have role models and mentors who are closer in age and with whom they may relate better. Children will also see that adults are not the only people who can offer things of value. In addition, children gain confidence and insights by serving as a mentor and guide while also reinforcing the knowledge, skills, and attributes already developed. The adults benefit by seeing just how capable children can be when given the right opportunities and circumstances.

The SLC learner journey

In the traditional system, all children enter formal schooling in kindergarten on a certain date. For the SLC learner, that journey begins at birth. For the SLC learner, there is no "first day of school" because there is no kindergarten—nor are there any grade levels. Rather, when a student is ready, she or he begins to establish individual learning goals guided by the child's support team.

For purposes of state-required student data and assessment reporting, there are administrative means for sorting students in more traditional ways, but these labels are not placed on the students in day-to-day learning. Instead of being beholden to these assessments and grade levels, children determine their own goals. In that way, they have true ownership and power and will take responsibility for their learning. One of the support team's roles is to help each child understand why certain skills and subjects (such as math or reading) should be included as elements of achieving their goals.

> ### ARE SUCH YOUNG CHILDREN READY TO SET THEIR OWN GOALS?
>
> While it may seem impossible to put such a high level of responsibility in the hands of a young child, the reality is that children have always done this; it just hasn't been formalized as part of their education process. When children pursue their own interests outside of a school setting—like hobbies and sports or even subjects like math, reading, and science—they will continually pursue more knowledge and skills and can be voracious learners. They may not set formal goals, but they don't have to; they are simply striving to learn and improve and continuing to stretch themselves.
>
> It is only when others—teachers, parents, and school boards—dictate what students must learn, how they will learn it, and how they will demonstrate their learning that children become disconnected from the process. Once their learning is controlled by someone else, they may even lose any personal interest they once had in a subject. By putting the children in charge of all of their learning, we let them take ownership and pursue the learning with a passion.

Having goals is only the beginning of the learning process and one of the three critical learning elements over which students are given substantial control. The second is determining how achieving the goals will be demonstrated. With guidance from support teams, students must explain how they will show mastery of each objective. Finally, the student works with the support team to figure out how to achieve each goal. This ensures that the activities and experiences in which the student participates are those that best meet the student's learning traits and current readiness to learn.

Once SLC students determine how they want to pursue the knowledge and skills that are part of their goals, the SLC brings all its resources to bear on making the plan a reality. That doesn't mean students are doing entirely individual activities. In fact, most learning activities are done in groups; however, the activities are designed to achieve the specific learning outcomes of each student in the group rather than deliver some specific instruction.

Although SLC students learn academic skills similar to what students in traditional schools are being taught, they do so in support of more complex learning driven by their interests and passions. The SLC students know specifically why they are learning something rather than being taught things just for the sake of learning them or "because they'll need them in the future." The SLC is adamant that students understand and agree with the reasons for pursuing a learning objective; students must have an intrinsic motivation to learn if the learning is going to be long-term and transferable. (See the case studies at the end of this chapter for examples of what this might look like.)

The nature of the activities through which students learn is incredibly diverse. There are some but not many formal, traditional classes with a teacher delivering instruction to students. These might occur where a group of students is pursuing high-level, complex learning in a particular subject and where the students are capable of learning effectively in that setting. Because the students in such a class are there by choice and to pursue their own learning goals, the classes are dynamic and very effective with deep student engagement.

There are many "seminars" led by learning facilitators who have the requisite knowledge and experience to help students achieve their learning outcomes. These tend to be short in duration and offered as needed with adults or students serving as facilitators. The students are expected to lead the seminar discussions and activities. The facilitators help to ensure the discussions and activities achieve each student's learning outcomes and only actively participate in ways that contribute to the learning. This may, at times, include delivering instruction, but only if that will best meet the students' objectives.

Beyond the seminars and an occasional "traditional" class, numerous other activities are used in the SLC. Students use individual or team projects to develop, apply, and demonstrate skills. They do service projects or develop enterprises. They use technology to access online courses, including those designed for K–12 students, college students, specific professions, and hobbyists. They contact people with particular expertise or experiences that will help fulfill a learning objective. Students use work-based learning activities such as workplace visits, job shadowing, worker interviews, internships, and partnerships.

HOW IS THIS GOAL-SETTING DIFFERENT FROM THAT DONE IN A TRADITIONAL SCHOOL?

This entire process would suck all or much of the joy out of learning for children if it was done with a rigidity and uniformity similar to that of traditional school structures. As with just about everything at the SLC, goal-setting is done with immense flexibility. Some children have an inherent desire for structure and order; they may embrace clearly developed and laid-out goals and benchmarks. Other students may have difficulty forming concrete goals and determining related benchmarks, and trying to do so may hinder the child's innate desire to learn. Such a student's support team will then work to establish the measures necessary for quantifying student learning and growth and ensuring the student is approaching and expanding his or her potential while also honoring the student's personality, strengths, and readiness to learn.

Meaningful, student-driven transitions

Because there are no grade-level designations, nor are students assigned to a particular school, there are no transitions between grades or schools. However, SLC students encounter significant and definitive transitions with greater frequency than students in traditional school districts. These transitions occur based on individual student-centered reasons rather than a policy-established date on which all students will transition.

The SLC students plan, prepare for, and execute transitions to achieve their learning goals. This helps prepare them to be confident, self-directed adults. They always have their support team and mentors available to guide and assist, but the power to try something new and different always lies in the student's hands.

Here is an example of what this might look like. A twelve-year-old student has been learning to play flute and becomes interested in writing and producing his own musical scores. The student decides he wants to develop a new learning goal related to this interest. He meets with his support team and revises his learning plan, which now needs to include exploration of writing and producing music. This, in turn, requires the student to tie the new plan elements into his other goals and activities and plan and execute the new elements. The changes require the student to add new information sources and, most likely, new people who will have roles in his learning. He will need to adapt and coordinate his schedule to accommodate those who will be part of this new area of learning. All these steps are transition elements for which the student will be responsible.

Coalitions and community: the foundation for expanding student potential

One critical outcome sought for every SLC student is the development and practice of skills needed to be part of a community. Toward this end, students become part of coalitions whose purpose is to help every member of the coalition achieve their goals and develop their related skills. This goes beyond lending an occasional hand; coalition members become advocates and champions for each other. They come to each other's aid when challenges arise regardless of when or where those challenges occur. They help each other figure out how to overcome even the biggest challenges that, in a traditional school, could result in a student dropping out or falling terribly behind. Of course, the coalitions also celebrate each other's successes.

The sense of community found in the coalitions also increases student learning and the overall performance of all SLC students. The relationships, trust, and support of the coalition provide a sense of safety, which is crucial to students being able to take risks; and it is the ability to take risks that allows students to reach toward and expand their potential. When community members have true faith that others in the community will be there for them no matter what, they will push themselves higher and further than even they are certain they can go.

The infrastructure

The facilities within the school district were designed and built to support the traditional school model. These buildings are used regularly for SLC activities, in ways very different from how they were intended. All the facilities are considered SLC resources, and they can be used to meet not only SLC student learning needs but also other needs within the community. Students work with their support teams and SLC staff to determine the most appropriate setting for a planned learning activity. If an SLC building has the necessary setting, then the facility is reserved. In many cases, spaces in the buildings have been renovated to increase their flexibility and usability.

The result of the SLC approach is that every facility has a very diverse clientele. That is, the buildings may at any time include infants, teenagers, and adults of all ages. These adults may include parents, instructors facilitating seminars or other learning activities, entrepreneurs who are incubating a business with some SLC connection, and lifelong learners who are attending a seminar or other activity to learn along with the younger students.

Due to the dynamic nature of the system, the SLC makes effective use of existing school buildings. Unlike traditional systems which operate during restricted hours, days, and months, the SLC is able and willing to operate 24-7, 365 days a year if needed to meet student needs. Consequently, the facilities are in use much more frequently than in a traditional school district, making them much more cost-effective. This has allowed the SLC to avoid expensive construction projects despite having significantly increased enrollment that would have exceeded their available space in a traditional system.

Discipline and code of conduct

Although somewhat expected, the degree to which student behavior concerns decreased in the new system was a surprise. Once given power and control over their educational journey, students also took responsibility for their overall conduct and performance. The SLC no longer has any sort of code of conduct or set of rules students must follow. Essentially, the expectations that have been established for students relative to participating in the community and setting and achieving their learning goals have eliminated the need for a set of behavior rules.

Because families are an integral part of the SLC, they are aware of the expectations and how they affect student conduct. Everyone holds themselves and each other accountable. This has created a collaboration of expectations that is not possible in a traditional system. Many of the conduct challenges in traditional systems are driven through competing interests of the many stakeholders, creating a web of "us versus them" and "me versus them" situations. These don't occur in the SLC because everyone is working to help everyone else achieve their best relative to their individual potential rather than relative to others, and this is true of adults and children alike.

That doesn't mean the SLC is completely free of conflict, but the guiding principles and the overall integrity of the system allow nearly all conflicts to come to a win-win resolution. This is also one of the primary reasons for not having a specific code of conduct or set of rules, which almost always bring with them an inherent lack of integrity because they fail to take into account unique circumstances. It becomes nearly impossible to apply the rules and codes in ways that everyone views as fair. When conflicts arise in the SLC, the parties involved work to ensure the outcomes of the conflict and the conduct moving forward support the overall SLC principles.

> ## ADAPTING TO THE NEW SYSTEM
>
> As could be expected, children born into the new system and who have not known the traditional educational model feel comfortable and can function at a high level within this system. Children who have spent several years in the old model have a much bigger challenge adapting. However, their challenge is not as great as that of the adults, who constantly fall back on old paradigms and expectations and then set the bar much too low for students.
>
> Most students, once they realize the SLC is serious about giving them power and responsibility, adapt rather easily. They become critical leaders of the entire change process because they are still learning and growing and don't have the institutionalized paradigms of the adults. Some students, often those who were the biggest behavior challenges in the old system, do at times see how far they are allowed to push their power. In almost all cases, they find no limit because, ultimately, the responsibility for the results falls back on them rather than on someone else, as had been the case in the old system.
>
> The biggest challenges faced by the SLC come from parents and other family members. Children learning to push themselves and take corresponding responsibility often face old, low expectations at home as parents struggle to adapt and let go of compliance-based rewards and punishments they have relied on for years. Part of the transition is preparing students to help their parents work through these situations. The SLC also provides forums for parents to meet and talk about how they are working through these things in their families.
>
> Working through challenges as families is nothing new. But in this case, unlike most traumas faced by families, it is a challenge of choice, with the possibility of significant positive outcomes. The families discover that working through this transition is an incredible growth opportunity that leads to much stronger relationships within the family as well as with others in the community.

The biggest challenges arise from students who enter the SLC after having spent time in a traditional school or another environment where compliance was driven through rewards and punishments. Such students don't immediately believe they will be granted significant amounts of power and control; they don't have a sense of trust in the system or other people. The SLC takes steps to transition students in such circumstances. These end up being valuable learning opportunities for current SLC students. It helps them better understand how to help others build trust while experiencing the challenges that a lack of trust can create.

For longer-term members of the SLC, relationships developed across the community provide significant resources for assistance with challenges that arise. Rarely are challenges solely school-related. Rather, there are almost always out-of-school events or circumstances that affect behaviors and performance in school. Because connections between families and the SLC begin early and are fostered continuously, those in the SLC can more easily and effectively reach out to families and work with them to develop solutions.

The bottom line is that the community and all its members are working toward mutually supporting outcomes. Consequently, everyone wants to support each other and seek outcomes to challenges that are in the best interest of the community as well as those directly involved. Conflicts and challenges are opportunities to learn and grow.

Athletics, clubs, and extracurriculars

In traditional schools, clubs, athletics, and other extracurriculars are offered to fulfill student interests that aren't met through academic instruction and to create an incentive for adequate academic performance and appropriate conduct. They are also meant to help students develop and practice teamwork and leadership.

In the SLC, activities are offered specifically to fulfill students' learning, growth, and development needs. They never exist as incentives. Activities must have inherent value if they are to be offered. In some cases, this might include activities that are also available in traditional schools, in particular where this is the means by which the activities are networked to more substantial opportunities. For example, the SLC may offer various career and technical student organizations (such as FFA, DECA, and

SkillsUSA) so that students may participate in their corresponding state and national leadership development and competitive events.

The same is true for sports. The SLC offers some traditional team sports that are part of an area conference and the state athletic association. Participation in sports is integrated into student learning plans so that it enhances and never detracts from a student's learning goals. The SLC had to work through challenges ensuring students met state athletic association requirements (in part because the SLC does not label students with grade levels and doesn't provide academic grades or traditional academic credits). The SLC also assists students in finding ways to participate in athletics that it does not normally offer or where not enough students want to participate to form a team.

Transportation

While it seems providing transportation for students on a variety of schedules would be a challenge, from the beginning the SLC saw this as a great opportunity. In most districts, the challenge is having to transport all students attending a certain school at the same time and having to deal with significant congestion at the school twice each day. This can result in students spending considerable time on buses and the need for supervision and a placc for students to hang out as the buses make multiple trips. With a traditional schedule, students riding the buses have to arrive or get picked up over a period of time (forty minutes or more for some schools), and parents of students not riding buses must be flexible enough for the students to arrive and get picked up during designated windows of time.

At the SLC, transportation is just another factor being considered as students develop their learning plans. As students determine the learning activities they will use to achieve their learning goals, they take into account where these activities take place or could take place as well as when they will or could occur. The locations and times can be fixed and regular or varied and flexible.

Then the students determine their options for getting to and from these locations at the necessary times. The SLC does provide some organic transportation assets that students can schedule, such as vans and buses. Rather than being used for regular daily transport, these are scheduled as needed. Students can also use alternatives such as parents, car pools, biking, and walking.

The SLC paradigm that learning can occur any time and that planned learning activities may then occur 24-7, any day of the year, has opened up incredible opportunities and contributed a great deal toward ensuring opportunities are equitable. By including transportation in this paradigm, the SLC ensures all children in the community, regardless of their family situations, have equitable opportunities to participate in any activity required to meet a child's learning needs.

Technology and devices

The SLC recognizes that using technology simply for the sake of using technology holds no direct learning value. Technology use is dictated by student's learning goals and the activities through which they will pursue those goals rather than being directed by the school. Essentially, students justify their use of a technology as a means of achieving their goals. Students with similar goals may choose very different means of achieving them, with some students making extensive use of electronic technology while others make minimal use of it.

At the same time, the SLC does not restrict the use of technology and devices. It is up to students to police themselves on appropriate and responsible use. They may enlist others' help in doing this if they feel unable to resist the lure of easy access to a device or certain apps (such as social media, videos, or games). One goal of the SLC is to prepare students to thrive in a world that is dynamic, uncertain, and filled with readily available distractions. The best way to prepare students to thrive in such a world is for them to practice doing so throughout their SLC activities.

Because students are committed to and invested in their own growth and development, they rarely seek distractions. SLC students receive intrinsic "rewards" for the learning, growth, and development they achieve. These are similar to rewards received through social media, such as the dopamine rush from getting a "like" for something. Student disengagement in traditional classrooms and the subsequent need for distraction are the primary reason traditional schools ban devices. With SLC students deeply engaged nearly all the time, there is no reason for devices to be banned.

Security and safety

The SLC is as concerned about student safety as any other school district, but the structure of the SLC means safety and security look very different. At traditional schools, with large groups of students located in rooms with limited access on a predictable schedule, security tends to consist of locked doors and a secured entrance. The dynamic nature of the SLC means people are coming and going at different times and school-related activities are taking place in dozens of locations. Consequently, it is difficult to similarly restrict access to outsiders.

At first, the SLC staff looked into technology to ensure student security. Ongoing conversations with students and parents, however, led to the decision that the SLC community would be collectively responsible for safety and security. The dialogues centered on the fact the SLC is preparing students to thrive in a world where personal liberty is valued above nearly all else and where overt security measures—like limiting access, security guards, metal detectors, and transparent bags—compromise liberty.

It is imperative that everyone in the SLC feels safe, so safety and security are points of discussion with children, families, and staff. Rather than implement overt, blanket security measures, everyone expresses their personal needs for being able to feel safe and secure. In practice, the sense of community present in the SLC tends to create a nearly universal sense of security. Everyone knows they are looked after and supported by everyone else—and will protect each other should the need arise.

While this approach may not provide the direct protection afforded by a locked building, those physical barriers have not always proven effective when someone has chosen to act violently. The SLC has come to a consensus on accepting the risk in exchange for the rewards of the environment it allows to flourish.

"Graduation" and beyond

The SLC believes in lifelong learning and is committed to supporting everyone who was ever a part of the SLC on this journey. At the same time, the SLC is preparing children to be leaders and contributors to society beyond the SLC. Consequently, the learner's journey within the SLC continues until the child determines she or he is ready to move on and the student's support team decides that their goals have been met. If there is consensus among the student and their support team, the student is granted a diploma and a transcript of demonstrated knowledge and skills and all notable accomplishments and experiences. The diploma is provided primarily for those institutions and organizations that require one. The transcript, however, is a show of mastery rather than a list of courses attended and credits earned.

The SLC wants recognitions and ceremonies to have integrity and real meaning for the students, so instead of one graduation ceremony for everyone on the same date, the SLC acknowledges and celebrates when each student transitions to whatever will come after the SLC. The scope of the celebration, along with the attendees and related activities, will be up to the student. Other meaningful student accomplishments are acknowledged and celebrated when they occur throughout a student's learner journey.

Because the SLC sees its purpose as preparing every student for success in the future, the student stays connected to the community as they move to their next destination. SLC members are expected to continue serving on support teams in whatever ways are reasonable and beneficial to both the continuing and the transitioning students. In addition, SLC alumni are tapped for continuous feedback on how well they were prepared and what the SLC could do better to ensure success of future students. It is common for SLC alumni to provide support and assistance to the SLC and its students for many years after they move on.

Getting into college

One common concern about the SLC model is that students will jeopardize access to their college of choice. This is one reason many parents kept their children in the old model during the transition years. But thanks in part to charter schools with nontraditional transcripts, nearly every college and university today is open to students without a traditional transcript. In fact, many give priority to students who come from innovative schools. To date, no student has been rejected from the college of his or her choice based on the education, diploma, or transcript offered by the SLC.

Students at the SLC apply to far fewer colleges because they have a clear picture of what they're looking for in a college; they know college is a means toward an end, not an end in itself. So they only apply to those colleges that will prepare them for the future they envision and, in many cases, only apply to one college that they are confident they will get into. Because the SLC has prepared students to be strong self-advocates, they figure out how to get accepted where they want to go.

Graduates from traditional schools often meet the readiness requirements on paper but don't have the actual knowledge, skills, and attributes to be successful at the college level. SLC students have everything they need to succeed and the authentic confidence that comes from having already used and demonstrated it.

Further, SLC has prepared students who truly understand the costs of attending college—both in terms of finances and opportunities. SLC students consider the financial costs of their choices, how these can be met and their long-term effects, and what benefits they will receive in exchange for those costs. The students also consider the opportunity costs of attending college immediately compared to delaying college or pursuing other options. They make decisions and develop plans that keep them from getting trapped by student debt or other circumstances that will severely limit their future options. SLC students enter their future with eyes wide open and a strong support network in place.

Standards

The SLC does not deliver a standard curriculum to its students, nor do the students take many standardized classes to which a standardized assessment might be connected. However, the SLC does use various standards, and the students participate in state-required standardized assessments; they are just viewed and used very differently than in most school districts.

The SLC believes that many existing standards are well done and have real value but are not useful as age-based benchmarks. As students create goals for the knowledge they want to acquire and the skills they want to develop—as well as attributes they want to foster and strengthen—they need to establish personal standards as a part of the goals. SLC students establish culminating and foundational standards and benchmarks that lead to those standards. In many cases, standards and benchmarks already exist that students can use to establish their goals and develop their plans. These existing standards and benchmarks may come from state and national education agencies, industry organizations, or previous SLC students. Through their support teams and mentors, SLC students come to recognize the importance of academic standards and the need to include them in their goals and plans. Consequently, they take ownership of achieving them rather than doing so for some extrinsic reward or punishment.

Standardized assessments

The SLC believes state-required assessments have little inherent value. They provide only a snapshot of students' abilities in a limited scope of knowledge typically not relevant to the students. There are numerous factors that can affect a student's performance, further reducing the accuracy of these assessments. However, the SLC willingly participates in the state-required assessments because they validate the approach to education being used in the SLC. The state assessments demonstrate that SLC students can perform well and often exceptionally with no specific test preparation.

SLC students' individual standards and learning activities are not aligned in any direct way with state assessments, and students can choose to opt out of these assessments. In addition, SLC students do not go through any sort of test prep. There are no "test weeks" or "test days" on which measures are taken to improve the environment and make sure students are truly ready. There are no SLC-developed incentives for students to do their best.

The students know the state assessments have no impact on them. The students are asked to put forth the amount of effort they think is warranted. Because SLC students are committed to the school and want it to look good, most try to do their best. They also want to show that SLC students are better prepared than students in other districts. When SLC students do well on standardized assessments, despite no preparation or prioritization, it ensures no one can challenge the SLC approach to student learning.

World-changing students

Simply put, the SLC prepares its students by putting them in an environment and situations that are truly reflective of the adult world outside of the SLC and then fostering in them the ability to thrive in that world. The SLC is not content preparing students who will "fit in" and become another cog in someone else's mechanism. The SLC strives to prepare students who will challenge the status quo and lead change in every aspect of the world as well as being able to thrive in that dynamic world.

Where did the courage to do this come from?

Most people who learn about the SLC are amazed at what's been built and wonder how such a big risk was taken. How was a system so completely different from a traditional school system established?

The people in Summitville came to realize there was a crisis in our schools. The children's most important years for learning were being squandered. Residents trusted that, in diving into this effort, the community would come together to make sure the children—and consequently the community—would thrive.

In reality, there was no risk. They knew most people in the community would step up to ensure success. No one wanted to see the children receive less than the best possible opportunities to grow into successful adults. Once the people of Summitville chose to trust in that reality, they could focus on creating a learning community that would stand as a beacon of what's possible for the rest of the country.

Student case studies

These case studies provide examples of activities through which students will learn, grow, and develop along with samples of the standards they would achieve through the activities. The website knowresponsibility.com provides more comprehensive case studies to more fully illustrate what it might look like to attend SLC. The first case study below (Thomas) provides a sample of specific standards for one of his activities. To save space and avoid redundancy, the remainder of activities provide only an overview of the sorts of standards an activity would support.

Case Study 1
Thomas, 16 years old

Thomas has a wide range of diverse interests and so has a wide range of both standards and means of achieving and demonstrating those standards. These are some activities Thomas is undertaking along with a sample of standards he will achieve and demonstrate:

- Thomas will conduct research on the nature and scope of injuries related to soccer, hockey, and track, three sports in which he participates. He will then present his findings to his teammates, their parents, and the coaches. He will also execute a means of sharing the important elements of his research with youth sports players and their parents. This is a small sample of core academic standards to be demonstrated by this project:
    - Synthesize the key elements of multiple texts to support a common argument (ELA)
    - Prepare written arguments supporting findings and claims (ELA)
    - Prepare written report using proper conventions that is readily understandable by the target audience (ELA)
    - Present and support synthesized findings, claims, and arguments of research project (ELA)
    - Make inferences and justify conclusions from sample surveys, experiments, and observational studies (math*)
    - Use probability to evaluate outcomes of decisions (math*)
    - Differentiate between causation and correlation (science)
    - Predict effects of changes in variables on outcomes (science)
    - Evaluate the possible interpretations and impacts of claims and arguments on various audiences (social studies)
    - Using scientific practices, conduct research related to a problem or issue affecting individuals and/or society (social studies**)

- In addition to core academic standards, Thomas will demonstrate standards in computer science, health science, information and technology literacy, and physical education.
- Thomas will develop and demonstrate numerous physical education and nutrition standards through participation in soccer, hockey, and track through documentation of training, diet, and performance.
- Thomas will develop and demonstrate numerous world language and social studies standards through participation in a local organization made up of students and community members that immerses members in French culture and language several times each week.
- Thomas loves math and science and so is taking self-paced, online classes and more traditional college classes. Due to his personal interest in these subjects, he learns effectively and is meeting numerous math and science standards in these courses.
- Thomas is involved with math- and science-related competitive teams made up of SLC students and is meeting numerous math- and science-related standards through these teams.
- Thomas plays flute and saxophone with two different local groups that include current and past SLC students and a few community members. Thomas gets both individual and small group lessons to supplement the bands.

*Taken from Wisconsin Common Core Essential Elements for Mathematics (Wisconsin Department of Public Instruction, 2014)

**Taken from Wisconsin Standards for Social Studies (Wisconsin Department of Public Instruction, 2018)

Case Study 2
Anna, 17 years old

Anna describes herself as a "gearhead." She has always loved anything mechanical and has developed activities that leverage that passion. Here are two activities Anna is undertaking and examples of standards they will achieve and demonstrate:

- Anna is "restoring" a classic muscle car while converting the car into a hybrid vehicle. During the project, Anna is submitting articles documenting and reflecting on the project to a car magazine while also serving as the subject of a documentary film being produced by a team of fellow SLC students as one of their activities. In addition, Anna and the documentary team are producing regular "how-to" videos to post online for others interested in pursuing a similar project. This activity includes standards in ELA, math, science, information and technology literacy, and technology and engineering.
- As an adjunct project, Anna is analyzing the financial and environmental cost-benefit ratio of the car conversion. This will be used to determine the feasibility of an enterprise for similar conversions on a custom basis. This activity includes standards in ELA, math, science, business and information technology, environmental education, marketing, management, entrepreneurship, and personal financial literacy.

Case Study 3
Brecken, 7 years old

Brecken loves comic books, playacting, and cooking. These are some activities Brecken is undertaking and examples of standards they will achieve and demonstrate:

- Brecken found other students who also like comic books and playacting. Together these students are writing and producing plays, videos, and animations based on their favorite comic books. The process of translating the static comic books into dynamic performances, whether live action or animated, is exceptionally complex and providing opportunities to achieve and demonstrate diverse standards in ELA, math, art and design, computer science, dance, music, information and technology literacy, technology and engineering, and theater.
- Brecken and many of the students involved in the previous activity are also involved in a related marketing enterprise. They are looking at the opportunities for earning an income from collecting and selling comic books and memorabilia as well as the possibilities of marketing their video and animation productions. This activity allows Brecken to achieve and demonstrate standards in ELA, math, art and design, business and information technology, marketing, management, entrepreneurship, and personal financial literacy.
- Brecken is creating a cookbook and producing a web-based cooking show which allows him to achieve and demonstrate diverse standards in ELA, science, agriculture, food science and natural resources, family and consumer sciences, art and design, nutrition, music, and theater.

CHAPTER 17

TRANSLATING THE SLC TO OTHER COMMUNITIES

Regardless of whether a community is similar to or very different from the example, no one should try to create the Summitville Learning Community. The only aspects of the SLC that anyone should consider "replicating" are the goal of ensuring every child in the community is able to approach and grow his or her potential and giving students authentic power over their learning. Eventually, elements of the SLC example may emerge to become elements of actual learning communities, but this must occur organically as the community determines what will best meet that community's needs.

The SLC was imagined to be a school community nearly any parent would want their child to attend, while also being entirely doable (as further explored in parts 3, 4, and 5). It was not, however, imagined to be a model for all schools and communities. Designing a model for all schools and communities is how we ended up with the system we have today. School models need to be designed for the communities they serve and must be dynamic to adapt as communities change. Human beings (students, parents, staff) are at the heart of these models, which means none are the same, so standardized and static systems will not work.

At the same time, there will be elements of school models that work similarly in multiple communities. That's okay, as long as the whole of the model was designed to meet the needs of the community it serves. Use the SLC as an example of what's possible when communities are willing and committed to the challenge of reinventing the way their children will learn, grow, and develop.

The question for you, whatever roles you occupy in your community, is this: Do you want all the children in your community to be able to pursue their true potential? If yes, then answer this follow-up: What role will you play in exploring educational models that would allow all the children in your community to pursue their true potential?

These are, essentially, the questions at the start of part 4 of this book, but they are also crucial as you consider the SLC within the context of your community. The SLC example is meant to break readers free from the blinders of our institutionalized education paradigms. It shows how limiting the current model can be by showing what is possible if we set aside the assumptions and limitations contained within it.

The question is not "Could an urban, suburban, or rural community implement something like the SLC?" The question is, "What do the children in a particular urban, suburban, or rural community need?"

Many elements of the SLC are based on research into how to improve learning. These are elements that many traditional schools try to implement. Unfortunately, in traditional schools, these changes can't be instituted in a way that leverages their benefits to maximize learning. So, while they may be partially implemented and may even benefit some students, they won't fulfill their potential. The SLC shows how these could be implemented if not limited by the traditional model and paradigms.

Therefore, if you want to imagine how a truly effective learning community could be created in your county, city, village, town, or neighborhood, go to parts 4 and 5 of this book. There you will be taken through a process of determining who you are—as a community—in order to determine what a truly effective school model would need to look like for your community. Then it will take you through a process of imagining that learning community and beginning the process of creating it.

You can use chapter 16 to reflect on what would be possible outside the limitations and paradigms of the factory model of school. But keep your mind open to all possibilities and know there really are no limitations.

If you can imagine it, there will be a way to attain it, if enough people in your community are committed to doing so.

PART 3

HOW TO REPLACE A CENTURY-OLD INSTITUTION

PART 3

HOW TO REPLACE A CENTURY-OLD INSTITUTION

"We are incredibly heedless in the formation of our beliefs, but find ourselves filled with an illicit passion for them when anyone proposes to rob us of their companionship."

—James Harvey Robinson, American historian

Part 1 of this book provides twenty-six reasons we must replace the model of education we've used in America for 126 years. This section of the book will address the arguments and excuses people typically raise or are likely to raise for why this change will take years to occur (or couldn't occur at all). Each chapter in this section will look at broad categories of reasons people might argue we can't immediately and quickly replace the factory model of schools. Chapter 23 consists of "Frequently Asked Questions" with responses to questions and challenges I have heard from people as this book was being developed as well as questions I anticipate will arise.

As noted in part 1, Tim McDonald and his book *Unsustainable* present an excellent approach to implementing innovative change in schools. (McDonald, 2011) Many aspects of his approach will be reflected in this section of my book as well as in parts 4 and 5. However, I am advocating for a much more comprehensive change than what McDonald calls for, so I encourage you to use his book as a supplement to what is included here.

CHAPTER 18

THE RISKS FOR OUR CHILDREN INDIVIDUALLY

This and the following chapter discuss risks. Really, the entire premise of this book is predicated on risks. What are the risks of continuing the current system and model of school relative to the risks of replacing it with a different system? Alternatively, this could be framed as the costs and the benefits of these options. Whether framed as risks or costs and benefits, these will be different for everyone and will depend on each person's various positions and roles, such as student, teacher, administrator, parent, and taxpayer.

Risks will likely be the highest hurdle of accepting the need for change. Most of us prefer the certainty of what we know—even if there are shortcomings—over the unknown. These two chapters will illustrate why we should all be relatively comfortable embracing this proposed change.

Risks of a new system vs. the existing system

Risks to our children, and the best interests of future generations, should always be at the forefront of our minds when we consider any changes. We must look out for children who are vulnerable and who depend on the adults around them for safety and security. So how do we quantify and consider the risks of a proposal like what is contained in this book, especially when the scope of the proposed changes is so substantial and far-reaching?

The simple answer is that these risks are actually quite small and reasonable once put into context and given a little thought. It comes down to putting more trust in people than in institutions. At the heart of the changes advocated for in this book are people who want what's best for the children in their community. The risks in this change are no greater than the risks we currently accept when we enroll our children in school or day care.

Almost all parents, sometimes when their children are only a few months old and sometimes when their children are a few years old, eventually put their children in the care of someone else for many of their waking hours. Parents are comfortable doing this because it's what nearly everyone else does and has been doing for decades.

If we put our children in day care or preschool, we are trusting that the people there will always act in our children's best interests. Prior to enrolling them, we will likely do research in hopes of getting them into the setting that will serve them (and us) best, but in the end, we must have faith in the people running the facility. We do this because we won't be able to continuously monitor the day care or preschool, nor will we expect a detailed accounting of everything that occurred each day.

Once our children are school-age, nearly all of us enroll them in a local public or private school. We may have chosen where we live based on the schools in that community, but as with the day care and preschool, we must put our faith in the people running the schools and teaching our children. If we don't trust them sufficiently, we look for other school options or homeschool them.

What would happen to our trust if we could not interact with our children's teachers and the rest of the school staff? I don't believe we would so readily enroll our children. That's because our trust is in the people, not the institution. And because the model and structure in nearly every school—public and private—is the same, everything comes down to the people.

Part 1 of this book breaks down the institution of schools to look at what is there beyond the people. It demonstrates the immense risk we are facing—that is, the cost of retaining the current model. The benefit that comes with those risks and costs is the comfort of a system that is familiar. Yet it's not really the system or institution that provides comfort; it's the people.

This book's proposal—replacing the factory model of school with a model designed in the twenty-first century for each specific community—holds no more risks or costs than the current model. In both models, parents must trust that the adults implementing the model will do so in the best interest of each child. In the current model, the implementation is pretty much the same for every child, with the instruction and activities aimed at averages for the given age group. One of the greatest risks of the current model is that a given child will not fit comfortably into the nature and rate of instruction and will then choose not to be engaged in the various activities. The new model, built on empowering all children and ensuring they approach and grow their potential, does not hold this risk.

I really want to emphasize this point—the risks of retaining our current educational model are far greater than the risks of implementing a completely new educational model. The only caveat is that the new model must be designed and implemented with a genuine intent of meeting the needs of every child in a given community.

Every parent hopes their child will be one of those who thrive in school, but most also know there's no guarantee. Parents whose children have some sort of individual challenge—a disability, economic insecurity, traumatic events in their past—will likely have more concerns about their child thriving. Parents do all sorts of things to give their child an advantage but then worry that it won't be enough.

Those are the very real risks parents face in our current educational model—and we simply accept this because it's all we've ever known. So what exactly are the risks of replacing this model with a new model? If you're absolutely confident that your child is or will be one of the high fliers on the continuum of success, you may feel there's significant risk to making a change. However, how confident are you that your high flier is really approaching his or her true potential? Is it possible that, while your child is doing well within the current model, the current model is actually limiting their growth and development?

Part 2 of this book, through the example of the Summitville Learning Community, illustrates the possibilities that a new model might bring in the long term. This example shows how, once established, nearly all the risks of the current model have been eliminated. There is no success continuum because the system is designed to move everyone toward their individual potential (and push to continuously increase that potential) without concern for comparisons to everyone else. Students will not be limited, because the system will adapt to accommodate high fliers. In addition, supports for students struggling to reach their potential are designed into each student's program rather than being interventions tacked onto a standardized program.

The current model, with its dependence on standardized instruction across every class—and in many cases across entire schools and districts—must by design limit how well it can facilitate high achievers and how much attention it can give to students who are struggling. So there is a significant risk that a child in the current system will not achieve her or his full potential in a given subject area or class. The risk that a child in the current system is able to achieve his or her full potential across all classes and grades is significant.

Risks during the transition to a new system

Of course, the more immediate concern of most parents will be the disruption in learning they expect during transition to a new model and system. Even parents who accept the need to replace the current model may prefer that the change occur slowly or after their children have graduated. Alternatively, they may advocate for a "split screen" approach, through which the new model gets implemented while the current model continues, with students opting into one or the other.

I would argue, however, that this is not a risk but an opportunity. Using the guidance in this book, students participating in the transition to a new model will learn, grow, and develop significantly more than they would in the current system. Their participation will provide incredible learning and growth opportunities as well as self-assurance and ownership.

There are two primary risks about which most people—parents especially—will likely be concerned during a transition. The first is that the students' learning and academic performance will suffer. The second is that the students' qualifications for getting into the college of their choice will suffer. There are two other related risks about which some parents will be concerned—qualifying for various honors while in high school (such as cum laude and valedictorian) and qualifying for financial aid and scholarships. Let's look at each of these risks.

Learning and academic performance will suffer

The concern here is that all or some students' learning would decrease during the transition. Remember, though, that in the current model, *learning* is not the main focus. The current model is focused on delivering instruction. And while access to some instruction could be jeopardized during the transition, that doesn't mean that student learning would suffer. Those planning the transition could, in fact, make it a priority that learning would actually increase.

The focus during transition should be on the learning outcomes that the instruction is supposed to achieve. The students, working with teachers and others, would develop benchmarks for the outcomes as well as the means for achieving them. This approach of students taking ownership of their learning would lead to development of skills and confidence that would likely not occur in the current system. Students would also be leaders in the development of a new educational system for their community, which would instill a sense of being a part of something more meaningful than just their own education.

As long as those who are collaborating on the transition are committed to the best interests of all the students—which they certainly will be if they've chosen to be part of such an effort—they will ensure that every student going through the transition learns, grows, and develops more than they would have in the old model. These folks all have a significant stake in the outcome of this effort, so they will be committed to making it successful for every student.

Students' qualifications for getting into the college of their choice will suffer

Many charter schools have moved away from traditional instructional models and transcripts, which has paved the way for regular schools and entire districts to reinvent themselves.

Most colleges and universities receive significantly more applications than available seats. In fact, the ratio of applications to acceptances is often used to rate the prestige of colleges; those with the highest ratio (that is, the most rejections) are the most prestigious. These institutions must sort all these applications, and this is typically done using the traditional college entrance criteria. The institutions sort through all the *typical* applications based on credits earned, courses taken, class rank, GPA, ACT/SAT scores, etc. This creates a ranking from which acceptance letters can be generated.

So what happens with non-typical applications? They must receive individual reviews. Colleges have figured out that meeting traditional requirements is not a guarantee of readiness or future success and that applicants who traveled a nontraditional route are often better prepared and more likely to be successful. Thus, colleges look more closely at nontraditional applications to get a better sense of the student and his or her experiences. In addition, many nontraditional high schools have developed a reputation for students who are better prepared and more likely to successfully complete college, so those applicants get greater consideration.

All this tends to be truer for the most selective colleges. These colleges are striving for greater diversity and want to attract students who will make significant contributions within their fields of study. They seek diversity not just in race and ethnicity but in every respect, so they typically embrace students with nontraditional backgrounds, including that they didn't attend a traditional school and don't have a traditional transcript. In addition, these colleges realize such students are more likely to break the bonds of conformity and push themselves to greater accomplishments.

Students who have participated in this transition will have greater self-confidence and will have developed other crucial skills that will contribute to college success. They will be aware of their abilities and have the confidence to pursue entrance to the colleges that will help them meet their goals. The likelihood, therefore, that students can get into the college of their choice—or be ready and able to pursue other options in the future—are greater if they are part of this transition than if they remain in a traditional school.

Qualifying for honors while in high school

If, as I strongly advocate, a new school model is designed for every student to approach and increase her or his potential, offering traditional academic honors will be a legitimate concern. Nearly all traditional academic honors and recognitions are based on comparing students using grades, class ranks, test scores, and other measures, which would not exist in a school model focused on pursuing the potential of each student. What will be lost if these honors no longer exist?

Some people argue that academic honors and recognitions demonstrate the value of academic performance. However, do these honors result in meaningful, long-term learning? As noted in chapter 13, research on motivation is clear that rewards are not effective motivators for intellectual and creative endeavors. Thus, these honors might be impeding student learning. This will be especially true for students who strive for honors due to pressure from parents or others rather than due to personal desire.

Another consideration is that academic honors tend to derive more from compliance than from motivation to learn. As Eric Barker notes in *Barking Up the Wrong Tree*, longitudinal research shows that high school valedictorians and salutatorians do well in their fields but don't usually become leaders or world changers. Many even report they were not the smartest in their classes but were simply the most willing to follow the rules and fulfill the expectations (Barker, 2017). Even if these honors serve as motivation, they will only motivate a small number of students—those who are willing and able to meet the requirements within the current model. It is true that academic honors may enhance a student's traditional college application, but as the previous section explains, a nontraditional application will likely be an even greater benefit.

Academic honors may also be tied to scholarships or other financial resources. No one wants to see these jeopardized, so this would need to be addressed during transition planning. (This is looked at more fully in the next section.)

All this being said, honors and recognitions *can* exist in the new system and during the transition. The key is to ensure they are truly meaningful to students and better illustrate what students have accomplished. They can also reflect students striving to achieve and push their potential rather than showing that they happened to outperform some other students, which may or may not have been all that challenging.

Qualifying for financial aid, including scholarships

College costs have increased substantially over the past couple decades, and affordability is a legitimate concern for students and parents. Many students need to qualify for financial aid or scholarships to be able to attend the school of their choice. Qualifying for federal financial aid will not be compromised by changing the system as long as the district retains the ability to issue high school diplomas. But some scholarships have a requirement for providing a GPA, class rank, or traditional transcript, and these could be at risk for students in the new system.

It is possible, however, that those providing scholarships would be willing to adapt their requirements to ensure students going through the transition and those in the new system remain eligible. This is another path where charter schools have paved the way, as most have figured out how to ensure their students remain eligible for available scholarships. Where possible, scholarship and aid eligibility should be addressed during the transition planning. Of course, some scholarships will not be influenced locally and will be unwilling to adapt, so they may become unavailable for students going through the transition and in the new system. The transition planners should determine how to ensure there is no decrease in access to financial assistance for any students.

Some scholarships are based on performance on certain exams or on other criteria that would not be directly affected by the transition to a new system. If students believe these scholarships may be within their grasp, they could include learning goals that would enhance their chances of earning these.

While decreased eligibility for scholarships is a legitimate concern, the risk of not qualifying must be put into a larger context. Very few students earn full scholarships. Where these are available and within a student's reach, steps should be taken to avoid compromising these opportunities. However, the vast majority of scholarships students receive are for a small portion of their overall college costs. That means the vast majority of those costs will be paid by the student, the parents, or through student loans. This is another place where a new system and the process of going through the transition may actually reduce the financial risks of pursuing a college degree.

DUAL ENROLLMENT OPPORTUNITIES

Over the past couple decades, many states and local districts have established "dual enrollment" (a.k.a. dual credit) programs for their students. These programs allow students to earn college credits while still enrolled in high school. They typically provide the college credits for free or at a substantially reduced cost. The rationale for these programs is typically a combination of making college more affordable (students will have fewer classes to pay for later), shortening the time it will take students to earn a college degree following high school graduation, and giving students an opportunity to experience college-level instruction and expectations.

These programs are valuable, but as with most "add-ons" to the factory model, their benefits are limited. Some students are able to leverage these classes to great advantage, but most students do not utilize them. Those that do often find they can't use the credits earned or the class didn't provide the expected benefits. It is likely many of these dual-enrollment programs would not continue in their current form under a new model of schools, but all the benefits they offer could be designed into the new model while limiting or eliminating the shortcomings. As with all elements of preparing students to attend and pay for college, earning college credits prior to transitioning out of the public school district could be made an option for every student.

Within the current school model, most students and parents get the same information about college finances and then try to make sense of it. They encounter similar paradigms about attending and paying for college—including beliefs that students need to go straight from high school to college, that four-year colleges are more valuable than two-year and technical colleges, that certain colleges are more prestigious and more desirable, and that there are limited ways to cover the costs of college.

One way that students and parents try to outdo each other in our current competitive model is through their choices of and acceptance into more prestigious institutions, often without thorough analysis of the costs and benefits of the choices, the readiness of a given student, or how a given institution aligns with the student's long-term vision and goals.

Students that went through the school model transition would be better equipped to make decisions about their higher education. In determining their planned learning outcomes, they would need to consider their vision and plans for after high school graduation. They would be guided through an analysis of their many options, the costs and benefits of these options, and other factors necessary to make thoughtful, objective choices. They would also be guided through the financial aspects of their choices, including their long-term risks and benefits.

These students will be developing and applying critical-thinking skills, leading to better-informed decisions. Financial aid and scholarships will become meaningful elements of a comprehensive plan for choosing, pursuing, and paying for a post–high school activity furthering each student's long-term vision and goals.

Here again, the risks of qualifying for financial aid and scholarships that allow a student to afford college and minimize corresponding debt are actually greater under the current model than they would be during the transition to a new model—as long as those collaborating on the transition are committed to the best interests of all the students.

Other individual student risks

The four risks addressed above are likely to be the most common for individual students and parents, but readers with school-age children likely have other concerns as well. Many may fall under the collective risks discussed in the following chapter, while others may be covered in chapter 23, "Frequently Asked Questions."

CHAPTER 19

THE RISKS FOR OUR CHILDREN COLLECTIVELY

This chapter looks at collective concerns, though they will also be concerns of many individual students and families. The collective risks may appear greater than those in chapter 18; however, these must be considered with the benefits a new model would bring to decide if they offset the risks.

Safety

Shootings and other violence at schools have affected our sense of security at schools. In response, most schools are implementing more substantial physical security measures. However, the additional security—more rigid structure, more oppressive rules, and intermittent intruder drills—can increase student stress and lead to reductions in learning. In addition, these measures aren't always effective, as several school shootings have occurred where more rigorous security measures were in place.

The challenge facing schools is balancing safety and effective learning. Our current, inflexible school model was not designed with security concerns in mind. Consequently, imposing security measures almost always compromises learning at least to some degree. Maybe most concerning is that the current model is not conducive to strong relationships and a sense of true community, both of which are critical factors in avoiding school violence. Calvin Morrill and Michael Musheno explore this in their book *Navigating Conflict: How Youth Handle Trouble in a High-Poverty School* (Morrill, 2018).

In designing a new model of school, the desired levels and nature of physical security can be a priority consideration and can be integrated into the design. Safety measures can then meet the unique needs of each community while determining how to balance safety and learning.

Of course, the new design should also contribute to an increased sense of community both in and out of the school. This is one of the most effective tools for providing physical security; essentially, it increases the number of people who are looking out for the school and its students. It is also the most effective way of identifying people who may pose a threat of violence within a school because people know each other better and are more likely to say something when they sense a threat.

The current school model may be easier to physically secure from an external threat, but that comes at a substantial cost to the learning that is supposed to occur. In the broader sense of safety and security, however, a school model could be developed that would be safer and more conducive to learning than what is possible now.

Access to athletics

Availability of athletics is important to many students and parents. Through athletics, students can learn and practice valuable skills such as goal setting, teamwork, and communication as well as developing attributes like determination, patience, and thoughtfulness. Sports also provide health and wellness benefits for students. Many communities rally around their high school sports teams, and they become a vehicle for bringing people together. Athletes and their teams are often involved in local service activities.

Consequently, there are legitimate concerns that athletic opportunities might be lost during the transition to and within a new school model. As with safety, the risks will ultimately come down to those planning and implementing the transition. There is no inherent reason that athletic offerings or sports participation would decrease when moving to a new school model. However, if the new school model expands the full range of student learning opportunities, sports teams may need to be more explicit in showing how participation will contribute to student learning, growth, and development instead of taking student participation for granted.

As part of the school design process, athletic opportunities can be incorporated to ensure they are being offered for the right reasons and to enhance overall student opportunities. Currently, academics and athletics are not typically linked in meaningful ways. Most schools require athletes to maintain certain grades to participate in sports, and some offer study sessions and other academic supports for athletes. However, these are not the same as making athletics an integrated part of a student's overall goals and learning objectives. By taking this into account during the school design process, athletics can become more beneficial for participating students.

Of course, the purpose of designing a new school model is for every student to approach and increase her or his potential. This should not be limited to academic potential and can readily include approaching and improving athletic potential. In many sports, improved thinking and learning enhance performance—such as learning complex plays, reading opposing offenses and defenses, and making quick decisions. Finally, because students who choose to participate in athletics will do so more thoughtfully, they may be more committed to their teams.

Access to academic opportunities

As with athletics, access to academic opportunities is a significant concern for many parents, and there is a risk that transitioning to a new school model will reduce traditional instructional offerings. For example, a new model may not offer, directly at the school, as many traditional honors and Advanced Placement (AP) courses or as many foreign-language classes. In fact, a new model may do away entirely with traditional classes offered through a menu-like course handbook.

Loss of instructional opportunities, however, should not be the concern. Rather, parents and students should focus on what *learning* opportunities will be available. The new school system's design team may strive to retain these courses in some form, but they should prioritize student learning over instructional and traditional academic opportunities. In other words, they may choose to lose course offerings to provide opportunities through which students will learn more and develop their college and life readiness much more fully.

Rather than be limited to opportunities the school could previously offer within the old structure and its available resources, the new model should open up a world of new opportunities that could be nearly limitless. Whereas the school may currently offer three or four foreign languages and a dozen AP courses, the new design may offer access to learning dozens of foreign languages and advanced learning in thousands of subjects, some of which may come with corresponding college credits.

Access to extracurricular opportunities

The risks to extracurricular and cocurricular opportunities are similar to the risks to athletics and academic opportunities. Some current opportunities may be lost in exchange for access to broader and more diverse opportunities. As with athletics and academics, what remains must contribute to the school's overall mission and purpose. If an extracurricular activity has real value for students, then it should be accommodated in the new design.

Very few extracurricular activities are dependent on the traditional school model. Those with inherent value should remain in some form. Those without such value may be displaced as students meet their needs in other ways. Here again, the scope of available activities may appear to decrease on paper under a new model, because the list of standing clubs and activities may be shorter than it is now. However, the actual number and scope of opportunities will likely be far greater than in the current model. They will just be tailored to each student based on need rather than existing in perpetuity.

Role of the school in the community

Local schools and their sports teams are often integral elements of a community. In many communities, especially smaller, rural communities, a significant portion of the local population attended and graduated from the local schools and now have children or even grandchildren enrolled there. Often, the identity of the community is intertwined with the identity of the local schools.

Choosing to pursue a redesigned school will not threaten these connections. In fact, they can be leveraged to ensure the best possible redesign of the school system. Where such connections are not as strong, the pursuit of a redesigned system should strengthen them; if it doesn't, then the community is missing out on one of the most important reasons for the redesign.

That's not to say the connections will make the redesign easier, just that they can make the redesign better. The challenge will be getting people to avoid glamorizing their memories. They will need to realize that the system that created those great experiences is now limiting the opportunities and the growth potential of current generations. Once they come to terms with this, they should become strong advocates for ensuring the final design provides the absolute best opportunities for all the community's children.

Where schools are a central part of the community, the risk is not that the new design will threaten that role but that the close connection could make overcoming the inertia of the old system more challenging. (More on this in chapter 22.)

Other collective risks

As with the individual risks covered in chapter 18, there are likely other concerns not covered in this chapter. I've tried to address many of these in chapter 23.

CHAPTER 20

THE FINANCIAL COST OF REINVENTION

One of the most common arguments against substantive change in education is the cost. Because the cost of implementing change in the current educational system is typically high, there is a perception that changing to and operating a new system will be prohibitively expensive. However, this is not necessarily the case.

Ongoing costs of a new model of education

Here again, Tim McDonald's book *Unsustainable* does an excellent job of illustrating how cost *ineffective* our current system is. The title of McDonald's book stems from the idea that, because we have already squeezed as much effectiveness as possible out of the current model, achieving additional growth in student performance will require increasing influxes of money and resources. The current educational system is too expensive to operate. Doing so, and expecting to get better outcomes, is futile—and there is an excellent and affordable alternative (McDonald, 2011).

To improve student performance while lowering the financial cost per student, we must design a new system that leverages available technology and the community in which the system will operate. The current system was designed in and for nineteenth-century society. There is simply no way to cost-effectively leverage modern technology within this model.

A new model could leverage technology and the community to their fullest extent, leading to improved student outcomes at a lower cost.

These would provide tools allowing personalization of learning-focused activities for each student. Learning activities would be developed and enhanced through technology and access to community collaborators who have experience, expertise, and resources.

> ### FAILURE OF TECHNOLOGY TO REDUCE EDUCATION COSTS
>
> While advances in technology have reduced the costs of thousands of products and systems in our world, they have not done the same with education. The reason is that other products and systems changed and adapted to leverage new technologies, leading to reduced costs. In education, we rigidly retain our existing system and model and try to force the technology to work within those limitations. The result is that new technology continually increases the costs of education—or redirects resources that are needed elsewhere—without seeing a corresponding, proportionate increase in academic performance or providing other relative benefits to schools or students.

While there will be costs for technology and facilitating collaboration with community assets, schools already have many of these things in place but aren't able to fully leverage them. Because teachers—with support from aides and various specialists—are the primary means of delivering instruction, up to 80 percent of a school district's budget is for personnel costs. The new model will be designed to more effectively use the skills, knowledge, and dedication of current educational staff to guide and mentor students toward meeting their individual learning goals.

Some students require lots of guidance and assistance in a few narrow areas while needing very little in others; others need small amounts of guidance and assistance across a broad range of areas; and still others need significant guidance and assistance across many areas. These needs will change as the students grow, learn, and develop while also changing as students strive to challenge themselves.

The current model can't direct each teacher's full range of abilities to meet these dynamic student needs. A new model could ensure all teachers' abilities are used effectively to have the greatest impact. In addition, the new model can direct teacher expertise or ability toward students with the greatest needs for that expertise or ability.

Although delivering instruction to large groups of students collectively gives the illusion of efficiency, this method is actually very inefficient because it can't meet each student's learning needs and does not result in meaningful, long-term learning. The new system should be designed to offer diverse and personalized activities that would result in significant, meaningful, long-term learning.

Most important in reducing costs of a new system is empowering students to be responsible for their own learning. In our current, compliance-centric factory model, students have little real power, so they have little reason to take on responsibility. That means schools must have sufficient staff to continually try to engage students while also ensuring they are in compliance with all the rules. Once staff no longer need to worry about supervising and engaging students, they can focus entirely on guiding and mentoring them as they pursue their learning objectives.

This, in turn, means each staff member can contribute to meaningful growth, learning, and development of significantly more students, not by delivering instruction to many students at once but by being available to assist on an as-needed basis. A collaborative local community and a technology-accessible global community will be the primary sources of student learning. The learning that could occur with current staffing levels will increase beyond what most anyone can currently imagine.

In addition to making staffing more cost-effective, the new model can be designed to make more effective use of existing infrastructure, facilities, and equipment. Usage of buildings can be adapted so existing space is used far more than is typical in most schools (as illustrated in the example in part 2). Student transportation can also likely be conducted more cost-effectively than current busing in many districts. Districts can design the new model to be flexible such that facility use can adapt to changing student enrollments without opening new or closing existing schools.

Costs of transitioning to a new model of education

The costs of planning, preparing, and transitioning to a new model can also be quite reasonable, though it can depend a great deal on the district, the community, and the approach being used. There are three primary costs for implementing or changing programs in a school: equipment, training, and additional staff. Not all initiatives have all these costs, but they are typical. We'll look at each as they relate to transitioning to a new model of education within a school or district.

Facilities, equipment, and material costs

There is nothing inherent in designing a new model that requires equipment and materials beyond what is already available in a school or district. Although a community could choose to design a new system that requires expensive new equipment or facilities, this is not necessary. The design process could instead include constraints that would require the new model and the transition to operate within existing facilities and use existing equipment. The transition process—from early notifications of stakeholders, to recruiting of people who will participate in the planning, all the way through implementation—primarily requires space for community and team meetings to occur and, probably, a web-based system for doing surveys and collaborative work. Nearly all districts will have these things readily available.

The only additional costs within this category for most districts would be refreshments and such for participants, if desired. Such costs, however, would not be prohibitive and, in most communities, could likely be donated or the costs covered by community businesses and organizations who want to be part of the process.

> ## THE COST INEFFICIENCY
> ## OF OUR CURRENT SCHOOL MODEL
>
> Although factories can be a cost-effective way to mass-produce goods, the factory model of school is very inefficient. To deliver instruction in the current model, all students must be present the same hours on the same days. Consequently, most students must be transported within a relatively narrow window of time, requiring multiple buses and drivers that will only be used for two to three hours each day. It would be more cost-effective to use a smaller number of buses and drivers constantly throughout the day.
>
> A similar situation occurs with facilities. Most classrooms in a school are used for about six class periods a day. The rest of the time, the rooms are used very little. It would be more cost-effective if the rooms were used nearly every hour of the day between, say, 7:00 a.m. and 10:00 p.m. In this way, significantly more students could be using facilities that, in the current model, would be completely overcrowded.
>
> Although holding school-related activities so early or late in the day may seem extreme to some, many students already participate in sports and other activities that go beyond these times. Designing a new model of school opens up cost-saving opportunities that are just not possible in the current model.

Training and staff development

There is nothing inherent in designing a new school model that requires expensive staff training and professional development. A community *could* spend significant amounts on training and staff development for the redesign process, but it is not necessary, nor will it guarantee the best possible design in the end.

There are several factors that allow a community to design a new school model on a very reasonable budget. Primary among these is that a community will only undertake this effort if it is committed to doing so for its own sake. It will be pursued by people who recognize the need and believe in their ability to succeed (as explored in depth in part 4 of this book). Those who get involved will do so for generally altruistic reasons and not to receive compensation. The foundation of this effort will be people striving to benefit their community and its youngest residents, so the cost should be low.

The exception would be a local school district serving as an active partner and leader in the school design process. School staff may need to be compensated in some way for their time or, if the district provides release time to work on this, the district will need to cover their regular responsibilities. This should not be an excessive expense, however, compared to the amount districts typically spend on staff training and development.

Because this will be a local effort, there does not need to be a budget for travel. A team may want to visit other communities, which would incur some costs; however, the primary benefit of such visits is confidence that comes from seeing a similar team charging ahead. Educators might also learn about another community's process and apply some of their methods to what they are doing, but they must be careful not to use such visits to shortcut their own process. This must be a local effort, not a replication of another community's work.

Another factor in maintaining a reasonable budget is not needing to hire an outside organization or expert. The designers of the new system may want some outside help and guidance, but their local team should already be experts on the most critical element of this process—their community. Designing the best possible model of school depends on an intimate knowledge and understanding of its community and residents combined with a commitment to the community and its children. These should be things they already have in abundance.

The "expertise" that could be contracted to an outsider is guiding the team through the process of self-discovery, exploring, visioning, planning, and implementing. Someone will need to ensure that efforts stay on track, stay on target, and retain their integrity. There are benefits to having an objective outsider take on this role. However, there may already be someone in the community who can fulfill this role and do so as well as a paid outsider.

Staffing

In many respects, the previous section on training and staff development addresses the staffing aspects of this process. As noted above, some communities may choose to contract someone to lead all or portions of the planning and transition process. Beyond that, it is possible the design team would choose to hire or contract with someone to maintain records or facilitate the administrative aspects of the process. These, then, could be costs for the transition and would need to be taken into consideration.

Part 4 of this book delves deeper into the sorts of roles the team would need, but most of these should be filled by community volunteers. All or most people participating should want to be a part of an exciting effort to improve their community and the opportunities afforded its children. Consequently, they will not expect compensation.

Part 4 also explores the role of students in the design process. They should be deeply involved throughout and will provide another source of "free" assistance and expertise because their stake in this effort is probably greater than anyone else's.

The rewards of a shoestring budget

Although having access to funding can be helpful, it is possible to maintain a reasonable budget in going through this school model design process. There will inevitably be funding needs that arise throughout the process, and being able to address these without taking time to find money may keep things moving more smoothly. On the other hand, one of the most powerful benefits of going through this school design process is that all aspects of a community will be integrated and focused on the learning, growth, and development of every child in that community.

Going through this process on a shoestring budget may result in much deeper and more meaningful connections being developed—and therefore a better initial design and plan—than might occur if an abundance of funding were available.

CHAPTER 21

EDUCATION LAWS AND RULES

Nearly all federal and state laws and rules related to public education are framed in the factory model of school, and most contribute to perpetuating this model. Even as state legislatures, Congress, and the federal government strive to foster innovation in education, they expect that it will occur within the existing model. A few states have enacted legislation meant to encourage innovation, such as allowing or even requiring districts to award credits and diplomas based on demonstrated competency rather than seat time. Such legislation may encourage schools to try a new model but is not premised on doing so.

State laws and rules

Although there is typically a great deal of flexibility available to schools—sometimes within education law itself and other times by receiving a waiver to a law—that flexibility can be hard to find when districts want to implement innovative practices. Wisconsin's Department of Public Instruction made a specific effort to help with this through publication of *Fostering Innovation in Wisconsin Schools* (see sidebar on page 175). I am not aware of other states replicating this effort, but such flexibilities likely exist in other locations.

While laws and rules can create challenges, they should not stop efforts to design new school models. Rather, they should be worked around or changed. State education agencies are a good place to start when trying to determine flexibility within a given law or rule. In some states, school board associations will help districts analyze laws and rules to figure out what is required and what flexibility exists.

I hope this book will prompt increased interest in and movement toward innovative education practices and that this, in turn, will lead other states to develop materials similar to Wisconsin's. In addition, as districts, schools, and communities push against existing laws and rules, I hope state legislatures will revise them to be more flexible and reduce the effort needed to comply. Maybe some states will even replace current laws with laws and rules that foster the replacement of the factory model of schools.

THE WISCONSIN GUIDE TO LOOPHOLES IN EDUCATION LAWS AND RULES

A few years ago, a number of Wisconsin school districts were working to implement innovative practices in their schools. Many of these districts contacted the Department of Public Instruction (DPI) concerned that some practices might not comply with state education laws and rules. These queries prompted the DPI to create a team to explore flexibility within the laws and rules, and they included on this team many of those who had been asking the questions.

The result of this effort was a document called Fostering Innovation in Wisconsin Schools, which lists eighteen different "flexibilities" within current laws and rules, cites the related statutes and rules, and provides examples of how the flexibility can be applied to allow various innovations. Some of the flexibilities require formal requests to the DPI, such as requesting a waiver of a rule, but most are within the control of the local school board. Essentially, the document reveals that almost anything a district wants to do that will benefit students is allowable—including a complete redesign of the current factory model.

At the same time, working to create this document did reveal rules that are nearly impossible to bend. For example, students must take a state-mandated civics test to graduate, although passing is not a requirement. Fortunately, the inflexible laws and rules would not preclude a district from creating a new model of school. In the case of the civics test example, the new model would simply need to ensure all students knew the test must be taken at some point and then facilitate doing so.

Federal laws and rules

Although there are federal education laws, these rarely apply directly to schools. Rather, they provide requirements to states that result in state laws and rules for local districts. That means districts that adhere to state laws should be in compliance with federal laws. Civil rights laws are an exception. All schools that receive federal funding must comply with federal civil rights laws. Fortunately, these should rarely interfere with implementing innovative practices or designing new school models.

> ### LESSONS AND EXAMPLES FROM CHARTER SCHOOLS
>
> The subject of charter schools can elicit a wide range of opinions. I won't enter into a debate on the educational value of charter schools, but they do provide a good example of state policies that can support innovative practices and approaches. Charter school laws and rules differ substantially from state to state. In general, however, charter laws provide relief from a range of school requirements so that a charter school can implement practices that might not otherwise be allowed.
>
> The willingness to provide the flexibility needed to create charter schools demonstrates that policymakers in most states are open to allowing innovation if they are confident the resulting school will serve students at least as well as the current schools. In some states, charter school laws will open the door for the new school design.

Local school policies

Local policies are typically furthest reaching and, consequently, most limiting when it comes to implementing innovative practices. Many communities wanting to replace the factory model will need to seek changes to or waivers from local policies. The good news about this, of course, is that these policies are within the control of the local community.

Local policies may create bigger challenges in large school districts, such as in urban or metro areas. In such districts, there may be challenges to one subset of the larger district that wants to implement a new model. This will be especially true if the district governing body is not open to significant change. Parts 4 and 5 of this book provide guidance on how to approach change within such districts.

I'm not trying to gloss over the challenges that federal and state laws and local policies can create in designing a new school model. In some cases, these challenges will be significant. However, they are not an adequate reason to forego designing a new school model for your community.

CHAPTER 22

INERTIA AND MOMENTUM

The greatest challenge to replacing the current factory model of school is inertia—the institutionalization of the factory model. This model has consistently resisted the best efforts of thousands of people and organizations over the past few decades. Federal government agencies, US presidents, advocacy groups, wealthy individuals, and education foundations have at various times called for reinvention of the school system. Educational researchers and professionals have revealed the hundreds of ways the current model fails to meet the learning needs of our students. Thousands of initiatives have been implemented attempting to compensate for the current model's shortcomings, to improve student learning, and to close achievement gaps.

Yet the factory model persists.

This chapter will explore why things can be truly different this time. If I didn't believe we could make this change now, I wouldn't have bothered with this book. The landscape has changed, and this can happen. A key difference is our awareness of the changing world around us. Even those of us who have been successful after attending factory-model schools realize that our education did not prepare us for many aspects of the new world.

My generations—I'm on the cusp between boomers and Gen X—have openly embraced technologies we never could have imagined existing. We have realized things that are new and different aren't always bad, even when they replace things we previously cherished. And each subsequent generation is even more open to change. Consider racism and sexism.

Know Power, Know Responsibility

While racism and sexism remain far too prevalent, and there have been recent increases in open displays of both, our overall population increasingly rejects these beliefs. Hopefully these open displays of hostility are the last gasps. In the fall and winter of 2017, the frequency of sexual misconduct and assault came to the forefront. The resulting groundswell led to the fall of numerous celebrities, elected officials, and other powerful people. There has also been growing acceptance of the LGBT population as well as increased support for extending marriage and other rights to same-sex couples. Again, open hostility and subtle discrimination do continue, but society as a whole is becoming more accepting.

In this environment of societal upheaval, people are showing their willingness to work for change when the reasons are truly compelling. They are even willing to abandon institutionalized paradigms if they understand the benefits these changes will bring for themselves and their communities. Such changes can occur through sheer volume of support or by the actions of a powerful few.

The challenge of changing our entire educational system is that there are hundreds of anchors holding people to the old model. At the heart of this resistance is the message of the quote that leads this section of the book: "We are incredibly heedless in the formation of our beliefs, but find ourselves filled with an illicit passion for them when anyone proposes to rob us of their companionship."

I am confident that the vast majority of people in our country want the best possible schools for all our children and are willing to consider new and innovative ideas to make this happen. I am further confident that, given the opportunity to thoughtfully consider a change of this magnitude, most will support it and many will even passionately embrace it. At the same time, I am aware of the challenges.

In their book *Switch: How to Change Things When Change Is Hard*, Chip and Dan Heath discuss the three elements of driving change: appealing to reason, appealing to emotions, and providing the necessary context and environment (Heath, 2010). In this book, I aim to address all three of these—with parts 4 and 5 laying everything out for those who are ready to go.

To overcome the inertia of our current educational system and develop the momentum to replace it, we must begin by calming the emotions of those for whom the current model is a big part of their lives and who can't imagine anything different. Concurrently, we appeal to the emotions of stakeholders by showing how the current system falls far short of what is possible. We help them see how entire generations and society as a whole are being shortchanged by the factory model, which prevents students from approaching their true potential.

We then appeal to people's reason by providing the rational, logical arguments for changing our educational system. We explain the ways the current system is unable to truly meet the needs of almost any students and then illustrate how a new model can address the shortcomings. It's not just showing a pie-in-the-sky vision; it's giving readers the recipe necessary to make it a reality.

Finally, we explain the environment and circumstances needed to bring about this change and provide guidance on creating these in any local community. I've laid out numerous resources in this book, but I cannot provide the will and courage to begin the effort. That must come from the stakeholders in each community. I know this won't be found in every community at first, but there are those who will start these conversations and find the courage to begin the process. These people will become examples and catalysts for others in the future.

A tipping point will be reached when there will be no stopping this change except in communities where the anchors are especially deep. Even these, however, will eventually succumb as they realize their children are missing out—or their children are opting out and moving to or attending those districts where the change has already occurred.

Is this a naive vision? Have I lost touch with reality? If you've read this far, then maybe I'm onto something.

CHAPTER 23

FREQUENTLY ASKED QUESTIONS

Chapters 18 through 22 address challenges and concerns I believe are most likely to arise. This chapter uses an FAQ format to addresses a number of other challenges and concerns likely to surface.

1. Numerous past attempts at education reform have failed; what makes this proposal different? How will this succeed where others have failed?

There are three primary reasons this effort will succeed. The first is that we live in a different time and culture. Until very recently, people remained wary of *institutional* change. With so many other things changing, people sought the comfort of stability wherever they could find it. Schools that looked and felt like those we attended provided such comfort that changing them was simply not a viable option. I believe the majority of people now accept that even institutional change is inevitable, so it's the ideal time to show how they can influence such change in something as important as education.

The second reason this effort will succeed is that it reflects an understanding that education and schools are human systems that are extremely dynamic and absolutely unique; no two schools or communities are alike, and none will remain static. Past efforts at education innovation sought to find one model or approach that would work everywhere for everyone. This effort recognizes and leverages the dynamic and unique nature of every community. It acknowledges that the outcome will look different in every community and will have to be flexible and resilient to endure. What doomed past reform efforts is now the driving force of this approach.

On a related note, the third reason this effort will succeed is that it takes a bottom-up rather than top-down approach. Many past reform efforts tried using laws and policies to drive change, while others tried to direct replication of some model. This effort recognizes that every community needs to determine for itself that change is needed and what that change must look like. The local community must be the driving force. As communities jump into this effort and begin implementing new models, others will take notice and follow suit. Eventually, a tipping point will be reached and the factory model will become the exception rather than the rule.

2. School attendance and being on time have been shown to correlate with student performance; what role will these have in the new school design?

While such research is valid, the results are due to the current model being focused on delivery of instruction rather than learning. The role of attendance and timeliness will depend on the school model that a community develops. In developing its model, each community will need to determine the purpose and value of tracking attendance and timeliness and then the means and scope of that tracking.

Some communities will adopt a model that treats attendance and timeliness different for each student based on individual learning plans developed with the student and his or her family. As with nearly everything else that may be monitored within a learning community, attendance and timeliness should be considered based on how they contribute to the learning, growth, and development of each student.

3. How will breakfast, lunch, and snacks be provided?

Food service will be handled differently in every school based on the needs and circumstances of the school and its students. In many schools, there will no longer be a traditional school lunch offered. Instead, meal planning, preparation, and service will be incorporated into the learning plans of the students. It is possible that schools will be able to offer meal options more cost-effectively because food preparation could be made to align more closely with what students will eat and so there will be less waste.

4. What about students on free or reduced lunch?

This will simply be another element in the design. All student needs, including those related to socioeconomic status, should be considerations during the overall school design and when developing student learning plans. Since student learning is inhibited when nutritional needs are not met, this has to be an element of the overall school model.

5. How will health services be provided?

Many current schools don't have nurses available at all times; instead, they have plans in place to provide health services when needed. Similarly, new school models would need to figure this out. A school design with strong, extensive community collaboration should be able to readily meet this need.

6. How will schools ensure students are learning the knowledge and skills the district and community think are important?

While districts in the current school model dictate that certain content is *taught*, they have little say in what students actually learn and retain. In designing a new school model, a district and the community can influence the structure and processes so that their priorities are emphasized. They can establish sets of beliefs, values, and outcomes they want the new model to support and reflect. They can even set certain learning requirements, though they must do this very thoughtfully.

The best way to get students to learn anything is for students to decide it is worthy of being learned. The community will need to demonstrate to students why they believe certain knowledge and skills are important, and they must do so with integrity. When given power over their learning, students will honor, embrace, and pursue community priorities if guided by trusted mentors. The evidence will be in the success students find in the future and the sorts of citizens they become.

7. How does a school or district ensure career and technical education, music, or other content important to the community is included in the new model?

If a content area is truly important to the community, it will be included in the school design created by the community. Going through the process of designing a new school model allows a community to reflect on what is important, why it is important, and how to ensure access remains in the redesigned school model. Often, schools and communities focus on certain content areas and offerings because they've always done so. By reflecting on what is important and what will be best for students, the areas that are truly important will be validated and emphasized.

The current model limits student choices because any subject that a student is interested in must fit into a structured schedule. A new model could provide vast flexibility that allows students nearly unlimited options in developing a learning plan. It is in designing the new model that the community will demonstrate those things they feel are of greatest value.

8. How will career and guidance services be provided?

How this will look in the new school model will be determined by the design team. These services could be included in ways that look similar to the current model, or they could be completely integrated into each student's program in some way. If these services are deemed important in the community, the design team will ensure they are included in the new model such that they will be able to meet every student's needs.

9. How will student performance data be collected and reported?

This is another concern the new school model design team will need to take into account. They will need to look at the state's collecting and reporting requirements and ensure their model will allow performance data to be collected unless there are available waivers or alternatives. The key is that the design team does not allow the data collection and reporting to interfere with the ability of their design to meet the learning needs of all their students.

10. Won't designing schools that cater to students just spoil them? Don't children want and need structure and discipline?

Yes and no. The intent is not to design a new model that caters to student wants, but rather to their needs. The structure and discipline will be self-imposed as students take ownership of determining what they need to pursue their long-term wants—their future visions.

The freedom and power advocated here will come with tremendous responsibility. If a design team heeds the points laid out in this book, they will be raising student expectations to an incredible degree because students will now become responsible for their own learning, growth, and development. They will be accountable to themselves for their performance rather than being accountable to someone else for their compliance. And they will become responsible for their own structure and discipline.

People point to "out-of-control" children in unstructured settings as proof that children want and need structure in order to behave. I used to believe this too. But I now realize that external structure leads to bad behavior and lack of control in unstructured settings because the children have not developed self-control and responsibility. When the shackles are removed, the children exploit their freedom because they know it won't last.

When students are provided significant freedom, power, and control over their own conduct and behavior—when they are treated with respect and trust that they can and will make good choices—they will prove themselves completely capable of doing all this. Those who recognize their own challenges in these areas will seek external assistance to stay on track, which is far different from having controls imposed on them.

11. How will parents who have only known the traditional school model adapt?

It will be a challenge. Like everyone else, parents will constantly fall back on old paradigms and expectations, and their actions will reflect this. And like everyone else, they will have to be "trained" in the new model. They will mess up and learn from their mistakes. The key is for the design team to include concerns about parent adaptation in its design. The Summitville Learning Community example in part 2 provides an idea of how this might play out, while parts 4 and 5 include information on addressing parents when seeking to plan and implement a new design.

12. Won't this be impossibly difficult?

If I believed that, I wouldn't have written this book. Like most things that have become ingrained in our being, the change will be difficult. So you can choose to change now because you know it is needed, or you can wait until the challenges of the current model reach crisis level. It's like weight loss, improving physical fitness, or giving up sugar, tobacco, or soda before they become deathly hazards. It will be hard, and there will be substantial discomforts along the way.

Throughout the process, people will constantly be asking, "Is this worth the effort?" And like those individual changes, it is easier when you are going through it with others. People in your community will have to encourage each other and work together when facing challenges. But it is absolutely not impossible—and, if you've read this far, then you must believe that too.

13. What are the downsides to this whole effort? Who will be the losers if we make these changes?

The losers in this effort, I believe, will be those who make money off of education without bringing any proportional value to the learning process. These people and companies will find themselves without work. Anyone whose highest priority is improving student outcomes will willingly adapt; if they make a living from public education, they will either need to figure out how they can provide value to students or will have to accept that their employment cannot be part of the new model.

PART 4

BUILDING A CHAMPIONSHIP CHANGE TEAM

PART 4

BUILDING A CHAMPIONSHIP CHANGE TEAM

"A small body of determined spirits fired by an unquenchable faith in their mission can alter the course of history."

—Mahatma Gandhi

If you've read this far or jumped right to this section, you're hopefully ready to begin revolutionizing education in your community. You're not alone. Thousands of organizations, agencies, and individuals have called for significant changes to our education system, and I've not come across one person who thinks our current system works adequately.

The reasons no real progress has previously been made have all become irrelevant with the passage of time. We must begin in earnest designing the educational system that is possible in the twenty-first century, but change cannot happen through state or federal legislation. It must start at the district, school, or neighborhood level.

Parts four and five of the book will guide you through the process of replacing the factory school model with one designed specifically for your community to prepare students to thrive in the twenty-first century. It will not, however, provide a blueprint. Instead, I hope to prepare you to face the unknowns and conquer the challenges yourselves. Like Grasshopper in the old television series *Kung Fu*, you can "flashback" to this section of the book to recall the lessons learned and consider how to apply them. The book will provide numerous tools that can be used to address the challenges, but which tools and how they will be used will differ for every community and school.

That being said, there are places I have tried to provide more specific guidance and examples where I think they could be helpful. Even these, however, are still just suggestions. You will need to determine whether, how, and when to use each of the tools here. You and those you enlist to help with your efforts will be the change agents in your community. Don't let that intimidate you. It is in working through these challenges that you will lay the foundation for the future success of your community's children.

YES, YOU CAN: THE EXAMPLE OF THE PARKLAND, FL SCHOOL SHOOTING SURVIVORS

While writing this part of the book, I kept hearing your voice—the voice of the reader. I could imagine the doubt of well-intentioned skeptics, including many colleagues. "There's no way a community could just get together and do this," you said.

I truly understand such doubt. The proof of what's possible is all around us, but it usually requires a crisis to surface. Following the February 14, 2018, school shooting in Parkland, Florida, that killed seventeen people, high school students became nationally recognized advocates for imposing restrictions on firearms. They had no background or expertise; they simply knew they had to speak out. Numerous people stepped forward to assist them, and a national movement resulted.

Whether or not you agree with the actions being advocated by the Parkland survivors, you can learn from the example of their dedication to creating change. After tragedies, people step up and demonstrate how capable they are because the alternative is unacceptable. You and others in your community are absolutely capable of leading this effort. There will be naysayers and detractors—just as there are for every worthwhile, groundbreaking endeavor. This has been true about those students from Parkland. They didn't let it stop them, and neither should you.

CHAPTER 24

FINDING THE WILL AND BATTLING SELF-DOUBT WITH AND THROUGH INTEGRITY

Integrity

This may be the most important chapter in the book. It describes one of the biggest challenges you will face and will require reflection and thought. The concepts in this chapter, like a championship team's training and practice, will lay the foundation for your success.

I am convinced that the most important element for an individual or team of any sort to achieve their potential is integrity—and that compromised integrity is one of the most common reasons organizations and initiatives fail to achieve their potential. Integrity means that our actions, decisions, and words align with our stated intentions and beliefs. I believe nearly every person wants to live with integrity, yet this is extremely difficult in our dynamic and complex world. The two ubiquitous ways that integrity is compromised are through arguing that the ends justify the means and through misaligning words, actions, and decisions.

The ends justify the means

There is a pervasive attitude throughout our culture and institutions that the ends justify the means. This usually doesn't entail an obviously horrific action taken to achieve a desired outcome; rather, we accept some small level of compromise on our beliefs and values if the end result is desirable. Often, the compromise is small, and we hardly even think about it. But each small compromise of our values and beliefs slowly, and often unnoticeably, erodes our integrity.

When we allow a result to justify the means by which it was achieved, we have made a compromise. We face such situations regularly, and sometimes they are a necessary choice we have to make. But when the alternatives to compromise are worse and some compromised action absolutely must be taken, we need to understand the longer-term impact and take every precaution possible to mitigate the damage. If we don't pay attention and take these precautions, here is what happens.

COMPROMISE VS. COMPROMISED INTEGRITY

A compromise of ideas and methods is desirable, especially in an endeavor or process like overhauling a large system. However, compromising an individual's or organization's values, beliefs, or integrity must be avoided or mitigated in some way. The challenge, of course, is when there seem to be conflicting values and beliefs among the members of a team or organization. That's why it's so important to have consensus on the vision and beliefs of the team pursuing the new school design, as addressed later in this section.

Fortunately, there is significant consensus among people throughout the world on foundational values, as noted in chapter 7 and explored in depth in Rushworth Kidder's book *Moral Courage* (Kidder, 2005). This consensus means a team is unlikely to face regular situations where there is significant conflict among values and beliefs.

Every time we allow the ends to justify the means, we create barriers to trust and diminish the ability to achieve our individual and collective potential. In every system that involves humans, whether a family or a federal government, allowing the ends to justify the means (even just a little) erodes trust among the people who make up the system or organization. It's often not noticeable, which makes it even more dangerous.

Over time, this mindset—that sacrifices will be made—becomes part of a system, and its members realize they might be among those sacrificed. People begin to wonder if they are at risk; maybe they will somehow be caught up in the next *means* that lead to some necessary *end*. Compromises become normalized, leading to more severe compromises later as trust erodes. Without the full trust of its members, an organization cannot achieve its full potential.

When there is no option that is clearly and completely within the scope of their values and beliefs, organizations and all their members must be open and honest about the situation and any compromise it requires. They need to be clear about the choices being made or actions being taken, their justifications, and the steps that have been taken to find acceptable alternatives.

Our hierarchical systems too often value leaders who "make the hard choices" without providing their rationale or showing concern for those who may be harmed. But organizations with integrity must take these steps if they want to achieve their potential. Often, in the process of trying to mitigate these actions, new solutions arise that no longer require compromising integrity. (For an example, see the callout box on Barry-Wehmiller.)

> **BARRY-WEHMILLER: BUILDING A BETTER WORLD THROUGH BUSINESS**
>
> In his TED Talk on circles of safety, Simon Sinek shares a story about the Barry-Wehmiller Companies, a group that supplies technology and services to the manufacturing industry. Sinek explains how the recession in 2008 took a toll on orders for this company. After seeing a 30 percent drop in orders, the company knew it had to reduce its payroll by $10 million to survive. The board of directors wanted to lay off a portion of its workforce. Company president Robert Chapman refused.
>
> Instead, everyone in the company had to take four weeks of unpaid furlough. This was not ideal, but it spread the pain among everybody rather than force select people to face the overwhelming burden of losing their jobs. What happened next, as Sinek explains, was rather incredible.
>
> People throughout the company realized some could readily afford a longer furlough, while others would struggle with the lost income of even four weeks. So these people started trading. Those who could afford to do so took a longer furlough so others could take a shorter leave. The company ended up saving $20 million and weathered a horrible situation while coming out stronger in the end by refusing to compromise its integrity (Sinek, 2018).

Misaligned words, actions, and decisions

Integrity is also frequently compromised through a misalignment of words, actions, and decisions. As with "the ends justify the means," this misalignment is usually not blatant and is often not even realized. Rather, it is usually due to lack of deep thought and critical thinking about how words, actions, and decisions align. When an organization has a set of stated beliefs but implements policies that are counter to them, integrity is compromised.

For example, many organizations express the importance of their employees or members and say they value their opinions, ideas, initiative, and commitment. Then they create volumes of rules, policies, procedures, and consequences meant to ensure compliance. Despite their claims to care about the ideas of their employees, their organizational structure severely limits all but a few people from making meaningful contributions beyond their assigned duties.

This misalignment has become so institutionalized that we must proactively counter it. It is not enough to tell team members that we welcome everyone's opinions, ideas, and initiative; rather, we must seek out the opinions, ideas, and initiative of every team member and then listen and act on them. We must also acknowledge that those who are less vocal and forthcoming often have some of the best ideas and solutions. Such an approach strengthens the commitment of everyone on the team, which will be necessary to weather the challenges to come.

Building a foundation of trust

So what does any of this have to do with finding the willpower and courage to design and implement a new model of school? This enterprise will challenge stakeholders, who have different and sometimes competing needs and priorities, to abandon the only school model they've ever known and collaborate on developing something completely new. There can be no doubt about the sincerity and commitment of the team members. Everyone must trust everyone else, and everyone must be confident that there is integrity in their collective efforts.

Further, to achieve this collective trust, individual members of the group should know themselves and why they are involved. They need to have individual integrity. Individuals shouldn't give up their personal needs and priorities or those of organizations they represent; rather, everyone must be aware of and acknowledge each other's needs and priorities. Everyone should know where everyone else stands; they must have enough trust that they are willing and able to be vulnerable with one another.

If your team has a foundation of integrity, then you can develop the collective courage, willpower, and confidence to follow through on the design and implementation of a new school model for your community.

There are substantial rewards for maintaining your integrity. Besides contributing to the success of your efforts, being part of a team with real integrity and a shared sense of purpose is invigorating and exciting. You'll find yourselves looking forward to the work you're doing.

Courage

I have had the privilege of being in the presence of thirty-seven winners of the Congressional Medal of Honor—the highest award offered to members of the US military. I have read countless stories of Medal of Honor winners and the citations from their awards. The standard for receiving this award is the very definition of courage. A service member must have performed substantial actions that protected and saved others while facing a clear threat to his or her own safety.

Unfortunately, the Medal of Honor is often given posthumously because the acts for which the medal was awarded cost the life of the recipient. Medal of Honor winners, however, don't see themselves as heroes or their actions as necessarily courageous. Rather, they all say they were just doing the right thing, what they knew their fellow service members would have done in the same situation.

The world is filled with similar courageous acts by firefighters, search-and-rescue teams, police officers, parents, teachers, neighbors, friends, and total strangers who step in without thought for their own safety to do the right thing. In most cases—whether rescuing a fellow service member or fighting racial injustice—the cause being fought for is often clear and the alternative is unacceptable. However, in the effort to design a new school model, the alternative of keeping the current factory model *seems* acceptable to most people. Therefore, those who choose to become part of this movement will need the courage of their convictions that not only is this a righteous cause but also that the status quo is unacceptable.

If you and your team are not convinced the current model is substantially inadequate for the twenty-first century, you will much too readily give up. That is the fate of most significant initiatives—an acceptance of the status quo or an easier alternative when challenges arise.

On the other hand, if you're convinced this change is necessary and our current model cannot meet the needs of our students, our communities, and our world now or in the future, then you know that replacing the current model is absolutely the right thing to do. That is where you will find your courage. Think about the children who have already been shortchanged by an out-of-date model, and consider how much potential has already been lost by graduates of factory-model schools and the loss to society of what they may have accomplished. Use these thoughts to strengthen your resolve and commitment.

Real courage comes from your personal convictions and is based in integrity. If you truly care about something, then you will live out that belief through your actions. If you believe in the abilities and incredible potential of all children and want to help unleash them because it's the right thing to do, then you will find the courage when you need it.

Will and willpower

Most of us think of willpower in the context of self-improvement—eating better, exercising more, saving money, etc. When we or someone else is successful, we often credit willpower. However, the critical element of willpower is *will*. Will is a reflection of the degree to which we believe in something. The greater our commitment to a value, ideal, belief, or idea—or a corresponding action or activity—the greater our will and our readiness to act accordingly. If we have sufficient will to accomplish something, we will find the willpower necessary to see it through.

Here again, integrity comes into play. Where there is strong, consistent integrity, the will of our convictions will be sustained and bolstered. When integrity is compromised, will and willpower falter.

Finding the will to soldier on in the face of adversity starts by figuring out who we are and what we truly believe. Unfortunately, we often allow our roles in life to define us, and we often allow others to define those roles. We may base our actions and decisions on what others want or how we think they'll respond; or we act as we've seen parents, teachers, or mentors act. Over time, we adopt that definition without having given it much thought. In most circumstances, this works out fine, but the changes outlined in this book require objective reflection—a sort of internally directed critical thinking.

The will to design a new school model for your community will come from your belief in this cause combined with the integrity to make it part of your identity. You need to identify yourself as a "change agent" and become a champion for bringing improved learning, growth, and development opportunities to children in your community. You don't have to be highly vocal and visible, but you should be willing to use your talents and resources to further the effort.

When challenges and adversity arise, this identity will provide the willpower to keep going. The integrity of wanting to do the right things for the right reasons at the right time will overcome doubts and desires to quit.

The big concepts covered in this chapter—integrity, courage, and will—are bolstered through the support, example, and assistance of others. When we are part of a group committed to a common cause and to one another, the collective strength of the group becomes the strength of each member. The group becomes its own catalyst for ensuring integrity, courage, and willpower are always available in abundance.

Thus, it becomes essential that the team taking on the challenge of designing a new model of school for their community is formed with integrity and maintains integrity in all they say and do.

CHAPTER 25

THE PEOPLE

There is only one essential resource in the process of designing a new model of school for your community—people. This is a human system, and people will make or break the effort. All other resources will be meaningless if people are not at the center, committed, and collaborative. Recent history is filled with education improvement initiatives that had millions of dollars in funding or were provided extensive infrastructure and technology but mostly failed to deliver more than incremental improvement. Human systems require an investment of human capital, so that is where this process must begin. We'll start by looking at the makeup of the leadership team and then at ways to attract people to this effort.

The leadership team

In his book *Good to Great: Why Some Companies Make the Leap . . . and Others Don't*, Jim Collins discusses how great leaders understand that change and improvement don't begin with a great vision but with building the right leadership team. (Collins J. C., 2001) This team, then, helps to create the vision, instead of the other way around. In his book *Leading Change: An Action Plan from the World's Foremost Expert on Business Leadership*, John Kotter includes building a guiding coalition as the second step of an eight-step process for leading organizational change (the first step being to create a sense of urgency) (Kotter, 2012). Although both authors are addressing change in existing organizations, the same principle applies for the creation of a new organization or team.

The first step, to use Collins's analogy, is to gather the right people on the bus. To do this, you might need to create a sense of urgency. Although the specific size and makeup of the team will vary with each community, there are certain skills and attributes that the team will need collectively. You don't want to fill each role with only one person, nor do you want each person to fill only one role. Each person will fill portions of multiple roles; they will each contribute to multiple collective skills and attributes. Keep that in mind as you build your team.

Here are the skills and attributes you should collectively strive to include on your leadership team:

- Commitment—Although their reasons for involvement and their priorities will vary, each person on the leadership team must be committed to designing a new school model for your community.
- Critical Thinking/Devil's Advocate—Everyone will need to think critically throughout the process. However, it is important that one or more people regularly and vocally play devil's advocate. These people will ensure the integrity of the group and the process. They will not let the group or the process get away with unrealistic assumptions or gloss over challenges or oversights.
- Networks—Not all community stakeholder groups have to be represented, but there must be regular, meaningful communications with each throughout the design and implementation process. Therefore, the leadership team must have sufficient networks and connections to maintain communication and collaboration with all groups who have a stake in the learning, growth, and development of children in the community.
- Trusted Spokesperson—You will need at least one person who is respected in the local community and is willing to serve as a spokesperson to various organizations and stakeholders.
- Community Pulse—There must be a combination of people who

have the pulse of the community. The team needs to be aware of challenges and opportunities that are likely to arise so they can prepare. They also need an ongoing sense of how the work of the team is being perceived and discussed in the entire community, including areas that fly under the radar.

- Historian—A person with a strong working knowledge of the history of the community can be invaluable in providing insights and cautions and simply serving as a resource. The importance of this role will vary, but it will be crucial in those communities where traditions are valued or where there have been past strife and conflicts over education, politics, development, or other elements of the community.
- Survey Facilitation—Make sure someone is able to develop, disseminate, and collect surveys of various groups and populations within your community and then summarize and report the findings. This should not be limited to web-based surveys. The integrity of your efforts requires consideration of honest opinions and thoughts, which can require in-person collection from some groups within a community.
- Cheerleader—Ideally, the leadership team will be upbeat and enthusiastic and keep a positive outlook even in the face of adversity. Even so, it is helpful to have someone or a small group to monitor the mood and sense of the team and strive to maintain energy and a positive outlook.
- Diversity—The leadership team should reflect the diversity of the community beyond gender, ethnicity, and race. Strive to have representation or at least the perspectives of those who are often less visible in a community, including those living in poverty, the homeless, small minority populations, LGBT individuals, and transient and migrant populations.
- Diverse Ideological Mix—Strive to maintain a balanced or neutral ideological makeup. That is, try to avoid having a liberal or conservative bias. The nature of the community will dictate, to some degree, the importance of ideological diversity as well as how challenging it

may be to remain balanced or neutral. The key is to avoid creating a leadership team that would be viewed as political or aligned with an ideological extreme.

> ### WHAT ABOUT EDUCATION-RELATED SKILLS AND ATTRIBUTES?
>
> While this seems like a glaring omission, it is intentional. This will be a pioneering effort, so there are no experts. It is unlikely you will find anyone in your community who has expertise in learning and brain development outside a factory school model. Also, most relevant research is fairly recent and very accessible. Your team will benefit by collectively digging into this rather than relying on one or a small number of experts.
>
> Essentially, those you would consider experts on education are only experts within the old model. They can still bring important insights to your efforts, but they wouldn't necessarily bring the sort of expertise needed most. Thus, this is not among the traits needed when building your team. Instead, everyone on your team should learn what they can about these topics and bring to bear reflections on their own experiences learning, growing, and developing or those of children they know.

Beyond ensuring your team covers the skills and attributes noted above, and within the context of the previous callout box, there are certain groups who should be directly represented or somehow closely networked:

- Teachers and School Administrators—Because this entire effort is aimed at replacing the current school model, it could be perceived threateningly by those who are part of the current local schools. Even educators who recognize the need for change may feel anxiety and concern about what it will mean for them. Some will want to fight against the effort. The best way to reduce the educators' anxiety and avoid conflict is to make them part of the effort. Where possible, include educators who are well respected among other educators.

- Private and Home School Representatives—Try to include people who bring these perspectives and who will help ensure these institutions and groups do not feel threatened or overly anxious about the purpose or outcome of the redesign efforts.
- Current and Past Students—In designing a new school model, students should have a strong voice. Recent graduates as well as current students should be regular members of the leadership team, while additional input and insights should be sought from other students when needed. In seeking out student and graduate voices, include those who have been successful in the current school model as well as those who struggled and those who are or were viewed as troublemakers. Students who are currently at risk of not being able to graduate or move to the next grade level can help ensure the new model design will better contribute to their success. The same is true of bringing in students who have dropped out of high school.

Of course, the leadership team will need people who can help ensure administrative functions are covered, such as planning meetings and setting agendas, publishing meeting notifications, record keeping, and budgeting. These roles are important to ensure the team's efforts are legitimized and fulfill any and all legal requirements. Transparency and openness in all team activities will contribute to the integrity of the team and the work they are doing.

Here are a few other considerations when developing your leadership team:

- Consider people who have been vocal about concerns with the current schools and system, but be careful about bringing on people who are overly critical or negative. Be sure team members with concerns also want to contribute to solutions.

- Visit local churches and service organizations to seek recommendations for people to serve on your leadership team.
- Try to find the entrepreneurs and business-oriented risk-takers in your community to see how their views could best be represented on the leadership team and how they might directly contribute to this entrepreneurial-type task.

EVERYONE—INCLUDING THE CHILDREN—WILL NEED HELP SHIFTING PARADIGMS

Although people might expect students to come up with the wildest ideas for school design, they are often trapped in the same factory-model paradigms as everyone else. I once helped host an event with the state superintendent of public instruction spending a day with public school students to hear their concerns and gather ideas for improving education.

There were presentations by students from several innovative charter schools talking about how different their schools were from traditional schools and how this improved student opportunities, learning, and performance. All the students were then divided into teams to "design" schools they would want if they had complete control with no limitations or constraints. Every group of students came up with some variation of the existing school model. They added various flexibilities and ways to increase student choices, but the designs almost entirely fit within the traditional confines: classrooms full of students taught by one teacher, meeting five days a week, for a typical length school day and during a regular school year. They were trapped in the paradigms just like adults.

Getting people on the bus

It's one thing to know whom you want on the leadership team; it's another to get them on board. One key purpose of this book is creating a sense of urgency. Ideally, several community members will read the book and begin a dialogue. This would be an organic way of starting to develop a leadership team. However, it only takes one person to get the ball rolling in a community.

As you review these steps, keep an open mind. Some suggestions may seem quaint in their simplicity and old-school approach, but not everyone uses social media or e-mail, and you don't want to miss important parts of your community who may be influential, be able to provide assistance in a variety of ways, and have great ideas to contribute. At the same time, consider the approaches that are most appropriate to your community. Not all are necessary, nor will all be effective in every community.

Recruiting other interested parties

Attracting others can begin by simply sharing what you read and seeking the reactions and thoughts of others. Ask people if they are willing to talk about local schools and education, then share your insights from reading and reflecting and ask them to weigh in. Discussion with others will help you clarify your own thoughts, build on what you've read, and identify people who may want to become involved in this effort. Those who respond positively and enthusiastically would warrant additional conversations, which could morph into discussions about building a team to explore creation of a new school model for your community.

If you're uncomfortable approaching people out of the blue, start with someone you trust. If you're not shy or timid, you could choose just about anyone to start with. The key is simply to get the ideas out in the open and see where the dialogue goes. If the conversation goes well and you sense some agreement about the need for school change, bring up the idea of drawing others into the conversation. Ask those you talk to if they would be willing to join a larger group discussion and would they be willing to invite some other folks.

As you do this, draw inspiration from the knowledge that just beginning these dialogues in your community will have value regardless of whether you achieve a full school redesign. These are important conversations about schools and learning that rarely occur. No matter how things play out, your efforts will not be wasted.

> **HOW THIS PLAYED OUT FOR ME**
>
> While forming the foundation of this book—in particular the many reasons the current model of school needed to be replaced—I thought I was crazy. I wondered if anyone would agree that we needed to replace the factory model and certainly doubted they would agree that it was possible.
>
> In my roles as an education consultant, army officer, parent, school district committee member, and youth hockey coach, I was surrounded by educators and parents. I had regular conversations about school, students, children, learning, and behavior into which I interjected the thoughts that make up the foundation of this book. I was surprised to find nearly universal validation of my ideas. People agreed wholeheartedly that the factory model should be replaced and, once giving it some thought, agreed we should be fully able to develop a much better model. Although the initial reaction was often that we were stuck with what we had, a bit of dialogue quickly convinced nearly everyone that change was possible.
>
> This validation was the catalyst for the book. As I've continued sharing these ideas and told people about my book, many have responded enthusiastically and anxiously. It's become clear there is a significant strong desire for change in public education. When people realize others feel the same and there may be ways to bring about this change, many begin chomping at the bit. These are the people who will join community leadership teams and help build the necessary momentum to bring about change.

Growing your pool of recruits

Once you have a handful of interested people, plan some gatherings to dig deeper into the ideas already discussed. You want to work toward a shared sense of urgency and begin identifying common beliefs about the possibility of designing a better school model within the local community. This will lay the foundation for bringing about change.

These gatherings could be at someone's home, a local community room, a restaurant or hotel, a church, or a school. If you are going to invite a broader community audience, make sure the location would not exclude anyone or make anyone feel uncomfortable. The more welcoming your early efforts, the greater the diversity of your team. This also helps avoid creating opposition by people who feel excluded from the effort.

When you are ready to bring a group together, use existing networks and forums to invite those who have read this book or who are simply interested in improving local education opportunities.

- Talk to your immediate family, friends, and social networks and have others do the same.
- Post notices on community bulletin boards in stores, churches, and libraries.
- Look for social media forums for your community. Facebook and other sites often have groups based on geography through which you can post notices and seek out people who have common interests.
- Contact your local school or the school district and let them know what you're doing. They may be willing to host a discussion and could send out a notification through their networks.
- Post notices in your local newspapers.

Sharing and discussing

Bringing people together to talk about local education and schools—and the possibility of reinventing them—is the formal start of this process. Attendees should recognize that everything is still on the table; nothing is certain. This process is as much about discovery and the journey as it is about the destination. These early gatherings should help each person reach her or his own conclusions about the need for change and the scope that may be needed.

Eventually, you'll need to move toward creation of a leadership team. Consequently, the discussion will need to include the idea of designing a new school model for the community. As you initiate this dialogue, keep in mind that emotions can vary significantly. Be sure to honor these emotions and be prepared to help people come to terms with them. At the same time, look for opportunities to move toward the actual design process, which is covered more in the next section.

There may be some who don't believe the current model needs to be replaced. Ask such people if they would still consider a role in the group's efforts, possibly serving as a "devil's advocate" on the leadership team. Remind them and everyone else that your intention is to ensure the children in your community truly have the best learning opportunities possible. Some may choose not to participate; you will need to move on without them, though they may reconsider down the road.

AVOID GOING NEGATIVE

Throughout this entire process, avoid criticizing the schools and those associated with them. Yes, this book and the changes being pushed are due to shortcomings of the current model, but it is not meant to demonize schools. Whenever and wherever possible, praise the schools for the efforts they've made and recognize the positive things they're doing. Then draw attention to the ways the current model limits the schools' efforts. Be clear that it's the model being used that is the problem, not those trying to function within that model.

Even further, stress the desire to collaborate with the local schools, district, and educators. If your efforts draw people who have been critical of schools and educators, ask them to set aside their vocal criticisms in order to foster cooperation and inclusivity. Focus your efforts on the idea that you want to build the best possible opportunities for future generations and not dwell on the past. Use the past for the lessons it provides—and, where appropriate, honor events and accomplishments from the past—but retain your focus on the future and the incredible potential that exists within your community and its children. Tapping into that potential is what this is all about.

Creating the leadership team

During your sharing and discussion sessions, you need to determine when there is consensus to begin forming the leadership team. Periodically ask what concerns still exist and talk these out. Those who have been involved up to this point should become the initial pool from which the leadership team will primarily be created. There are countless ways of creating and organizing that team. The key is to do what will work for your group and community. A team that forms organically through dialogue and consensus will have more success than one formed to meet someone else's vision.

The same is true about the "governance" aspects of the team. A good example is when a group of parents creates a charter school. This typically starts with parents who feel their children's needs are not being met in the current school or have learned about innovative schools elsewhere. These parents have discussions, which draw additional parents and other interested parties into the conversation. They explore various means of meeting their children's needs and decide that creating a charter school is the best option, so they begin planning and preparing to do so.

The parents agree to take on various roles and responsibilities based on their interests, passions, and experience. As the process progresses, these roles and responsibilities may morph into formal positions on the charter school's governance board which, in turn, may be formalized through a set of bylaws. Throughout this process, additional parents and others who have interest and needed expertise may be brought in to fulfill certain roles and responsibilities.

Those working to design a new school model can use a similar approach. Once there is sufficient interest and support, begin filling the skill and attribute needs identified earlier in this chapter. You can collaborate on how you want everything structured and the level of formality needed to function effectively. There is a good chance someone will step up to take on a more comprehensive leadership role. Some will self-select roles to fill the skill and attribute needs. Others will say they are ready to help when needed but don't want to commit to any specific role.

Organic growth and development of the team will result in a more authentic and trusted outcome than trying to fit into a prescribed structure. If the initial pool of participants was truly representative of the community, then the resulting leadership team and its structure should reflect the nature of the community. Even so, it's important to ensure the diversity of the community is reflected in the team's makeup. When identifying skills and attributes still needed, strive to ensure diverse representation when recruiting people to fulfill those needs.

Once the leadership team makeup is set, work on formalizing the structure. Those with experience leading teams can work together to establish some operational processes, with input from the rest of the team. If it is necessary or you think it helpful, bring in a consultant of some sort to help with this step. Having your leadership team organized effectively will make everything else go more smoothly.

Next steps for the leadership team and others

There are two tasks the leadership team may want to consider prior to starting the community school design process that begins in chapter 28. One is to establish a set of ground rules for the leadership team. These are not formal rules and procedures but rather guidelines meant to foster and maintain trust and open communication. You may determine these are unnecessary or at least can remain unwritten if trust and open communication are clearly evident without them. Just be sure everyone on the leadership team agrees.

The second task is determining the ongoing role of those who are not part of the leadership team and how to keep them engaged. You want to keep them constantly informed of the leadership team's work and include them wherever appropriate. You can also have them serve as an ongoing conduit to the broader community and as continuous recruiters trying to grow the base of support for these efforts.

INTEGRITY AND HARNESSING THE ELEPHANTS IN THE ROOM

In the school model design process, there will be interpersonal issues that need to be addressed. These can include biases, prejudices, loyalties to other teams and groups, and prior conflicts among team members, as well as personal challenges and situations that may distract from the team's work at some point, such as health, finance, job, or family situations. If not addressed, these issues erode trust and interfere with communications, leading to compromised integrity. The only solution is to identify and acknowledge these "elephants in the room."

The caveat is that those who "own" the elephants must be the ones who expose them. This is not a hunt for others' elephants. Rather, this is show-and-tell, with team members introducing their elephants so others can feel safe in their presence. This ensures everyone knows, truthfully, where everyone else stands, which strengthens trust. An environment in which people feel safe to talk about the elephants in the room affirms that your team will be respectful and foster trust no matter what situations arise. It also reduces the chance of repressed factors that can destroy trust and derail a team's work.

It's not important to rid the room of elephants, as long as they are being acknowledged. These issues belong to people, and usually the only way they leave is with their owners. Instead, expose them, embrace them, and harness them to help pull your team toward its vision. And if some elephants vanish on their own—maybe two team members who have often been at odds work things out and build a strong, mutually supportive relationship—that's okay too.

CHAPTER 26

CRITICAL ROLE OF CHILDREN

Children are at the heart of public schools and must be central in designing a new school model. It's not enough for designers to just keep children in mind. Rather, children themselves must have substantial active roles in every aspect of the effort to design a new school model. This will bring integrity to the process and lead to a significantly better design.

The premise of this book, based on research and experience, is that our students will exceed our expectations if we give them the power to direct and pursue their own learning. That means the adults must relinquish most of their power and move to a guiding and mentoring role in order for students to grow, develop, and learn at their full potential. Stixrud and Johnson explore this very effectively in *The Self-Driven Child*, where they suggest parents serve as "consultants" to their children (Johnson, 2018).

Start by identifying and recruiting students from your community to become a part of this process and orienting them just as you would the adults who are joining the effort. While this may seem a monumental and somewhat scary prospect, it also has a significant and exciting reward—the students who become integral parts of this process will simultaneously become the validation of your efforts. These students will become the proof that they are capable of wielding this power and can serve as the spokespeople for the change.

Here are the considerations you'll need to address in bringing children on board your team:

- Don't limit involvement to high school and middle school students; consider younger students as well. When put in an adultlike role and treated with the same expectations, elementary school students are capable of acting more responsible than many adults.
- To maintain your team's integrity, accommodate the students' needs the same as everyone else on the team. Work with their schools, parents, and others as needed to connect the design work to their learning goals, and try to work out a system so they can earn credits for their help as an alternative to attending all their classes. This can provide them the time and energy to fully participate on the team and has the added benefit of trying out things that may become part of your new school model.
- Strive to treat children the same as you treat adults on your team. No one on your design team should speak condescendingly toward any other member, whether adult or child. Treat them with respect and trust just like everyone else on your team. Treating everyone with respect and trust means adapting your relationships and communication to account for each person's qualities, concerns, experiences, and personalities. This holds for children and adults alike.
- Be up-front with the children that the adults may need reminding if they fall back on old behaviors based on traditional adult-child roles. Tell the children and adults to feel free to provide gentle reminders when needed.
- Some children will be ready to actively—maybe even assertively—participate as team members. Others will need coaxing and may participate less until they are certain there is sufficient respect and trust; be prepared to encourage them as needed. This is also true of adults on the team.
- Children are people; they just have less life experience than adults. That also means they have fewer preconceived notions and inflexible paradigms. This is a huge advantage your team should leverage.

- Don't simply put out a call for student volunteers or approach those who are more active or demonstrate leadership in school. Rather, seek out students who will bring diverse perspectives and insights to your team. This includes at-risk and special-needs students as well as gifted and high-achieving students. Your design team would ideally include athletes, musicians, and dropouts as well as students that are minorities, LGBT, homeless, home-schooled, or from private schools in your community.
- While you are striving to respect the children, honor their individualism, and build trust with them, remember they are still children and thus are probably not treated this way in other settings. Be prepared to help them navigate this possibly confusing situation and the challenges it can bring.

CHAPTER 27

BUILDING A BASE OF KNOWLEDGE ABOUT LEARNING, GROWTH, AND DEVELOPMENT

The Committee of Ten did include some elements of pedagogy—how instruction should be delivered—in their recommendations of 1893, but they did not include anything else relative to ensuring students effectively learned the content. This is understandable, given there was relatively limited knowledge at that time about learning, growth, and development.

Today, there is substantial knowledge and research available, yet they have not been leveraged to create a model of school that effectively allows students to approach their potential. And as noted throughout this book, applying the research and knowledge within the constraints of the current model yields relatively small improvement compared to what is possible.

A new model of school, therefore, must be based on what we now know about learning, growth, and development. It's not necessary everyone becomes an expert in everything. Rather, key principles must be considered throughout the design process, while various members of your team can be designated to increase their expertise in select areas.

What I have found is that nearly all the current knowledge and research aligns with my own observations and experiences; that is, my experiences validate what I'm reading. I expect you will find the same thing. This helps improve comprehension of the research and conclusions and provides a strong base of knowledge for doing the design work.

> **TRUST YOURSELF, YOUR EXPERIENCE, YOUR INSIGHTS, AND YOUR GUT**
>
> As you dig into the resources in preparation for this endeavor, there is one significant caveat I need to make: Think critically about everything you read. Don't just accept it as fact and plan to apply it literally and as written. Rather, consider how what you're reading matches with your own experiences and observations. Think about what it means in the context of planning a new model of school. Reflect on how this new information validates or is counter to what you believe or know works. Then, mash up your own insights and experience with what you are reading to create a more full, complete, and accurate understanding of it all.

Divide and conquer

There is a lot of knowledge and research available. Rather than everyone reading everything, have individuals become experts on select aspects of learning, growth, and development, or create teams to be collectively responsible for knowing current, relevant principles regarding each of these areas. Meet periodically so people can share insights and discuss connections that crop up among the various areas.

Use the numerous available formats for accessing the research and knowledge. I provide a list of books I believe are excellent resources for building a base of knowledge, most of which are available in print, digital, and audio format. Many of the authors have produced TED Talks, Google Talks, and other video presentations that include the most important points. You can often watch these videos as a reasonable alternative to reading the books; you won't gain as much knowledge and insight, but you'll usually get the most important elements.

In addition to books, there is a constant flow of related research coming from numerous institutions and agencies. Do online searches to find the latest articles and reports. I've noted several journals that regularly include reports on recent research. You can subscribe to these or receive regular notifications of stories, and many allow free access.

Seek out people from your community with knowledge and expertise in some or all of these areas. Ask them to do presentations for your leadership team or sub-teams. Better yet, ask if those people will participate in the design process to ensure the model incorporates the associated knowledge and research.

Required reading for all team members

At a minimum, I strongly recommend all or most team members read the following books. I consider these critical to understanding the most important aspects of designing an effective school model. Full descriptions of each are found in their respective sections that follow:

- *Mindset: The New Psychology of Success* by Carol Dweck
- *The Self-Driven Child: The Science and Sense of Giving Your Kids More Control Over Their Lives* by William Stixrud and Ned Johnson
- *The End of Average: How We Succeed in a World That Values Sameness* by Todd Rose
- *Drive: The Surprising Truth about What Motivates Us* by Daniel Pink
- *Turn the Ship Around!: A True Story of Turning Followers into Leaders* by L. David Marquet

Leadership, planning, and change

The knowledge and research here are more about the process than the school model itself, except for *Turn the Ship Around* and *Blink*. If you want a better understanding of how a leader can bring a group together to effectively achieve a purpose such as designing a new school model, consider reading these books or exploring alternate versions of their contents.

- *Turn the Ship Around!: A True Story of Turning Followers into Leaders* by L. David Marquet—Navy Captain David Marquet shares the lessons he learned introducing an entire new paradigm of leadership aboard a US Navy nuclear submarine. These lessons are incredibly relevant to local efforts of designing a new school model as well as the school model itself (Marquet, 2012).
- *Leading Change: An Action Plan from the World's Foremost Expert on Business Leadership* by John Kotter—Kotter provides a model for leading change in an organization; this model can be adapted for leading a change such as designing a new school model. If you don't take time to read the book, visit Kotter's website on this change process: kotterinc.com/8-steps-process-for-leading-change (Kotter, 2012).
- *The Fifth Discipline: The Art and Practice of the Learning Organization* by Peter Senge—This is one of the earliest works on learning organizations and contains valuable resources and tools for creating and leading organizations striving to make change. It contains many excellent insights (Senge, 2006).
- *Switch: How to Change Things When Change Is Hard* by Chip Heath and Dan Heath—This book explores the science behind the difficulty of getting individuals and organizations to make significant changes. Dan and Chip Heath use effective analogies to help illustrate the challenges of change and ways to address these challenges (Heath, 2010).
- *Start with Why: How Great Leaders Inspire Everyone to Take Action* by Simon Sinek—In a book directed at businesspeople, Sinek demonstrates how the "why" of an organization is much more important to success than the "what" or the "how." The ideas here support the development of a vision and belief statements (Sinek, 2009). Sinek also has a website dedicated to the book's concept: startwithwhy.com.

- *Blink: The Power of Thinking Without Thinking* by Malcolm Gladwell—Gladwell explores the science behind intuition and demonstrates why we shouldn't always discount hunches, which can greatly influence our decisions and behaviors. This book also has value in the realm of learning (Gladwell, 2006).
- *Good to Great: Why Some Companies Make the Leap . . . and Others Don't* by Jim Collins—While not as directly valuable as some of the others, this book and *Great by Choice: Uncertainty, Chaos, and Luck—Why Some Thrive Despite Them All* look at the factors within an organization that can lead to success beyond that of peer organizations and then allow those organizations to sustain that level of success. Of particular interest are the insights on leadership for such organizations (Collins, 2001; Collins, 2011).
- *Simple Thinking: How to Remove Complexity from Life and Work* by Richard Gerver—Gerver led one of the most successful school turnaround efforts to ever take place in Great Britain. In this book, he talks about the many things that can lead to such successful outcomes without being overly complex. In fact, often simpler is better (Gerver, 2016).
- *Creating Tomorrow's Schools Today: Education – Our Children – Their Futures* by Richard Gerver—This is Gerver's story of bringing innovation to the Grange School and the many lessons he learned along the way. The most recent edition includes additional insights from his later journey working with schools around the world (Gerver, Creating Tomorrow's Schools Today, 2014).

Use of data, information, and averages

Data-based decision-making and using data for accountability are rather volatile subjects. Data use has been emphasized in education for decades and is regularly used to justify actions and decisions. One of the chief arguments against the use of data is the difficulty of collecting and applying it appropriately. Having a better understanding of this challenge will be helpful. Here are two books I recommend:

- *The End of Average: How We Succeed in a World That Values Sameness* by Todd Rose—This book exposes the perils of applying averages to humans and human systems. Rose details the ways that averages have been inappropriately used in all areas of our society and the many problems and challenges our reliance on averages has created (Rose, 2015).
- *The Signal and the Noise: Why So Many Predictions Fail—but Some Don't* by Nate Silver—This book helps readers determine when and how to use data to achieve a desired purpose while demonstrating the many ways that useful data is lost or obscured by other data and information (Silver, 2012).

The brain

Anyone designing a school model should have a basic understanding of the way the brain functions, grows, develops, and learns. Many of the books in the learning and thinking section below contain additional information on the brain.

- *Brainstorm: The Power and Purpose of the Teenage Brain* by Daniel Siegel, MD—This book addresses numerous myths about the adolescent brain and helps explain how understanding the teen brain can allow us to create circumstances and respond to teen actions and decisions that will lead to more positive outcomes (Siegel, 2013).
- *My Stroke of Insight: A Brain Scientist's Personal Journey* by Jill Bolte Taylor—This book, written by a brain researcher after having recovered from a stroke, provides great insights into how the brain functions, the ways the two hemispheres of the brain interact, and how all this can play out in people's personalities and traits (Taylor, 2006).

Motivation, willpower, and success

When people are motivated to learn, they retain knowledge better, can combine it with other learning, and can apply it in new situations. Pushing past challenges that occur when striving to learn may require willpower. These books help provide an understanding of motivation, how motivation occurs in individuals, and where willpower might come from.

- *Drive: The Surprising Truth about What Motivates Us* by Daniel Pink—Pink cites extensive research and examples that demonstrate the shortcomings of rewards and punishments for providing motivation. The book details alternative, more effective drivers of motivation (Pink, 2009).
- *The Marshmallow Test: Why Self-Control is the Engine of Success* by Walter Mischel—Mischel tracked numerous child test subjects over the course of several decades to see how early demonstrations of "willpower" affected their future education and professional paths. He provides research that shows that willpower is not simply a trait people have but is something that can be enhanced and strengthened (Mischel, 2014).
- *Barking Up the Wrong Tree: The Surprising Science Behind Why Everything You Know About Success Is (Mostly) Wrong* by Eric Barker—This book explores myths and facts about achieving success. The nature of Barker's research and writing is somewhat diverse, but the insights are individually and collectively very valuable (Barker, 2017).

Learning and thinking

This is clearly one of the most important and valuable elements when it comes to building a base of knowledge for school design, but it comes with a huge caveat. Most of the literature around learning—including books, journal articles, and research—frame the work and findings in the current model of schools. The authors and researchers take their findings and adapt them based on an assumption they will be applied in such a school model. That means, to get the most out of these materials, we must consider what the findings and recommendations would mean in a different model or, even better, how they can inform the design of a new model.

For example, in *How We Learn*, Benedict Carey spends a great deal of time on memorization of vocabulary lists, science terms, poems, and math formulas. The writing is framed with the expectation that a student is memorizing to prepare for an upcoming exam. The insights that Carey provides are valuable in a traditional school, where there are exams that rely on rote memorization, but they might be useless in other school models. Other parts of the book, however, note that knowledge will be learned more effectively and be more retrievable if encountered in a more meaningful, relevant, contextual manner (Carey, 2014).

Although many of the writers would likely agree their findings support a different model of school, their texts rarely consider a new design as an option. To best utilize these texts, we must look past the writers' biases toward the current model. Instead, we should focus on ways the findings and recommendations can lead to significantly better learning than the writers even considered.

- *The Self-Driven Child: The Science and Sense of Giving Your Kids More Control Over Their Lives* by William Stixrud and Ned Johnson—In this 2018 book, Stixrud and Johnson show how lack of power and control is a leading cause of childhood stress and contributes to numerous challenges. Stixrud is a clinical neuropsychologist who works primarily with children, and Johnson runs a tutoring service. They provide solid, research-based insights along with corresponding examples from their own work and experiences (Johnson, 2018).
- *Mindset: The New Psychology of Success* by Carol Dweck— Dweck, a Stanford psychologist, discusses the concept of mindset and research showing the powerful benefits of a "growth mindset." Even more

important is that Dweck illustrates numerous dangers of a "fixed mindset" beyond just learning and academic performance (Dweck, 2016).

- *Tapping the Power of Personalized Learning: A Roadmap for School Leaders* by James Rickabaugh—Rickabaugh, senior advisor at the Institute for Personalized Learning, provides a comprehensive look at what personalized learning is, the incredible positive impacts demonstrated through decades of implementation, and insights on implementing such innovative practices (Rickabaugh, 2016).
- *Why Don't Students Like School: A Cognitive Scientist Answers Questions about How the Mind Works and What It Means for the Classroom* by Daniel T. Willingham—Willingham is a cognitive scientist who wrote this book to help teachers better engage students by exploring the science behind the challenges they face in learning at school. The research and explanations, however, also provide valuable insights for how to design a new school model that will foster learning for all students (Willingham, 2009).
- *How We Learn: The Surprising Truth about When, Where, and Why It Happens* by Benedict Carey—This book dives deeply into centuries' worth of research on how we learn and what that might mean for the most effective ways of fostering learning for oneself or others (Carey, 2014).
- *How We Learn* audio course from The Great Courses, delivered by Monisha Pasupathi, associate professor in the department of psychology at the University of Utah—This course is made up of twenty-four lectures on how people learn and is based on a wide array of research which is presented in a clear, easy-to-understand format (Paupathi, 2012).
- *Outliers: The Story of Success* by Malcolm Gladwell—Though written for a business audience, *Outliers* provides excellent insights on the influence of environmental elements and the ways certain experiences can contribute to success, thus informing how we might design a school model (Gladwell, 2008).

Journals to further inform your work

Although the listed books are more comprehensive, journal articles have the benefit of being current. Also, because they are shorter than books, you can cover more ground in a shorter amount of time. Rather than list specific articles to read, I encourage you to seek out the most recent articles on a given topic and consider subscribing to or browsing through learning-related journals regularly for the latest research and perspectives. Here are a few I recommend:

- *Edutopia* (Edutopia.org)
- *The Hechinger Report* (HechingerReport.org)
- *eSchool News* (eSchoolNews.com)
- *Education Week* (EdWeek.org)
- *Educational Leadership* (ASCD.org/publications/educational-leadership.aspx)
- *THE Journal* (THEJournal.com)
- *The Education Trust* (EdTrust.org)
- *Education Next* (EducationNext.org)

The list continues

Even as we were preparing this book for publication, I found more books with great value. My website, knowresponsibility.com, will maintain an up-to-date list of resources, so check there regularly. Three additional works I found just prior to press were *The Coddling of the American Mind* by Greg Lukianoff and Jonathan Haidt (Lukianoff, 2018); *Dare to Lead* by Brené Brown (Brown, 2018); and *Free to Learn* by Peter Gray (Gray, 2013).

CHAPTER 28

BUILDING COMMITMENT AND ESTABLISHING A VISION

"People will become committed to that which they help create."
—Michael Beer

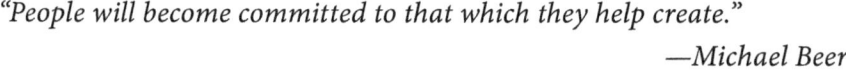

A ny organization striving toward its potential needs the commitment of its members. True commitment—where people have an intrinsic desire to further the purposes of their organization—requires that members are willing to act courageously when confronted by daunting challenges and refuse to quit in the face of naysayers and setbacks.

It is commitment that separates champions from also-rans, allows underdogs to overcome favorites, leads communities to come back stronger after being devastated by a disaster, and allows a small group of thoughtful citizens to change the world. Changing a 126-year-old institution requires commitment. Your team must truly believe in its purpose and vision and be ready to tap their courage and will.

This chapter will explore development of vision and belief statements. One critical element of gaining commitment is maintaining the organization's integrity and ensuring everyone has opportunities for meaningful input. When done, everyone should feel they truly contributed to the development of a vision for your team and were actively engaged in establishing your principles and belief statements.

> ### INTERNAL VS. EXTERNAL MISSION AND VISION STATEMENTS
>
> Many organizations publish their mission, vision, and belief statements to communicate important information about the organization. However, the statements discussed in this chapter are specifically meant for your internal purposes first. These will be critical tools for maintaining integrity and guiding your work. Once established and agreed upon, they may be adapted for external audiences, but those audiences should not be considered while developing the initial statements. Don't get bogged down in wordsmithing or compromising the statements to appease external groups.

Establishing a vision

People have mixed feelings about organizational visions and vision statements, usually based on personal experience. In essence, a vision statement created with integrity by a committed team will have incredible value; it will serve as a compass, sounding board, and litmus test for the organization and its members by ensuring they stay focused on the path toward their shared purpose. A vision statement should be a guiding light for the organization, not a marketing tool for outsiders.

As with everything else in this how-to part of the book, establishing a vision for your team must be done collaboratively and with integrity. It is the vision statement and the subsequent plan for implementing the vision that will bring cohesion to the design process. It also allows everyone involved to make decisions and take actions that will have integrity and contribute to achieving the team's purpose.

There are books, websites, and consultants available to help organizations establish a vision. However, you probably already have all or most of what you need with a little guidance and direction to get started.

The components of a vision statement

A vision statement should include three elements:

- a picture of the future desired by the organization (the "what")
- the purpose for which the organization exists (the "why")
- the means by which the organization will attain that future (the "how")

The elements don't have to be in any certain order. Rather, the order and the specific language used should result in a statement that is easy for everyone in the organization to understand and apply. While it is critical that everyone in the organization agrees on the true meaning of the statement, vision statements should not be overly detailed, specific, or complex. The statement should have meaning that goes beyond its precise wording.

Developing a vision statement

When you understand that the vision statement is for the organization and its members and not outside audiences, reaching consensus becomes fairly simple. If desired, supporting statements can be added that clarify the deeper meaning of elements of the statement. Prior to beginning this process, however, there must be trust and respect among the members and substantive dialogues must have occurred.

With all this in mind, the process of developing the vision statement does not need to be complicated. Here are a series of steps that can be used as a starting point for your process, which you can adapt as needed:

1. Determine who will have primary responsibility for developing the vision statement; this could include the full leadership team, select members of the leadership team, or others not on the leadership team.

2. Determine the degree to which input will be solicited from the broader organization.
3. Brainstorm and solicit input on each element—what, why, and how—of the vision statement. Ask questions along the lines of:
    a. "When our vision is achieved, what will our organization be doing? What will it look like for our students?"
    b. "What is the larger purpose for which we are seeking the vision? Why do we want the outcomes we've identified for our students?"
    c. "To what are we willing to commit to achieve the outcomes we've identified? How will we make these outcomes achievable?"
4. Categorize and combine the input you receive to reduce the total number of items while maintaining the essence and intent of all input to the greatest degree possible; if there is input with which there is disagreement, seek consensus now, or address it in the next step.
5. Research and implement a method to identify the items the selection team considers essential to the vision of the organization. (I recommend the Nominal Group Process.) The goal is group consensus on each item you retain and each you eliminate.
6. From the list of items for each element, develop language that would encompass or represent all the input items retained for that element. Remember, don't worry whether outside audiences would understand; rather, ensure that organization members will be clear on the scope of what the language represents.
7. Finalize the language of the vision statement so it is concise, easy to understand by everyone in the organization, and meaningfully representative of the full scope of the what, why, and how of the organization.

A LOOK AT THE SUMMITVILLE LEARNING COMMUNITY VISION STATEMENT

Part 2 of this book provides an example of a new school model; that fictional community has the following vision statement:

> *The Summitville Learning Community meets the learning, growth, and development needs of all children to ensure every child approaches and continuously expands their potential so that each is prepared for the paths they pursue in the future. Individually and collectively, they contribute to making our world a better place to live.*

In this statement, the picture of the future (the what) is that "every child approaches and continuously expands their potential"; the purpose (the why) is "so that each is prepared for the paths they pursue in the future" and "individually and collectively, they contribute to making our world a better place to live"; and the means (the how) is "The Summitville Learning Community meets the learning, growth, and development needs of all children."

An outsider reading this vision statement may have concerns that it is inadequate, too broad, or too general. That's okay as long as those within the SLC understand the deeper meaning the statement encompasses and the principles and beliefs of the organization that are inherently included in the statement.

For example, within the SLC, there is a clear consensus that the community is fully committed and will collectively take whatever steps are necessary to meet the learning, growth, and development needs of all children. Everyone in the SLC understands this level of commitment without the statement having to be clearer than that.

Another example is that those who are part of the SLC understand that "prepared for the paths they pursue in the future" means that each student who "graduates" from the SLC will have the skills, knowledge, and aptitudes to pursue any postsecondary options. That doesn't mean they meet every requirement for every college or career or other option but that they will be able to figure out what is required, develop a comprehensive plan for meeting those requirements, and have the confidence and drive to follow through.

8. Document the deeper meaning of the statement in a way that organization members (and outside audiences, if you so choose) can readily reference when needed or desired.
9. Post the vision statement in visible locations to help all organization members become familiar with it.
10. Regularly reflect on the vision statement to ensure that all decisions and actions of the organization support and align with the statement.
11. Don't be afraid to revisit and even revise the vision statement if situations change or if it is determined that something about the vision statement doesn't truly align with the purpose and internalized vision of the organization. This should not be done lightly, but it is necessary if some aspect of the vision statement is causing the organization to compromise its integrity.

Principles and belief statements

While not specifically part of a vision statement, establishing principles and belief statements can help maintain the integrity of vision statements. Organizational principles set constraints on what the organization will strive to do or will refuse to do. For example, US Army members take an oath of enlistment, in which they swear to obey the orders of the president of the United States.

Each team or organization pursuing design and implementation of a new school model needs to establish those principles that will provide needed guidance and constraints. Like the vision statement, these serve as a compass when approaching obstacles and forks in the road so that the organization continues toward its intended outcomes. They can also serve as a litmus test when confronted with a dilemma about some decision or action.

Like the vision statement, there must be consensus on the principles. Therefore, a similar process can be used in developing these as was used for the vision statement. Alternatively, use the input from the vision statement to develop a draft list of principles. Then use the process to narrow the list and seek consensus.

In many respects, belief statements are a variation of principles but add value through their language. Whereas the language of principles reflects the organization as a whole, the language of belief statements reflects each person in the organization. Though they are written in a "*We* believe . . ." format, each member should personally believe each statement.

Consequently, in carrying out their roles and responsibilities with the organization, each member is committed to the belief statements. For integrity, members should occasionally review and internalize the meaning of the belief statements and reinforce their commitment to them. Also, as with vision statements, it is appropriate to revisit and revise principles and belief statements with integrity and thoughtfulness.

Using a vision statement, principles, and belief statements

A vision statement, principles, and belief statements should serve as a compass, a sounding board, and a litmus test for the organization. That means that all become tools for the following and more:

- developing the plan for achieving the organization's purpose
- periodic checks on the organization's progress toward achieving its purpose
- ensuring resources are being directed appropriately
- ensuring decisions made will best move the organization toward its purpose
- maintaining the integrity of the organization and all its activities

If the vision, principles, and beliefs reflect the intents and purposes of the organization and its members, and if those members are committed to the organization, then they will be applying these automatically. During the early stages of the design process, it is useful to apply them more deliberately. Dilemmas and challenges may occasionally arise that can be addressed through a more deliberate consideration of the vision, principles, and belief statements. No decisions should be made or actions taken that conflict with or are counter to the vision statement or any of the organization's principles or belief statements.

PART 5

REINVENTING PUBLIC EDUCATION IN YOUR COMMUNITY

PART 5

REINVENTING PUBLIC EDUCATION IN YOUR COMMUNITY

This final part of the book provides a process for designing a new school model for your community. The process borrows significantly from the implementation of Academic and Career Planning (ACP) in Wisconsin. That process broke new ground that held important lessons for designing and implementing community-centric change by deviating significantly from the normal approach to implementing state-level initiatives and mandates.

Our Department of Public Instruction ACP team first developed the general ACP model for students. We knew that to have integrity, the ACP process had to honor the unique nature of each student and each school. Consequently, while there would be common threads and activities, the ACP process for each student should be unique. We applied this same belief and structure to ACP implementation at the school level, as the program had to be altered for each school's unique aspects as well. This same approach will allow your community to design and implement a school model specifically to meet the needs of your community.

This approach amounted to four steps. The first step, self-awareness, is contained in chapters 29 and 30. This is critical in developing and implementing any plan, but most organizations either ignore this step or do it with little to no integrity. One reason it is so important is it ensures you know your true starting point. Many organizations start new initiatives and activities without assessing their true readiness, which inevitably leads to failure of the initiative or activity to meet its potential.

The second step, exploration, is contained in chapter 31. This is about exploring all the possible ways you could structure and implement a new school model and all the ways you could then achieve the model you choose. This is where you'll really exercise your creative and critical thinking skills, throw off all the old limitations, and challenge all your old paradigms. The sky is truly the limit!

"SCHOOL" VS "SCHOOL MODEL"

Throughout the book I refer to the "school model" rather than just "school." The terminology isn't critical, but the meaning is. When we talk about a "school," we almost always think of a building and a relatively static structure. This traps us into discounting ideas that are incompatible with this paradigm. It also limits our thinking to ideas that are compatible with this static structure paradigm.

Using the term "school model" hopefully leads to a more open mind. What "school" should be for children is the collection of activities, experiences, and opportunities that foster learning, growth, and development. This is not limited to what happens in a physical building during set hours of the week. The term "school model" is meant to foster thinking and ideas that consider every location and every waking hour of every day as possible elements of a child's learning environment—in other words, his or her "school."

The third step is the planning itself and is contained in chapter 32. There, you will take the findings from your self-awareness step and mesh them with the outcomes of your exploration step to begin forming a school structure that will be ideal for your community. The value of this step is not in finalizing an actual school model and an implementation plan; rather, the value is the process you go through in developing these products.

The final step, implementation of the school model and the corresponding implementation plan, is contained in chapter 33. There you will begin to implement your new school model, but it will be a dynamic process. When working with human systems, everything is always in flux, so you must be ready to adapt constantly. Chapter 33 will dig more deeply into this reality.

While there is a logical order to the steps in this process, it is not absolute. You will be starting some steps prior to finishing previous steps. Don't hesitate to leverage opportunities that arise that seem to fit in a later step. And know that none of these steps is ever finished. You will constantly revisit and revise your self-awareness, exploration, planning, and implementation.

PLANNING YOUR ADVENTURE VACATION

To better understand the steps of the design process, think about planning a family adventure vacation—mountain climbing, white water rafting, or zip-lining through a rainforest canopy.

Step 1: Self-Awareness—You have to come to terms with who and where you and your family are. In this context, you need to figure out your family's readiness to participate in an adventure vacation. What is the level of interest? What is everyone's fitness level? What experience and expertise does everyone have? What resources (money, time, equipment) do you have available? What challenges might you face? How committed are all the family members?

Step 2: Exploration—You need to explore possible options, including types of adventure, locations, and means of accomplishing the vacation. You can keep this wide open or begin with known constraints, like staying within the continental US. Consider challenges you will face (costs, schedules, necessary preparations) to determine the breadth of "means" you will need to consider.

Step 3: Planning—With what you've learned in the first two steps, identify your selected adventure vacation and your honest starting point. That is, be realistic about your readiness for that vacation: Will you need to sell some on the idea? Will some or all family members need to improve their physical fitness? Will training need to be done? Will you need to save up sufficient money? Will you need to get passports? Will you need to align everyone's schedules? This type of questions will allow you to be realistic about when you can take the vacation and what tasks lie ahead. Then you can start to lay out the actual plan.

Step 4: Implementation—This is where your efforts in the first three steps pay off, but not in the way that may seem obvious. As soon as you begin to execute the plan, something will change, maybe to the extent that the plan is no longer doable as prepared. However, the process you went through in developing the plan will allow you to adapt to whatever changes are needed and continue toward taking that adventure vacation. Even better, some unexpected opportunity may arise that your early work allows you to leverage for an even better vacation than planned.

CHAPTER 29

SELF-AWARENESS: FIGURING OUT WHO YOU ARE

Given the nature and scope of designing a new school model, honest self-assessments are critical. First, determine the nature or "heart and soul" of your community. This is important in considering what you're working toward and tapping into all the valuable resources available to your efforts. I believe most people will be surprised by what they learn about their communities as they work through this process.

Begin by diving deep into your community. Often our impressions are not complete because we function in only some circles. Even if our impressions are fairly complete and accurate, it is good to validate them and have supporting documentation. Begin with information available from public sources, such as your local government or chamber of commerce; include demographic data, community profiles, business information, crime statistics, and any other information that seems relevant.

As you collect data and information, create lists of community resources and challenges. Resources are any current or possible assets for supporting student learning or meeting student needs. This includes faith-based institutions, service organizations, business and economic development organizations, youth sports organizations, philanthropists and foundations, and youth groups. If there is an entity or group about which you're unsure, include it in your list. Be as inclusive as possible.

Resources you find through these initial steps are, quite likely, the tip of the iceberg for your community. Most communities have a wealth of hidden resources that only emerge in a crisis or under certain circumstances. Never stop identifying resources, as needs will continue to arise.

Using networks you've been developing, identify individuals, organizations, and businesses who have previously provided assistance or resources in your community or who you believe may do so in this instance. Look for those who may have been contributors to your local library, sports complex, neighborhood or youth center, arts programs, or scholarships and include these among your identified resources. As this process continues, you will likely see additional resources emerge.

Challenges that can detract from the community or interfere with the learning, growth, and development of children could include crime, poverty, areas of neglect, drugs, homelessness, gangs, racial and ethnic conflicts, transitory populations, and broader economic issues such as shrinking revenue, unemployment, and closing businesses. You'll come back to this list in chapter 30 and when you begin to actually plan and design your school model.

Your list will likely be incomplete or may underestimate the scope of some issues. Relatively hidden challenges contribute significantly to many shortcomings that occur in schools, while many recognizable challenges have multiple, less obvious roots. Consequently, you will need to dig deep so that you are considering the roots and designing your school model with these in mind.

Your journey of community self-discovery will need to look at how the challenges in your community affect children's learning, growth, and development. This will help ensure the new school model is designed to counter the impact of community challenges to the greatest degree possible. To do that, it becomes necessary to have an accurate and complete understanding of these challenges.

Collecting and documenting resources and challenges in your community also provides insights about the nature of your community. Your team will discover those things that often give a community its heart and soul. You may find inspiring examples of people pulling together in times of need and strong community bonds overcoming differences, but you may also discover discrimination or ways that race, religion, or other differences affect people's treatment in the community. Such discoveries may be hard to face and address, but this awareness could be the opportunity needed to turn such situations around.

The self-evaluation and discovery processes never end. Instead, you will refine this picture as you continue the school model design and planning process. In addition, this picture could change if your community embraces changing paradigms as part of this process.

The key outcome of the self-discovery process is to answer several questions that will help inform the design and planning steps themselves:

- What things in our community contribute to *all* children reaching their potential?
- What things in our community contribute to *many* children reaching their potential?
- What things in our community contribute to *select* children reaching their potential?
- What things in our community deter *all* children from reaching their potential?
- What things in our community deter *many* children from reaching their potential?
- What things in our community deter *select* children from reaching their potential?

CHAPTER 30

SELF-AWARENESS: FIGURING OUT WHERE YOU ARE

To design and implement a new school model, you need to begin with a completely honest and unbiased determination of your readiness. This does not mean you delay your efforts until reaching a certain level of readiness; rather, you just need to know your starting point. For example, if you're planning a vacation to the Columbian jungle and are currently in Ames, Iowa, you can't plan as if you were currently in Bogotá. Your plans have to include getting to Columbia as well as getting to the jungle itself and following through on the entire adventure.

For the school design process, you need to determine the readiness of your team and your community to support and commit to this effort, as well as know the resources and challenges identified through the process in chapter 29. Designing a new school model encompasses many stakeholders, so this readiness check must be similarly broad. Those who are strongly committed need to assess their readiness for the task at hand, while the enthusiasm and commitment of others who will be part of or affected by it down the road must also be gauged.

I predict that most communities will discover they have significantly more resources and tools available than they realized but that there is a significant amount of inertia that must be overcome due to fondness for the current school model.

Determining the readiness of the broader community

The leadership team and those already committed to this effort will be doing the bulk of the work, but support or resistance in the broader community will make a substantial difference in planning and implementing your school model. Figuring out where you are in this context is a matter of determining two things: the scope or breadth of the various stakeholders who are likely to commit early on and the level of resistance that seems to be present among those not ready to commit.

Although you will not be able to get a precise measurement, you should be able to get a good estimate through dialogues with various audiences, including those whom you engaged when determining who you are as a community. Be honest in your assessment of support and resistance. Being too optimistic may leave you unprepared, while being too pessimistic may dampen your team's energy and enthusiasm.

In gauging the level of support, commitment, and resistance among stakeholders, you want people's deeper, more thoughtful opinions rather than quick, off-the-cuff responses. You can facilitate this through a two-step process. First, have people do personal reflection, and then use dialogues, forums, or surveys to gauge their level of support, commitment, and resistance.

Step one—reflective questions

Reflective questions help people determine their core belief about the need for change. In most new and different situations, our first response is driven by emotions rather than reason. Simply asking questions about the changes being considered can trigger emotions that may lead to resistance. Once emotion-driven resistance builds, often no amount of logic and reason can overcome it.

Starting with reflection allows people to consider the change from a personal, less threatening perspective. They are not responding to someone else's opinions and arguments but rather considering their own opinions. If doing this at a forum or group event, have people consider the reflective questions individually before moving on to the second step of this process.

> **REFLECTION TIME—MAYBE YOUR MOST IMPORTANT INVESTMENT**
>
> We live in a world of instant gratification, and we are under constant pressure to avoid wasting time doing things that have no clear value. Chapters 30 and 31 include several reflection activities that don't directly result in any tangible outcomes. It will be tempting, therefore, to minimize time for people to reflect. Don't do this!
>
> Reflection time is an investment that will pay fantastic dividends throughout this process. As you have people go through the reflection activities, create the space and time for them to truly think deeply about the questions they are asking themselves. And know that most of us will take a little while to be able to do this because we don't do it very often. Make this investment early, and you will see the rewards throughout the design efforts.

The reflective questions should be of two types. The first are questions that create context relative to each person's principles and values. These help prepare people to answer later questions based on their true beliefs, not what they think others want to hear or things others have already said. Remember, these are reflective and not to be answered aloud. Here are examples of questions that could be used:

- What are my principles and values? What sorts of things are most important to me?
- How do my daily actions and decisions reflect my principles and values?
- How do my daily actions and decisions conflict with my principles and values?

- How important is it that my actions and decisions reflect and support my principles and values?

The second type of reflective questions is related to education and learning. They will help people think more deeply about their own experiences and observations rather than what they've heard or read somewhere. Here are examples of questions that could be used; make sure to consider all levels from kindergarten through twelfth grade.

- What were the best parts of my time spent in school?
- How effective was the education I received?
- What sort of challenges did I encounter during school?
- How effectively did the schools I attended push me to reach for my full potential?
- How effective was the education of my children or other children I know?
- What sort of challenges have I seen children encounter during school?
- How effectively did the schools push children to reach their full potential?
- How effectively do I believe the current school structure uses available time and resources to facilitate student learning, growth, and development?

Step two—gathering thoughts and opinions

Once people have had a chance to reflect, gather their thoughts and try to gauge possible commitment. This can be done using surveys, online forums, or in-person gatherings such as a focus group. If you will have multiple people together (online or in person), you can include dialogues related to the reflective questions already asked. After the discussions, have people share some of their beliefs and levels of commitment.

Here are examples of questions that could be used during focus group sessions, in online forums, or as part of a survey; make sure to consider all levels from kindergarten through twelfth grade.

- To what extent do you believe our current schools are meeting the needs of all students?
- To what extent do you believe our current schools could be improved to meet the needs of all students?
- What things about our current school structure* do you believe work really well for all or most students?
- What things about our current school structure* do not work well for all or most students?
- Why do you believe we have the current school structure*?
- To what extent do you believe children have greater potential than what they are able to achieve in their current schools?
- To what extent do you believe some, many, or all students could learn more effectively in a structure very different from the current one?
- What degree of value do you see in considering new school models designed from scratch rather than adapting the current model?
- How likely would you be to support a local effort to design an entirely new school model meant to ensure all students can learn effectively?

*The term "current school structure" refers to the traditional calendar, schedule, K–12 grade breakdown, subjects being taught separately, etc.

Determining the readiness of your organization and leadership team

Those who have joined your organization or accepted a role on your leadership team should already be committed to this effort. However, there is immense value in each person reflecting in a similar way to that of the broader community. This process helps solidify each member's commitment while considering the thought process others will need to go through to accept and support this effort.

You might start by having the members go through the same questions and discussions used with the broader community. Then, drill down with a few additional reflective questions and follow-up dialogues.

Here are reflective questions to consider using with your organization members and leadership team:

- Why have you become a part of the process of designing a new school model for your community?
- What are your personal priorities, and where does the school model design effort fit within those priorities?
- What outcomes of this effort are you seeking in order to meet personal needs and wants?
- What biases do you have that could challenge you in maintaining an open mind about the model of school being developed?
- What priorities and loyalties could compromise your objectiveness as part of this effort?
- How open are you to candid discussions with those who have different opinions, priorities, and biases than you?
- How willing are you to put your trust in and be vulnerable with others who are part of this organization and the leadership team?
- What level of commitment are you willing to make toward this effort?

Here are questions you may consider as part of your discussions to follow the reflective questions:

- How can we help each other maintain open minds about the model of school being developed?
- How can we help each other account for our biases as we work together?
- How can we help each member of our organization address their personal priorities while maintaining the integrity of our collective purpose?
- How can we ensure our discussions and work are completely open and honest?
- What are the elephants in the room? How can we harness the power of those elephants or at least account for them in our work?
- How can we maintain our trust with each other under any and all circumstances?

Remember, all the questions listed in this and the following chapters are only examples. Use them only if you believe they will have value for your group, adapt them where necessary, and add your own.

CHAPTER 31

EXPLORATION: FIGURING OUT WHERE YOU WANT TO GO

Begin with desired student outcomes

Knowing who you are as a community and your readiness level, it's time to consider what a new school model might look like. This can be challenging because the current model is so dominant in all our minds. If you try to imagine the final design in its entirety, you'll likely end up with some variation of the factory model. A bit later, however, you will try to imagine a more complete model.

A better approach begins by thinking about the young adults you hope come out of the new model. Ultimately, this is what you're striving toward. You want to design a school model that results in every graduate having the traits, skills, and knowledge to thrive in the world of adults.

This approach has its own challenges. We still default to our own experiences and the traits, skills, and knowledge we had after high school graduation. That's an okay starting point, especially if you feel you graduated from high school with all the preparation you needed. If not, then you want to explore the traits, skills, and knowledge you wish you had when you were a young adult.

Once again, start with individual reflection. Each person working on the exploration step should take time to think about their own journey from childhood to the present. Take note of milestones, challenges, and choices that were encountered. Think about the people and events that influenced the journey. Then, reflect on questions such as these; for those related to school, make sure to consider all levels from kindergarten through twelfth grade:

- What formal instruction in school influenced your journey?
- What formal instruction in school helped prepare you for your journey?
- What extracurricular or informal events at school influenced your journey?
- What extracurricular or informal events at school helped prepare you for your journey?
- What events that occurred outside of the school environment influenced and helped prepare you for your journey?
- Who influenced or helped prepare you for your journey, and in what ways?
- When you encountered challenges during your journey, what were the traits, skills, and knowledge that helped you overcome them?
- Looking back on challenges you encountered, what traits, skills, and knowledge would have been helpful to have?
- When you faced important decisions, what were the traits, skills, and knowledge that helped you make good choices?
- When looking back on important decisions, what traits, skills, and knowledge would have been helpful to have?
- After reflecting on your journey and the questions above, what traits, skills, and knowledge would you want all young adults to have?

Of course, your reflections may lead to traits, skills, and knowledge related to specific jobs or careers; take note of these things, but then focus on those that would be beneficial regardless of one's path ahead.

After time to reflect, begin to generate lists of outcomes you want for the young adults in your community. As with the visioning process, start with a comprehensive list generated by many people, then work to combine the various items in a logical manner, and finally seek consensus on the initial collective list of traits, skills, and knowledge. This list should change as you continue with this process. The ongoing dialogues will trigger thoughts and ideas you want to work into your exploration.

Determine how the outcomes might be achieved

For this task, leverage your team's collective knowledge on learning, growth, and development, including personal experiences and what you gained from books, articles, and research as noted in chapter 27. Keep in mind that one of the biggest drawbacks of our current school model is trying to achieve nearly every desired outcome by *teaching* it—and that doesn't work.

This is why the research and your own experiences are so important. Both demonstrate that simply being taught something in a traditional sense will not result in long-term learning, development of skills, or adoption of attitudes or traits. To internalize the outcomes you listed, young adults will have to be applying them in situations and contexts that are meaningful and relevant.

In constructing your school model, you'll need to consider the opportunities students would need to learn, apply, and practice the traits, skills, and knowledge you have identified. Since this is the exploration stage, you don't need to place constraints on the ideas you generate. Consider any approaches or activities that might be effective, no matter how wild. Strive to be creative and push yourselves outside the box. When everything is done, the idea is to no longer be inside the box.

You also want to generate ideas from a wide assortment of people. Different experiences and perspectives will lead to different ideas. Remember, the ideas being explored must be capable of working for a diverse group of children, so they should come from a diverse group of participants.

The ideas you are generating—of experiences and activities that could be part of a new model—should span a full range of dates, times, locations, and situations in which they could occur. In other words, don't limit your ideas to things that could occur within the restraints of traditional schools.

This is also why, during your reflection time, you should have thought of times you learned something, practiced a skill, or adopted some trait outside of school. Many of our most meaningful lessons came during summer vacations, at sleepovers, on weekends, at home, in youth sports, listening to a grandparent's stories, at a job, or elsewhere totally unrelated to our formal schooling. Others happened at school but outside of the formal, intentional instructional process. If these provided meaningful learning opportunities, include them in the list you are developing.

Make sure you document all ideas. You will revisit this list once you begin the actual planning of your school model. As always, be ready to add to this list anytime new ideas occur.

Determining how to meet diverse student needs in order to remove barriers to learning

After generating your list of activities and experiences, begin figuring out how to remove barriers to learning for every student. In designing a new model, one of the most important considerations is that anytime a learning barrier arises, the new model allows it to be addressed effectively.

Toward this end, go back to your reflections and identify as many barriers to learning as possible. Look beyond your own experiences and consider classmates and other students and families you have known over the years. In addition, consider barriers to learning you identified in your research. Be sure to drill below the surface and try to identify root causes and not just symptoms.

For example, one of the most commonly discussed "barriers to learning" in the current model is attendance. There is significant research showing that, as student attendance drops, so does academic performance. Schools then attempt to improve attendance by instituting penalties for absences, rewards for attendance, and laws and rules that punish students and parents for chronic absences. But attendance is a symptom, not a problem. There are countless factors leading to student absences, not just students' desire to play hooky.

Although some schools try to address causes of absences, the school model itself is a significant contributing factor. As you work to design a new model of school, you can take the shortcomings of the model out of the equation and consider how to address every root cause of absences.

Take the time to think about all the barriers to learning. Also, go back and review part 1 of this book. Many reasons cited for replacing the factory model are based on learning barriers inherent to the model. These may help you generate a list of barriers you will want to be sure your model avoids.

Exploring leadership and administration models

Another element to explore is how leadership and administrative functions will be provided. Administrative functions are things schools must do to operate and meet legal requirements, such as record keeping, assessments, reporting, payroll and taxes, infrastructure, finance, billing, and other bookkeeping functions. Leadership, on the other hand, is largely what each school chooses to make it.

While legal requirements provide some limitations, most of the leadership and administrative structure is open to numerous possibilities. Students may even be able to take on many of the roles as part of their learning, growth, and development opportunities. Don't limit yourselves in how this might be structured. Rather, look at this element systemically with everything else. This is just exploration, so look into any and every possible approach. Eventually, you will want a structure that supports the learning model you envision while not creating learning barriers.

As you explore leadership and administrative models, don't look to schools for examples. Rather, look to businesses, nonprofits, and other organizations. This is where having entrepreneurs and other businesspeople on your team can be helpful. They will hopefully be familiar with contemporary models that have been implemented successfully in recent years and that could be adapted effectively for your school model.

Revisiting your vision statement, principles, and belief statements

During these exploration activities, you should occasionally revisit your vision statement, principles, and belief statements to ensure you are remaining true to them. You can also consider whether any changes are needed to reflect what you've learned about yourselves and your community.

Exploring how you could reach your destination

Your final exploration will be of various means for achieving your desired end state. What tools and activities could you use to implement your school model when the time comes? In the adventure vacation analogy, this is akin to determining your method and route of travel. Like a vacation trip, consider what you can gain from the travel experience beyond getting from point A to point B.

This aspect of exploration is a bit simpler. You already have an organizational structure (your design and leadership teams), but you will want to consider if that structure is what's best moving forward. You also have constraints to consider, such as the size of your community, your geographic location, and education laws and rules. In this part of the process, you are exploring the benefits and drawbacks of variables that will affect your plan and planning.

These are some of the key structural and implementation variables to explore, and you may come up with others:

- Leadership structure during implementation (may be different from final structure)
- Means of communicating with various audiences

- Overall implementation timeline
- Timeline for various elements of the process
- Contributions/roles of various stakeholders

As with so much else covered in this book, be open to a unique structure and make sure it is sufficiently dynamic. While there are numerous organizational and leadership structures taught in courses and books, they are all just starting points. They are also based, in almost all cases, on models from the past. You are preparing for a dynamic and uncertain future, so don't get caught with a model that will hinder your efforts.

CHAPTER 32

PLANNING

"I have always found that plans are useless, but planning is indispensable."

—Dwight D. Eisenhower

The most important outcome of this chapter is not a plan but rather the readiness to pursue your organization's vision. The reason for this seemingly counterintuitive statement is reflected in this chapter's epigraph, a quote from Dwight D. Eisenhower—a man who experienced the shortcomings of plans themselves in two extremely dynamic environments: combat and politics. Eisenhower would also have been familiar with the related military adage, "The plan never survives the first shot."

In other words, as soon as one begins to execute a plan, something is going to change. This is especially true in human systems like the military, government, or education. Human systems are infinitely dynamic because they are based on the interactions of unique human elements. Each of the elements is in constant flux, which means the interactions between them are in constant flux. Believing that one could successfully implement a static plan for anything of consequence in such a system would be naive.

Which brings us to the second part of Eisenhower's quotation: planning is indispensable. The value of planning is not the plan but, rather, being immersed in all the variables that make up the plan. Ideally, those doing the planning get to know all the parts and pieces, resources, potential challenges, and relationships. They should also become familiar with the landscape and environment, understand how the elements interact, and explore how these elements might respond in various situations and under different circumstances. In short, the planners become integral parts of the system for which they are developing the plan. Then, when they begin to execute, they are fully prepared to drive on, regardless of what challenges arise or how the landscape changes, and leverage unexpected opportunities that emerge.

That level of readiness is the outcome you want from this step of the process. That you will likely also create an actual plan is fine, and that plan can become the base from which you adjust as you begin implementation. It will also be a valuable historical artifact when people look back at how your school model was created. Just don't become too attached to it.

> ## "I CAN'T DO THIS. I'M NOT AN EXPERT ON ANY OF THIS STUFF!"
>
> You may believe you lack the expertise to help design a new school model. Although this is totally understandable, you're wrong. You may not have all the knowledge and understanding, but you definitely have some of what will be needed. The key is to realize there are no experts for this particular challenge; there are only experts on the current school model.
>
> This is even true of most current educators. Their experiences are relevant to the factory model of school. They may be excited about the possibility of a new school model, but they probably have little experience in that area. At the same time, educators open to a new model can be extremely valuable contributors. Their experiences may allow them to visualize new models that would address shortcomings of the current model with which they are familiar.
>
> I am not an expert on designing a new school model for your community. My journey, reflections, research, and experiences have given me valuable knowledge and insights, but they pale compared to a group's collective knowledge and insights. This book, combined with resources such as those in chapter 27, gives you all you need to take on this effort except for the most important thing—the knowledge and understanding of your community.
>
> Anyone from outside your community who says they know what your community needs or who wants to lead you to the solutions to all your problems should probably be dismissed—unless they want to take you through a process similar to what is detailed in this book. If you'll feel better having someone guide you through the process, that's okay; but know that you likely have all the expertise you need right there in your community.

One-pair-team technique for planning and design

Planning and design must be a team effort. The collective experiences, insights, and ideas of multiple people will always be better overall than one person working alone. However, it is critical not to lose valuable individual insights and ideas that will improve the final results. I recommend using a technique that will move between individual and group work, ensuring every person's ideas are shared while still being a collaborative process.

Throughout planning and design, each team member thinks through the steps individually and documents his or her ideas and thoughts. Then, team members pair up to share those ideas and thoughts with one other team member. The pair documents their consensus ideas and thoughts. Finally, the entire group comes together to share their paired ideas and thoughts and come to a consensus on that aspect of the draft plan.

This technique can be adapted in various ways based on available time, the way the planning and design process is broken down, and any number of variables. The key is to leverage the diversity of ideas that gives value to collaboration without the collaboration itself squelching individual voices.

Backward planning

"Begin with the end in mind." —Stephen Covey

To develop a plan requires knowing your destination or envisioned end state. Your destination is captured in your vision statement, your collection of student outcomes, and the ideas you generated about how students might achieve those outcomes. You will now backward plan from that destination. Each step back from your end state will provide a benchmark for your plan and may represent a task that will be part of the plan. As usual, you will need to constantly fight the biases and paradigms of the factory model, especially when trying to envision the more complete school model.

Begin with your vision statement. Have each planning team member imagine your community with a school model in place that would fulfill that vision statement. Try to imagine various aspects or elements of that school model based on previously developed student outcomes. Think about what students would be doing to achieve those outcomes, but don't get trapped thinking about when, where, and how current students attend school.

Imagine a variety of students—representing the diversity within your community—engaged in learning at different times, in different places, through various activities. Imagine the unique and most challenging circumstances of those students. Imagine how this school model would contribute to your collection of outcomes for that diverse group of students.

Use the one-pair-team technique. Each planning team member, on his or her own, will take notes or draw a diagram to document the school model they are imagining. They should go into as much detail as they like and record as many thoughts and ideas as come to mind. Each person should record questions that arise in their own mind as they go through the exercise; if they determine their own answers, they should note these answers, since similar questions will likely arise from others; if they remain unanswered, others may be able to help answer them.

Don't discard anything at this stage. Even ideas that seem detrimental for some students or that raise concerns may fill a need later or prompt another idea when shared. This step could be done with everyone together or on their own and then brought together later. Eventually, each team member should have some sort of "sketch" of their vision of the new model school and a list of the student outcomes that the person feels should drive that model.

One reason for addressing the vision of the school and the student outcomes simultaneously is they are likely intertwined in each person's mind. Another is that they address two different but inseparable aspects of school: the need for every student to achieve certain learning, growth, and development, and the need to ensure every student is ready and able to learn. The former is reflected in the student outcomes, and the latter is reflected in the vision of a school model.

> ### ELEMENTS, ACTIVITIES, EXPERIENCES, AND OPPORTUNITIES
>
> Throughout this chapter, I use the terms elements, activities, experiences, and opportunities. This may raise the question, "What's the difference among these?" In truth, there is a lot of overlap among these, and it's not critical to differentiate the terms. What is critical is developing ideas, "sketches," and mental models of the ways in which the children in your community achieve the outcomes you've identified.

Once each team member feels they have captured their thoughts adequately, pair up and share what you have. Then, bring the team together and share the collective findings. Document ideas and be sure to capture questions and answers people developed. Work toward consensus on the outcomes that will be the "starting" point for your backward planning and the elements that should be included in your design.

You may find your team works effectively and comes to consensus easily, or you may need to use a technique, like the Nominal Group Process, to narrow your list before seeking consensus. Whatever approach you use, ensure no one on your team feels their ideas, concerns, or input are diminished. Remember that maintaining integrity throughout this process is critical to achieving its full potential.

Outcomes—moving backward to move forward

At this point, your team should have consensus on a set of outcomes and a collection of elements for the new model. Both will almost certainly change as the process continues, which is fine as long as consensus and integrity are maintained. The next step is working backward from each of the identified outcomes. Here again, you have options for how to proceed. Everyone can be part of the process for each item, or smaller teams can be formed to focus on select items. Whichever approach you choose, try to use the one-pair-team technique or some variation.

Working backward from the outcomes leads to activities and opportunities your school model must facilitate for students to achieve those outcomes. This process is largely the same as that used for developing the vision and list of outcomes. Sketch out a way for each outcome to be achieved. Think about the experiences and learning a student needs to reach that outcome.

Nearly every outcome requires a student to have a variety of experiences, learn a variety of knowledge and skills, and develop and strengthen certain attributes. You are tracing a path backward from each end state outcome to the point at which students would enter the school model, and you are identifying key experiences and learning opportunities needed between those points. Then, consider how the school model can facilitate those experiences and opportunities. Along with the previously identified elements, this becomes the starting point for the actual design of your school model.

Designing your new school model

Your team will need to come to terms with what designing a new school model means. You need to decide the degree to which your model will have defined, specific elements as opposed to being more dynamic and flexible. For some people, a dynamic and flexible model is scary. But these models work better for human systems because trying to set strict definitions and structures on a human system will compromise the ability of that system to achieve its potential.

As an example of a highly defined and structured model, look at the current factory model:

- Age-based cohorts of students
- A defined age at which students enter the model
- A defined number of years during which students are enrolled in the model
- A defined number of hours during which students attend school each day and each year
- A defined number of class hours that earns a student a credit
- A specific location at which the majority of instruction takes place
- All or nearly all courses taught by individual teachers focused on a single content area
- A set of required credits to be earned and courses to be attended for a student to graduate
- A defined grading scale for all classes
- A curriculum for all classes that largely determines what will be taught and, to a large degree, when each element will be taught

Some factory model schools go even further by requiring school uniforms and implementing routines and structures that remove even more flexibility. On the other end of the spectrum, of course, would be turning children loose with no supervision or sets of expectations. You are seeking a middle ground that accounts for the uniqueness of each child while helping them flourish.

In the end, you will want to include in your model some version of the following:

- The relationship between the school community and the larger community in which it is located. This should include how that relationship is fostered and maintained over time.
- The relationship between the school community and families with children who will rely on the school community for a significant part of the children's learning, growth, and development. This should include when the relationship starts and how it is fostered and maintained.

- The means through which student learning, growth, and development will be monitored.
- The means through which student learning, growth, and development could occur.
- The means through which each student establishes learning, growth, and development outcomes and benchmarks.
- The roles of school employees in fostering student learning, growth, and development.
- The ways in which the school community will address the unique needs and challenges of each student.
- The locations in which school community learning opportunities might be provided.
- Which children are eligible to enroll in your school community based on age, readiness, or residency.

Some elements above, like the location of student learning, could be wide open. Others may have strict legal requirements. During the design phase, don't get bogged down in whether you've missed anything. You almost certainly have, and that's okay; you'll catch these things later.

> ### HOW LONG SHOULD ALL THIS TAKE?
>
> There is no set timeline for this process. You can move as quickly as your community and circumstances allow or as slowly as necessary to reach the point of having sufficient commitment, enthusiasm, and community readiness.
>
> This is not a race. Consider pioneers settling the United States. Some were ready and able to go further faster than most others. Others followed much later for a variety of reasons but benefitted from the trailblazers. While there may have been some advantages and bragging rights for the early settlers, those tended to become less relevant over time. The same will be true in this journey. That is why knowing your community and your readiness is so important. The best way to ensure your journey is successful is to first ensure your community is ready and then move at a pace that is right for your community.

Capturing ideas

Throughout this process, be sure to capture all ideas as they occur and are built upon. At some stages, ideas will start flowing rapidly. There are many ways to capture these, including shared documents, whiteboards, flip charts, and notebooks. You could assign people to capture ideas or ask everyone to do so. You don't want to miss anything, and you don't want to slow things down while trying to capture everything.

Take time to discuss what method will work best for your team. There is no one right way. Just be sure you have a means of capturing ideas and a plan for organizing them and putting them into a meaningful structure as the process moves along.

Getting inspired

Having identified and come to a consensus on your elements, activities, experiences, and learning opportunities, it is time to begin designing your school model. Anyone who's been involved in designing traditional school facilities may see similarities. The big difference is you are not designing a static facility, and you have very few constraints. Rather, you can consider nearly any option when determining how to provide one or a combination of your elements, activities, experiences, and learning opportunities.

These could occur in a school building, but they could also occur in the community, at a business, in a student's home, virtually, or across several places. They could occur during the day on a weekday or at night or on weekends or in some combination. They also don't have to occur the same for every student. Consequently, your "clean sheet of paper" for designing is much cleaner than that of people designing new school buildings, who really always start with significant limitations.

This exceptionally clean slate, however, is both an opportunity and a challenge. With few limitations, the options can seem overwhelming and it can be hard to know where to start. It is also easy to fall back on what you know, which is the factory model. Instead, trust yourself, your team, and your planning process. If your team is committed to a vision that was developed with integrity, the pieces of the plan will fall into place.

Also, remember that your efforts are an example for the children and everyone else in your community. You're taking risks to push learning opportunities to new heights. You're providing a leadership example by not settling for good enough. And you're demonstrating that the best learning and growth occurs following failure. Know that you won't design the perfect model school. You might miss the mark by a lot to begin with. Embrace that expected failure for what it is—the only way to keep improving.

> ## INSPIRATION FROM OLYMPIANS
>
> We all know Olympic athletes build their ultimate success on failures. They push themselves to ever greater limits, failing again and again until they succeed. Sometimes, their absolute best performance occurs after they are no longer in contention for a medal.
>
> An even greater source of inspiration are Paralympic athletes due to the challenges they must overcome just to compete. Interestingly, many Paralympic athletes would never have considered striving for world-class status prior to becoming handicapped.
>
> All these athletes know they will never see meaningful improvements without pushing themselves in ways they have never done before and without taking risks. You will not see the children in your community approach their potential unless you are willing to give them a school model that will challenge them in ways they've never been challenged—and implementing such a model will require risks. Even more than an Olympic medal, the future of those children is worth taking such risks and putting in the necessary effort.

Find inspiration in the heart of your team

Bring your team together and have people share stories of overcoming adversity and accomplishing significant achievements through risk-taking, stubbornness, and the support of someone who believed in them. These could include stories of overcoming learning disabilities, poverty, handicaps, oppression, or abuse, or even just of being part of an underdog team that finally won a game at the end of a horrible season. Also, if anyone has them, include stories of being the best or nearly the best and choosing to try to reach even higher heights. Share stories of being knocked down and getting back up to keep going.

The purpose of all this is to get excited about the next part of this journey. You are about to design an entirely new school model that will not compromise its values. You will not make choices because someone who knew nothing about your community gave you limitations or told you what you have to do. At some point, you will need to accommodate some constraints, such as legal requirements, but right now you can throw off the reigns.

Come to this process with heart, integrity, curiosity, and joy. You are on a mission to improve the lives and futures of every child in your community. Stand up to whatever fears or worries you have and go full steam ahead.

Scope

This process is all about reducing limitations. The one exception is not a limitation on your design, but rather the scope of your design process. You are designing a new school model. You are not yet designing the path to get to that model. You will do that, but for now, focus on the model itself rather than how you will achieve it. It is okay to capture implementation ideas and concerns, but don't let them bog you down, limit idea generation, or detract from the integrity of your work.

FINDING CONSENSUS: INTEGRITY, OBJECTIVITY, BIAS, AND OPINIONS

Reaching consensus on high-stakes items can be difficult, but it is much easier when there is real trust among those on the team. Consensus is reaching a conclusion that everyone can live with, though some may have preferred a different conclusion. To have integrity, everyone must have had an opportunity to voice their concerns and opinions and been truly acknowledged and considered.

At the heart of consensus is agreement that the conclusion reached will contribute to achieving the team's vision and outcomes. When individuals have a concern about a conclusion, they need to ensure their concern is objective. Personal bias and opinion can be legitimate reasons for concern and should be noted, but they should not trump objectivity and the need for the actions and decisions of the team to further the team's shared purpose.

Testing your wings

This is the point at which your team must truly trust itself. It's time to leave the nest. There's more guidance to follow, but at this stage, you have all the expertise you need. So this section will be pretty short. Prior to starting, have your team review your vision, principles, and belief statements so they are fresh in your minds as you proceed.

There is no best way to carry out the initial design process. It needs to be organic and guided rather than structured and managed. People must feel free to share any idea that pops into their head at any time, even if it may not be immediately related to the ongoing dialogue. Once the actual design process gets moving, it should gain momentum and largely steer itself. Then it's just a matter of capturing everything. The real challenge is getting the process started.

I will share a few options you can use, combine, or ignore, depending on what you feel is best for your team. If a method doesn't seem to be working, shift to another. It's also possible your team, once inspired, will just take off. If so, let 'em go and try to keep up. If not, here are some ideas to try:

- Collective student journey—Imagine children beginning their journey within your model. Start by thinking of your model integrated into the lives of these children. How would it enhance, build on, and leverage the natural learning, growth, and development already occurring with these children? Consider how most children would "enter" or "merge" into your model, and then consider others who would enter through other means (e.g., transferring from another community or a private school). Capture ideas for how the model would reflect all of this. These could become part or one of your final design elements. Now imagine these "enrolled" students encountering various elements of your model. What would that look like? How would the students progress through time? What would their learning, growth, and development look like? To some degree, this is the opposite

of the backward journey you made when identifying the elements to include in the school model.
- Individual student journey—Imagine one child being integrated into your model and then following this student on his or her journey of learning, growth, and development. Capture ideas for how the model would reflect all this. Use questions like those in the collective journey above but for the individual student. Then, repeat this journey as needed with other imaginary students who have different life circumstances and challenges.
- Element by element—Take one of your elements and begin building your model around it. Have your team explore various students interacting with that element. Then start to "sketch" how that element would look in your model. Take another element and repeat the process, but this time also consider how this element would connect with that first element. It might be a clear and direct connection, or you might add one or more things to bridge between the elements. Repeat this process with all the elements as your model starts coming into focus.
- Multi-element—This is similar to the previous approach, but start with several elements rather than just one. Have your team explore various students interacting with these elements. Then start to "sketch" how the elements would look in your model. Include the ways the elements interconnect and add "bridges" to appropriately connect the elements. You could repeat this process with other combinations of elements and then connect the different combinations, or you could take your initial collection and begin adding elements one at a time. Either way, continue until all the elements are integrated and your model starts coming into focus.

Once you've completed the process of working all your elements into your model—and likely made adjustments and added additional elements—do an integrity check with your team. Have everyone consider your draft model and see if they think it will accomplish all the outcomes you intended. Develop some "sample" students with a variety of unique circumstances and challenges and try working them through your school model. Would your model facilitate each of those students achieving your chosen outcomes?

Again, remember that your model is not static. The model itself is less important than the process you're going through. Your model will be adjusted and adapted, by your team and the rest of the community, for as long as it exists. Trust your team, the process, and your community. You won't fail the children as long as you keep their well-being and learning in mind.

Vetting your model

Once your model is sketched out, it is time to do a test drive. Bring in people who were not part of the design process and show them the model. You can begin with people who are part of your larger school model development team or organization, but make sure to eventually get input from people who have not been involved in any way. This will provide a real test of your model's completeness and the direction you are heading.

Explain the model as you would to a family moving to your community and inquiring about the school system. Ask the "test drivers" to give brutally honest feedback while you avoid getting defensive. Take note of not only the questions and concerns that you cannot address but also the ones you can, as you can expect these to come up again.

Although you want to address shortcomings that arise, don't compromise your model's integrity. Keep in mind that some people may understand the model but are not ready to accept it as a workable alternative to the current factory model. These people will need to see the model in action and how it's working for enrolled students before they accept it—and they still might not. Don't worry about placating these folks. You'll need to acknowledge them and their concerns during the implementation stage, but don't let them compromise the integrity of your model.

Planning the transition

You are now ready for planning and preparing to bring your design to life. It's one thing, of course, to have a conceptual school model complete; it is another thing entirely to make it a reality. That is why you must also develop a plan for implementation. Fortunately, designing the model prepared you to design an implementation plan. The process is very similar, just with a narrower focus.

Planning for the transition is just a variation of the design process, so this section is relatively short. It provides guidance while encouraging your team to take ownership of the process. You will leverage the trust you've built and the experience you've gained to this point.

With that trust and experience, begin developing a transition and implementation plan using the following considerations:

- Determine the degree to which students will have access to the new model. Will the model be piloted with a fixed number of students, or will you allow as many students as want to enroll?
- Establish the date by which you want to have your model in place and available to those students.
- Generate an estimate of staff members necessary to facilitate the model when it begins to operate; include the experience, skills, and traits these staff members will need.
- Determine how you will recruit and select the staff members needed.
- Determine how the staff members will acquire skills they do not have, individually or collectively.
- Ensure your staffing considerations take into account the dynamic aspects of your model; be sure you are considering the full scope of your design.
- Determine the infrastructure/facilities that will be necessary to facilitate the model when it begins to operate.
- Determine the stakeholders and audiences with whom you need to continue communicating about your efforts. (This could be a

continuation of the communications you've already been having throughout the design process, but discuss it to be sure; revise and adapt as needed.)
- Determine what will be needed to comply with state and federal laws and rules.
- Determine what, if any, local policy changes will be needed.
- Develop a budget reflecting the costs of operating the new model and projecting the income sources.
- Develop a budget for implementing the new model and transitioning from the current model; project how these costs will be covered.

As you develop responses to these considerations and others you create or that arise, begin to identify the actions necessary to realize those responses. Drill down with actions as needed to ensure little or nothing is overlooked. Then, put the actions in chronological order and build a corresponding timeline. Assign a person to each action who will then be responsible for ensuring the assigned action is carried out according to the timeline.

Here again, the process of developing the implementation plan is more important than the plan itself. In this case, however, your timeline and action steps will be of ongoing value. Be prepared to adapt as changes occur and to address unexpected challenges and leverage opportunities that arise. These opportunities may provide enhancements to your design and implementation or allow you to move up your timeline.

Having completed your initial design and your plan, you are ready to begin implementation in earnest.

CHAPTER 33

READY, SET, GO

You have a plan. Much more importantly, you have taken a team of people through the planning process. It's time to start implementation if you haven't already done so. Once you reach this stage, your team should have the knowledge, skills, trust, and confidence—along with the momentum of the work already done—to begin implementation. I'll just add a few quick thoughts:

- Maintain the integrity of your team and plan and work toward bringing integrity to everything in your community.
- Don't be afraid to adapt and don't be surprised if it seems you're adapting constantly. The planning process should have prepared you to adapt to a changing environment and circumstances, overcome challenges that arise, and leverage emerging opportunities. Look forward to opportunities to apply what you learned through planning.
- Don't be afraid to screw up. If you begin implementing your plan and everything is going smoothly and according to that plan, then you may be in denial or may not have pushed your model far enough. Remember, it's better to fail occasionally while implementing a model that can truly achieve your vision than to compromise your model to avoid failure and have no chance of achieving your vision.
- Keep your faith in your children and your community.

Really, that's it. The ball is in your court. You are taking actions that will change the future for every person who is part of your new school model. And those changes will have an incredible ripple effect for generations to come. Be proud of what you're starting.

> **YOUR TEAM IS ON A JOURNEY OF LEARNING, GROWING, AND DEVELOPING**
>
> You are in the midst of a journey very much like the one the children in your community need to take. Done right, a learning community continuously learns, grows, and develops along with the students and everyone in the community. The process of designing and implementing a new school model requires each individual on your team and your team collectively to learn, grow, and develop; and this will continue as the journey continues. You are modeling what you want for the children in your community. Reflect on that and allow it to further inform the work your team is doing.

CHAPTER 34

OTHER CRUCIAL CONSIDERATIONS

This next-to-last chapter of the book covers a variety of other considerations. There are far more considerations that could arise, but this book could only be so long. My website, knowresponsibility.com, will provide additional resources and considerations to help any community wanting to design a new school model, and more will be added regularly. Here are the items likely to be of more common interest.

What constitutes a community?

This book is meant to be applicable in any community, from small rural settings to portions of large urban settings. As used in this book, the term "community" refers to a group of people who are somehow interconnected and who will support and rely on each other. In some cases, such as small, rural school districts, the district and the community are one and the same. Larger school districts will have numerous smaller communities. In this context, "community" doesn't refer to an entire municipality or school district.

You and your team will need to come to a consensus on what constitutes the community for which you want to design a new school model. You might consider the people and places you would feel obligated to help in the event of a traumatic occurrence. For example, if a tornado caused massive destruction, what neighborhoods or other areas would you feel obligated to assist? Similarly, who are the people you would turn to if you were in dire need of help? Where or who are the families whose children you would feel obligated to provide the best possible learning, growth, and development opportunities for?

Of course, geography is a significant factor in defining most communities. Your community might align with existing boundaries, or you could create entirely new boundaries. My general recommendation is to use *common sense with heart*. Consider the natural, logical boundaries of your community and give greater weight to serving students who may be facing greater adversity.

Another factor may be the residency of those involved with this effort. Of course, they are going to want the defined community to include their school-age children. If defining the community to include all the families represented on your team would result in unnatural or illogical boundaries, consider designing multiple school models for the separate communities. While you could use one model for multiple communities, be certain to honor the reality that each community has unique qualities and challenges.

Alternatively, you could define your community in terms other than geography. This is common for people developing charter schools in large districts, where the school is able to draw from anywhere within the district. In such a case, you might not specify your community up front but begin to work toward it as you go through the design process.

Designing new school models in larger school districts

This book applies to any community in any size school district, but it does not give instruction on how to design schools for entire multi-community school districts. This is an important distinction because there can be vast differences among the many communities within a large district. One model is highly unlikely to work for every community.

Instead, a large district should pursue designing new school models for each of its communities, and I hope many choose to do so. Were that to happen, each community within the district would develop its own model based on its own unique characteristics. A community within a larger district could also pursue this book's school model design process even if the district itself is not doing so. They would follow the same process as any other community, but they would be navigating a more complex political and bureaucratic landscape.

Regardless of the district size, it will be necessary to convince a variety of audiences and stakeholders of the need for this work. This will likely be a larger endeavor in a larger district, but that won't always be the case. There are large districts that embrace innovation and will support this effort in a variety of ways, just as there are small districts that will fight tooth and nail against anything that challenges the status quo.

Those in larger districts need to figure out who needs to be kept informed and who should be collaborators. Whether a district is enthusiastic or opposed to your efforts, building and maintaining a working relationship with the district is crucial. Even if, in the end, you have to implement your model without the support of the district, leave the door open for future cooperation.

If the district is supportive, continuously work with the appropriate people in preparation for implementation. In working with the district, emphasize that compromising on the model can only occur if it does not compromise the integrity of your team or your efforts. Help the district understand why this is so important in creating a school model with the true faith and trust of students, parents, staff, and the community.

One of the biggest challenges to retaining integrity when working with a large district is defining the community for your model. It is likely the district will want to influence this and might make some demands. Some of their suggestions may be helpful, and you should accommodate those. Just make sure you can maintain the integrity of your design while doing so. As long as the district's wishes have the intent of offering the best possible opportunities to all students, do what you can to accommodate them.

Beyond the challenges noted above, larger municipalities and districts likely have more variables to consider when defining the community and going through the design process. For example, when exploring who you are as a community and where you are in terms of readiness, there will be far more elements included in your analysis. On the plus side, there will be a wider variety of resources available.

None of these differences changes the process of designing a new school model. If you recognize there is a need for a new model in your community and find others who agree, you will be able to make it happen.

Uncooperative or change-averse governing bodies

Some school districts may resist a new school model too strongly to overcome. But strong resistance doesn't mean that you should abandon hope. Those who overcome the greatest challenges during their journey often end up with the greatest outcomes.

Even if you struggle against resistance in your district, continue with everything laid out in this book—including maintaining communications and a relationship with the district to the greatest extent possible. I recommend approaching it with a sense of humor, keeping a positive attitude, and having fun. If no one working for the district is supportive, find those who are least resistant and use them as your liaisons. Send them witty yet accurate updates and continue to seek their involvement, even if you don't expect them to respond. Stay respectful at all times while trying to soften their resistance through your upbeat efforts.

Then, proceed with the planning process in every other way. Many people in the communities within this district will also be change-averse, but approach them anyway. If you can begin to convince a few resistant people to at least listen to your reasoning and then convince a few of those to become part of the effort—even if in the role of devil's advocate—then count those as small victories. Keep going even if the resistance must lengthen your hoped-for timeline.

Your journey may be longer and more difficult, but your outcomes may be much better because they will have to be. Your team will have to be well prepared when trying to convince others. Your ideas and products will need to be of high quality to withstand the scrutiny of the naysayers. Against this adversity, your team will need a higher level of commitment and enthusiasm to overcome the challenges.

If you do all this and still can't get the time of day from the district, explore the options available in your state. Yes, this will add more challenges, but the end result will be worth the effort. One possibility would be transforming your model into a charter school. Each state allows and regulates charter schools differently. A good first step is to explore current charter schools in your state and reach out to some for assistance. Also, seek assistance from charter school organizations in your state or elsewhere.

A second option is to see if another school district in your area would be open to helping implement your model. This may not be feasible if your model and community have important geographical components, but maybe your model could be adapted to make it work while maintaining its integrity.

Seek out organizations, foundations, and individuals who support innovative education and ask them for assistance. Some may have experience, resources, and influence that could help in getting your model implemented.

Let the students on your team become your spokespeople. They are much harder for adults to counter with the usual arguments, and they will be able to demonstrate much more effectively why the current model must change. This would also be a fantastic learning, growth, and development opportunity for them.

Don't give up! Your team came together because you all realized it's necessary for the future of your community and maybe our broader society. Keep working on and improving your model while seeking ways to get it implemented. It has literally taken decades to reach the point where some people realize the need for this reinvention, so taking a little longer in your community won't be tragic. Know that teams who successfully implement new models in other communities will become catalysts for your efforts. Change is coming; it will just take longer in some places than others.

Designing a new school model for an elementary, middle, or high school only

I have tried to keep this book grade- and school-level neutral. Since age-based student cohorts are one of our current model's biggest shortcomings, I wanted to avoid referencing that paradigm. However, your situation may only support a single school encompassing a limited range of student ages or, in its current form, grade levels.

If that is the case, then approach this effort with that self-awareness. Among the elements of knowing your community will be your students' starting points and where they will be going when they leave your school model. This approach is the same as for a school model that covers all grades, though your students' starting and destination points will be different.

If you are designing a model just for elementary-school-age students, then consider the range of situations of students entering your model and the corresponding transitions coming in. Then, consider the destinations when students leave your model and how to prepare them for that transition. If going to a traditional-model middle school, what must you do so they can be as successful as possible? How do you help students become resilient and flexible to adapt to that other model?

If you are designing for middle-school-age students, consider the elementary schools from which most students will come and the paradigms and preparation they will have when they arrive. Consider how to help the students transition to your new model school. Then, consider how to prepare them for the school they will attend when they leave your model. As with the elementary school model, if going to a traditional high school, what must you do so they can be as successful as possible? How do you help students become resilient and flexible to adapt to that other model?

If designing for high-school-age students, consider the middle schools from which most students will come and the paradigms and preparation they will have when they arrive. Consider how to help the students transition to your new model. Preparing these students for when they leave your model will be much the same as those designing a more comprehensive model that covers students of all ages.

Teams designing an all-age school model will also need to plan for transitions from the old model. In their case, however, it will be for the initial large-scale transition when moving from the current school model to the new model as well as for transitioning students who are entering from or leaving to traditional model schools.

Put on a happy face!

The contents of this section have been covered previously, but they bear repeating.

The effort to design a new school model will be a challenge for any community. Don't add to the challenge by creating animosity or friction. Being positive throughout this process will make your journey much easier. People are much more likely to join your team if you're having a good time. People resistant to your efforts will have a harder time opposing your work if you remain upbeat even when addressing their resistance.

Of course, it can be hard to appear positive when trying to convince people the current school model needs to be replaced, especially during discussions of that model's shortcomings. If you come across as negative, you will compromise people's trust and their belief that you are taking on this effort for entirely positive reasons. You need to build, not burn, bridges. Good, caring people you want and need supporting your efforts are the people who would question your motives and integrity if they see or hear you denigrate others, even if they agree with what you're trying to do.

Avoid blaming local schools for problems, and instead recognize ways local schools have done positive things within the limitations of the current model. Then, show how the current model limited these efforts as a way to illustrate why a new model is needed. Further, explain how nearly universal acceptance of the current model blinds most people to its shortcomings.

It shouldn't be difficult to stay upbeat if you focus on the end state you are pursuing. Think about your community filled with young adults who had the opportunity to truly pursue their potential and are now ready and anxious to go out and make the world a better place. That vision should get you excited, as it represents the future you are striving to achieve. Harness that, and let it be reflected in all your efforts and especially your interactions with others.

Finally, don't allow this to become political. The intent of this effort—to design a new school model that will help every child in your community pursue his or her true potential—should be universally supported. Some elements of the model you design, however, could be counter to things connected to a political ideology. Some people on your team could be viewed as partisan or connected to a particular political party. Do your best to sustain an ideological balance on your team and reflect a neutral approach to your work.

Of course, it is more important to maintain your integrity than to falsely put on a happy face or remain ideologically neutral. If you have people on your team who are somewhat gruff, have a more cynical nature, or are partisan in some way, own that and work it into your efforts. Those are some of the "elephants" noted on page 212. Acknowledge and harness them rather than trying to hide them and risking that all-important integrity.

"Training" parents and other adults

An important element of your design is addressing how your new model affects relationships between children and their parents and other adults whom children will regularly encounter. Most parents raise their children in ways that reflect the current model of school's use of rewards and punishments. They adopt a power dynamic in which the parents have most of the power and the children get little or token power, and they mostly reinforce the current compliance-centric approach of the schools.

This is not a criticism of parents; they are doing what has been done for a century or more and what is still the predominant method of parenting. However, if the schools start to change their model without considering the parent-child dynamic, it could result in challenges for parents and children.

I have been arguing that new school models must grant significant power to students and move away from rewards and punishments. Without steps being taken, parents could be in for a rude awakening when their children start to become empowered at school and resistant to rewards and punishments as well as the compliance mindset.

If you have been following the process in this book, families will be part of the design you put together. As they learn about the coming changes, they will see the changes needed to complement them. Making those changes, however, will not necessarily be easy, just as it will not be easy for school staff to adapt to the paradigms of the new model. Consequently, the design and implementation teams need to consider how they will help parents with this transition.

Similarly, the staff in the school and other adults with whom students regularly interact—coaches, employers, babysitters, guest speakers—will have these old paradigms. People who are not part of this design effort could have a similar rude awakening when interacting with students in ways they always have if that is counter to the paradigms of the new school model. They, too, will need to be considered in the planning process.

The key is not to criticize or be condescending with anyone. These are very new ideas for nearly everyone, so they will require time and patience. Acknowledge this and provide illustrations of how practices that have been staples of parenting (and staples of schools) for years turn out to have unintended negative outcomes. You might do this by reframing the many school examples in this book to relate them to parenting or the roles of other adults.

The bottom line is that everyone needs a foundation of understanding that paradigms about children and learning need to change. Expose them to the same information that led you and your team to pursue the new school model, but with additional insights and context. Specifically, explain how improving students' critical thinking and self-confidence will also improve their awareness of integrity and their desire to confront hypocrisy. As students are given greater power over their learning, growth, and development in school, they will want more control over these things elsewhere in their lives. They won't simply accept "Because I said so" anymore.

A great place to start is Johnson and Stixrud's book, *The Self-Driven Child*. Encourage adults to read the book and use elements from it when working with adults on these paradigm shifts. Beyond that book, the best tools for addressing this challenge are those at the heart of it: children. Ask for the children's help in delivering the messages and guiding the parents and others through these changes to the greatest extent possible. This puts power into the hands of children while also providing excellent learning opportunities and strengthening the integrity of your work.

These are the key points I would consider in developing this aspect of your design and implementation plan:

- Children must understand that adults will need time and assistance replacing paradigms about school, parenting, and adult-child interactions they have held their entire lives.
- Children can help with this process.
- Children must recognize some adults will support these new paradigms and treat children as equals to adults while other adults may be unaware of and not ready to interact with children as equals. Children must be respectful, patient, and understanding of adults who have not gotten used to the new paradigms.

- Children must recognize and adapt when interacting with adults who have no interest in changing their paradigms and in situations where candor would be more appropriate.

These are all variations of students applying critical-thinking skills to relationships and interactions. They should learn there are times it's okay to acquiesce, especially when the cost of doing so is minimal. Sometimes the best way to demonstrate one's power is to withhold it out of respect for someone or when realizing there is nothing to be gained by wielding it.

Finally, consider creating forums in your community for parents and other adults to get together and help each other adapt to the new paradigms and new school model. Simply getting together with others who are in similar situations and sharing stories, suggestions, successes, and challenges can be incredibly helpful.

LOVE AND LOGIC AND OTHER PARENTING APPROACHES

Numerous programs have emerged to help parents address common challenges, and many parenting programs have had positive results. However, like initiatives trying to address challenges in schools, the results have been limited by the underlying paradigms of parenting.

One widely adopted parenting program, which my wife and I learned and practiced with our kids, provides a good example. Love and Logic seeks to help parents put greater responsibility on their children, give them greater choice, and make use of natural consequences. We used numerous techniques from the program and were thrilled with the results. In retrospect, however, I realize the short-term positive outcomes probably contribute to longer-term negative outcomes.

With Love and Logic, adults retain nearly all the actual power. Like attempts to bring "voice and choice" to students in school without changing the underlying model, Love and Logic and similar approaches strive to create in children an illusion of control without the parents actually relinquishing power.

Although parents often see improved behavior and thoughtfulness, these approaches reinforce the power imbalance between the adults and the children. The children have some choices, but they know they still don't have any real power. The children embrace the choices they are given, but they aren't practicing the responsibility of having actual power.

The children whose behavior doesn't improve through these programs may be those who see this reality and refuse to go along with the illusion. Such behavior often leads to more significant restrictions, which confirm for the children their lack of power. Children constantly told to act responsibly without being given any actual power sense the lack of integrity. Remember, obedience demonstrated to receive a reward or avoid a punishment is not responsibility; it is just compliance.

Tracking student progress and success

Increasingly, our society uses data for planning, decision-making, tracking progress and performance, determining pay and bonuses, and establishing budgets. Data can bring objectivity and equity and can prevent our biases and prejudices from tainting our judgment. In some cases, we can use data to maximize performance and output by finding techniques and strategies leading to the highest performance and then replicating them.

However, because there is nearly infinite variability in human systems, most ways we use data in schools do little to identify specific student progress or techniques that will work for all students. As noted previously, the ways we currently use data in schools can actually be detrimental to students.

To determine if students are learning, growing, and developing, we can do what parents have done on their doorframes for centuries: measure children against themselves. In some respects, this is similar to what is done in the current school model—checking student progress against a variety of benchmarks. There are important differences, however.

In the current model, benchmarks are typically the same for every student and consist of completing assignments, passing tests, and demonstrating specific skills at predetermined ages. In the new model, all the benchmarks and timelines will be specific to each child and will consist of demonstrations of learning, growth, and development. Your model will need ways for each student to establish individual benchmarks and the means of demonstrating their achievement. Ideally, the students will have primary responsibility but will have guidance and monitoring by a mentor or support team that endorses the benchmarks.

Student progress will be tracked by seeing that every student achieves his or her benchmarks and then establishes new, higher benchmarks to strive for. With this approach, staff will ensure students set appropriately challenging benchmarks and push themselves to achieve them. Another staff role will be working to find and address the root causes when students fail to achieve these benchmarks. In a system with integrity, students will set the bar at realistic levels based on their perception of their ability—as long as they have the real power and are able to understand the value, to themselves, of establishing these benchmarks.

Students who would set the bar low are the same students who would be stressed and struggle with the standards established by others in the current model. This struggle is not usually student inability but developmental readiness, lack of confidence, and stress. This struggle, however, constantly reaffirms their negative perceptions of their abilities, creating a loop of poor learning, growth, and development. Here, data use becomes detrimental.

On the other hand, giving students ownership of this process and timeline (along with supportive peers and mentors and a model that truly facilitates learning, growth, and development) allows them to demonstrate—to themselves and others—they are fully capable of being successful. They will set higher benchmarks and push themselves to achieve them. They will need encouragement as they gain self-confidence, but once they do, they will exceed expectations.

Student success is the ongoing creation and accomplishment of benchmarks. Data that demonstrates student progress and ability will be collected from and applied to each student individually and can include the benchmarks for each student, how they have been accomplished, and how they have been set higher over a period of time. For a "snapshot" of student progress at a given point in time, just sit down and talk with the students. Ask what they've been accomplishing and what that means for them and their future. I have talked to self-aware students who have taken true ownership of their learning; no one would doubt their level of accomplishment nor their ability to succeed in the future.

Will Schaaf, a 2018 high school graduate I've known since elementary school, wrote this for his senior quote: "Sometimes you get so caught up in the data that you don't take a look at the human being in front of you that is uniquely capable of doing remarkable things." What might Will and the rest of the class of 2018 have accomplished in a school model that helped them truly pursue their potential?

Tracking school model performance and success

The ultimate success of a school model is that every student continually approaches his or her potential and then pushes that potential higher. If that is happening, the model is meeting the highest possible measure of performance and success. This result is neither data-centric nor immediate, which means it doesn't fit readily on a typical district or state school performance report. Even so, if you are tracking student progress and success as discussed in the previous section, this measure will be exponentially more meaningful than the measures used in the current model.

In the current model, graduation rates and standardized test scores—along with, to some degree, AP enrollment and AP test scores—are the primary means of measuring school performance. Some measures also look at the percent of graduates enrolling in college. These do not accurately demonstrate individual student abilities, learning, growth, or development. They also don't measure how close students have been to reaching their individual potential.

Instead, an honest measure of school model performance is reflected in individual student performance, as discussed in the previous section. In addition, evidence of school model performance—and, ultimately, what determines whether or not the model is successful—is what former students achieve after they leave. This measure is neither data-centric nor immediate. Rather, it is based on the opinion of each of those former students. Can they honestly say they were as ready as they could have been to pursue their chosen endeavors after leaving your new model school? If not, their feedback should be informing adaptations to the model.

The real question, then, is how to address those who are concerned about the required data-centric measures, such as state reporting. Simply put, in your design and planning process, be sure to address such requirements and develop strategies for both how to accommodate the requirements and how to respond to concerns the data may raise. Of course, don't assume the data will be negative, but plan for that contingency. More likely is that the data will be mixed and help demonstrate both the shortcomings of the factory school model and of the data collection requirements.

If you reach the stage where you are designing a new model school and planning its implementation, then your community—or at least a sufficient portion of your community—has demonstrated its support. That means they will be understanding about the disconnect between the new model and the existing assessment and measurement requirements. They will also be open to the measures of success that you are designing into your model, such as those previously noted.

With that being said, use students and parents as the primary drivers of how you will accommodate state testing and data collection requirements and how you will respond to the results. With knowledge of testing and data collection requirements and how the data will be used, students and parents can develop plans that take into consideration both the collective and individual impacts of both. Families should be well aware of any issues so they are not concerned about what the results portray. If statements are needed to address concerns and perceived issues, students will be the most convincing spokespeople to address these.

As far as standardized tests, students in new model schools will likely perform well and possibly excel at these. Their learning, growth, and development will be accelerated, so when they take a standardized test intended for students near their chronological age, they will likely be functioning at a much higher relative level. Even if they haven't been "preparing" for these tests the way students in other schools have, they will almost certainly do just fine. This will, however, need to be a consideration of the design team.

At the end of the day, the success of a school model will be evident if it looks like the vision being pursued for the community. It will also be evident, as noted above, in the long-term performance of the students as they move toward and through various adult endeavors.

ASSESSING PERFORMANCE WITHOUT FORMAL ASSESSMENTS

As noted previously, a number of schools have moved toward standards-based grading. Some do not use any regular assessments but instead track when students are able to consistently demonstrate the standards or competencies for the class. The following was related during a session of the Personalized Learning Convening a few years ago.

A suburban Wisconsin physics teacher decided to convert one of his classes to project- and standards-based with no formal assessments used for the entire term. The students were engaged and enthusiastic and demonstrated excellent learning and growth during the class. They liked it so much they wanted the teacher to convert more of his classes to this approach. Yet the teacher was curious how the students would perform on a formal physics assessment.

On the last day of the term, he gave that class the final exam that he was giving to his other, traditional physics classes. It would not count toward their grades or be for any purpose other than to see how they would do—to satisfy his curiosity.

The regular classes had been taking similar assessments throughout the term, so were accustomed to such exams. Those students were given a large review packet to prepare for the exam. Those students' grade would be impacted by the exam. The project-based students had none of this going for them. The average score for the traditional students was 92; for the project-based students it was 87. While the project-based scores were lower, that they performed that well validated his efforts, especially knowing that the project-based students' ability to retain and apply what they learned was significantly higher as evidenced by classroom observations.

CHAPTER 35

THE LAST CHAPTER

While this is the last chapter in the book, it is certainly not the conclusion. And, like little else in this lengthy tome, it will be brief. This entire book is meant to serve as the first chapter in a much more substantial effort—the effort to replace the current 126-year-old school model to which almost our entire population of children is subjected. It is the first chapter in a revolution of educational change through which each community designs its own school model.

If you have read this far, then I certainly hope it means you're champing at the bit to get started or you already have begun the process in your community. I know my work is also not done. With this book finished, it is my mission to provide assistance to those pioneers who will be leading this effort in their communities and blazing the trail for others to follow. Remember, I am not the expert—you are. So what are you waiting for?

ACKNOWLEDGMENTS

I offer my sincere gratitude to the following people, without whose assistance and support this book would never have come to fruition.

To Dara Beevas, chief strategic officer at Wise Ink and the person who took a chance on me and my crazy ideas for this book. Dara provided encouragement and inspiration throughout the writing and editing process and connected me to the folks who would help make this book a reality.

To Patrick Maloney, production director at Wise Ink, who personally took on the editing of my manuscript. His edits contributed to a substantially more accessible book while his guidance and suggestions helped significantly improve the overall text. His honest, candid feedback was essential to this final product.

To Roseanne Cheng, marketing director at Wise Ink, who provided my first real lessons in social media and marketing myself and my ideas. More importantly, Roseanne provided encouragement and guidance as the project was coming together.

To James Rickabaugh, founder and director emeritus of the Institute on Personalized Learning, for his invaluable assistance with so many aspects of this book. His critiques and feedback were absolutely critical to turning this into a readable and accessible tool for a broad audience, while his encouragement provided the confidence to keep going. Thanks also to Jim for turning me onto Rushworth Kidder, whose work on moral courage provided invaluable insights as I was doing my rewrites of the manuscript.

To the dozens of friends who served as readers and reviewers of my early manuscripts. Their feedback and ideas all contributed to making the final product significantly better.

To the teachers and students at Valley New School in Appleton, WI; Clark Street Community School in Middleton, WI; Etude Elementary, Middle, and High Schools in Sheboygan, WI; Endeavor Charter School in Watertown, WI; and Waukesha STEM Academy in Waukesha, WI—and to the countless other teachers and students who have helped form the insights and lessons at the heart of this book.

To the students in my Command and General Staff Officer Course (CGSOC) Phase 1 class at Camp Parks, CA, in March 2018. This incredibly bright group of (mostly) young officers were enthusiastic participants in deep discussions about critical and creative thinking that helped inform the writing in this book. They challenged me and each other, helping all of us, I believe, gain a better appreciation for critical thinking and the important role it needs to play in all aspects of our lives.

To the hundreds of other CGSOC students I have had the pleasure of instructing. All have been subjected to my evolving understanding of learning and thinking while contributing substantially to that evolution. These students, current and future leaders of US Army organizations responsible for our nation's security, are one reason I am so confident that our country and world will continue to flourish even in the face of crises and conflicts that at times can make the future seem bleak. We are in good hands.

To the many CGSOC instructors and leaders with whom I have had the pleasure to serve. They have taught me incredible skills and helped me to continuously improve my own teaching abilities while further adding to my understanding of learning and thinking. Their insights and influence have contributed in countless ways to the ideas and thoughts shared in this book.

To my teachers in middle and high school and my professors at the University of Wisconsin–Stout and University of Wisconsin–Madison. I learned lessons from all of them that were critical to developing the insights in this book.

To the teachers and students and all the other education professionals with whom I've worked over the years, for all the critical lessons you taught me that contributed to the insights in this book.

Know Power, Know Responsibility

To my parents, who modeled many of the concepts in this book, probably without realizing it. They allowed me to have more power and control than may have been smart at the time, but they also provided great guidance and mentoring so that I usually made good choices and demonstrated responsibility (while learning invaluable lessons from the poor choices). Also, to my mom for making me take a typing class in high school—one of the few times she did such a thing. "Typing" is one of the most valuable skills I've ever developed and has helped me become a better writer.

To my sons, Samuel and Matthew. They were the real guinea pigs as I strove to understand how we can ensure students develop critical thinking skills and the confidence to challenge the norms and paradigms of schools and parents. I hope they have benefitted from the early stages of my work on reinventing public education.

And finally, to my wife, Katherine, who I'm sure had no idea what she was getting into when she said, "Yes," she would marry me. She has stood by me as I left perfectly good jobs to continuously pursue a better way of improving our world through public education. She bravely faced the overwhelming challenge of raising two young boys while I was serving with the army in Afghanistan and graciously allowed me to miss countless events—weddings, funerals, birthdays, Christmases, anniversaries, and more—for other army-directed events. Probably most important to this book, she allowed me to parent our children in ways that were totally foreign to her—truly pushing power and responsibility to them and trusting they could handle it. It's been an incredible learning experience for us all.

REFERENCES

Anderson, N. (2018, June 18). "Several well-known private schools in the D.C. area are scrapping Advanced Placement classes." Retrieved from *Grad Point*: https://www.washingtonpost.com/news/grade-point/wp/2018/06/18/several-well-known-private-schools-in-the-d-c-area-are-scrapping-advanced-placement-classes/?utm_term=.d234559b30c8

Barker, E. (2017). *Barking Up the Wrong Tree.* New York: Harper Collins Publishers.

Brown, B. (2018). *Dare to Lead: Brave Work. Tough Conversations. Whole Hearts.* New York: Random House.

Carey, B. (2014). *How We Learn: The Surprising Truth About When, Where, and Why It Happens.* New York: Random House.

Collins, J. C. (2001). *Good to Great: Why Some Companies Make the Leap, and Others Don't.* New York: Harper Business.

Collins, J. C. (2011). *Great by Choice: Uncertainty, Chaos, and Luck: Why Some Thrive Despite Them All.* New York: HarperCollins Publishers.

Covey, S. R. (1989). *The Seven Habits of Highly Effective People: Powerful Lessons in Personal Change.* New York: Free Press.

Dweck, C. S. (2016). *Mindset: The New Psychology of Success.* New York: Ballentine Books.

Feinstein, S. G. (2009). *Secrets of the Teenage Brain.* Thousand Oaks, CA: Corwin Press.

Gerver, R. (2014). *Creating Tomorrow's Schools Today*. New York: Bloomsbury Education.

Gerver, R. (2016). *Simple Thinking: How to Remove Complexity from Life and Work*. Chichester, West Sussex, UK: John Wiley & Sons.

Gladwell, M. (2006). *Blink: The Power of Thinking Without Thinking*. New York: Penguin Group.

Gladwell, M. (2008). *Outliers: The Story of Success*. New York: Little, Brown and Company.

Gray, P. (2013). *Free to Learn: Why Unleashing the Instinct to Play Will Make Our Children Happier, More Self-Reliant, and Better Students for Life*. New York: Basic Books.

Hamzelou, J. (2017, November 28). "Teenage brains can't tell what's important and what isn't." Retrieved from *New Scientist*: https://www.newscientist.com/article/2154884-teenage-brains-cant-tell-whats-important-and-what-isnt/#.WiAza3ZAy0Q.email

Heath, C. and Heath, D. (2010). *Switch: How to Change Things When Change Is Hard*. New York: Crown Publishing Group.

Johnson, N. and Stixrud, W. (2018). *The Self-Driven Child: The Science and Sense of Giving Your Kids More Control Over Their Lives*. New York: Penguin Random House LLC.

Karklis, L. and Keating, D. (2017, September 27). *How Diverse Is America*. Retrieved from *Washington Post*: https://www.washingtonpost.com/graphics/national/how-diverse-is-america/

Kidder, R. M. (2005). *Moral Courage*. New York: HarperCollins Publishers.

Kotter, J. (2012). *Leading Change*. Watertown, MA: Harvard Business Review Press.

Lukianoff, G. and Haidt, J. (2018). *The Coddling of the American Mind: How Good Intentions and Bad Ideas are Setting Up a Generation for Failure.* New York: Penguin Press.

Marquet, L. D. (2012). *Turn the Ship Around: A True Story of Turning Followers Into Leaders.* New York: Penguin Group.

Marr, B. (2018, May 6). "Big Data: 20 Mind Boggling Facts Everyone Must Read." Retrieved from Forbes: https://www.forbes.com/sites/bernardmarr/2015/09/30/big-data-20-mind-boggling-facts-everyone-must-read/#10b84e8017b1

McDonald, T. R. (2011). *Unsustainable: A Strategy for Making Public Schooling More Productive, Effective, and Affordable.* Landham, Maryland: Rowman and Littlefield Publishers.

Merton, R. K. (1968). *Social Theory and Social Structure.* New York: The Free Press.

Mischel, W. (2014). *The Marshmallow Test: Why Self-Control is the Engine of Success.* New York: Little Brown and Company.

Morrill, C. and Musheno, M. (2018). *Navigating Conflict: How Youth Handle Trouble in a High Poverty School.* Chicago: University of Chicago Press.

National Commission on Excellence in Education. (2018, May 2). *A Nation at Risk - 1983.* Retrieved from U.S. Department of Education Archive: https://www2.ed.gov/pubs/NatAtRisk/risk.html

National Education Association. (2017, September 17). *Committee of Ten Report.* Retrieved from Google Books: https://books.google.com/books?id=PfcBAAAAYAAJ&pg=PA3&lpg=PA3#v=onepage&q&f=false

Paupathi, M. (2012). *How We Learn.* Chantilly, VA: The Great Courses.

Pink, D. H. (2009). *Drive: The Surprising Truth About What Motivates Us.* New York: Riverhead Books.

Rickabaugh, J. (2016). *Tapping the Power of Personalized Learning: A Roadmap for School Leaders.* Alexandria, VA: ASCD.

Rose, T. (2015). *The End of Average: How We Succeed in a World That Values Sameness.* New York: HarperCollins Publishers.

Schlechty Center. (2018, May 2). *Schlechty Center.* Retrieved from Schlechty Center: https://www.schlechtycenter.org/

Senge, P. M. (2006). *The Fifth Discipline: The Art and Practice of the Learning Organization.* New York: Doubleday.

Siegel, D. J. (2013). *Brainstorm: The Power and Purpose of the Teenage Brain.* New York: Penguin Group.

Silver, N. (2012). *The Signal and the Noise: Why So Many Predictions Fail, but Some Don't.* New York: Penguin Books.

Sinek, S. (2009). *Start with Why: How Great Leaders Inspire Everyone to Take Action.* New York: Penguin Group.

Sutcher, L., Darling-Hammond, L., and Carver-Thomas, D. (2018, May 7). "A Coming Crisis in Teaching? Teacher Supply, Demand, and Shortages in the U.S." Retrieved from Learning Policy Institute: https://learningpolicyinstitute.org/product/coming-crisis-teaching-brief

Sweeney, M. S. (2009). *Brain, The Complete Mind.* Washington, D.C.: National Geographic.

Taylor, J. B. (2006). *My Stroke of Insight: A Brain Scientist's Personal Journey.* New York: Penguin Group.

The Secretary's Commission on Achieving Necessary Skills. (2018, May 2). "What Work Requires of Schools." Retrieved from U.S. Department of Labor: https://wdr.doleta.gov/scans/whatwork/whatwork.pdf

Whalstrom, K. M. (2018, May 3). "Later start time for teens improves grades, mood, and safety." Retrieved from Phi Delta Kappan -

Kappanonline.org: http://www.kappanonline.org/later-start-time-for-teens/

Wikipedia. (2017, September 12). "Committee of Ten." Retrieved from Wikipedia: https://en.wikipedia.org/wiki/Committee_of_Ten

Willingham, D. T. (2009). *Why Don't Students Like School: A Cognitive Scientist Answers Questions About How the Mind Works and What it Means for the Classroom.* San Francisco: Jossey-Bass.

Wisconsin Department of Public Instruction. (2014, April). *Essential Elements and Alternate Achievement Descriptors for Mathematics.* Retrieved from Wisconsin Department of Public Instruction: https://dpi.wi.gov/sites/default/files/imce/standards/pdf/math-essential-elements.pdf

Wisconsin Department of Public Instruction. (2017, August). *Fostering Innovation in Wisconsin Schools.* Retrieved from Department of Public Instruction: https://dpi.wi.gov/sites/default/files/imce/cal/Fostering%20Innovation%20Credit%20Flexibility%202017.pdf

Wisconsin Department of Public Instruction. (2018, May). *Wisconsin Standards for Social Studies.* Retrieved from Wisconsin Department of Public Instruction: https://dpi.wi.gov/sites/default/files/imce/standards/New%20pdfs/2018_WI_Social_Studies_Standards.pdf

YouTube. (2018, May 6). *YouTube for Press.* Retrieved from YouTube: https://www.youtube.com/yt/about/press/

INDEX

A
Academic and Career Planning (ACP) 236
academic honors 28, 155-156
academic performance 51, 153-154, 185
achievement gaps 21, 22, 23, 26, 41, 74
Advanced Placement (AP) courses 162
age cohorts 32, 35, 39, 73, 282
allegiance 64, 66
American Dream 22
A Nation at Risk report 34
assessments
   of conceptual understanding 30
   lacking formality 293
   of long-term retention 30
   of new school model 291-292
   standardized tests 24, 30, 40, 137-138, 292
   tracking student progress 289-290, 293
athletics 131-132, 161-162
attendance 182, 253-254
averages
   and developmental readiness 42
   versus fitting each student 43-44
   problem with 40, 41, 74
   research on 221
   and school start times 43
   and standards 39
   use by military 39, 40

B
Barker, Eric 28, 156, 222
Barking Up the Wrong Tree (Barker) 28, 156, 222
Barry-Wehmiller Companies 195
behavior. *See* compliance
beliefs 193, 232, 233, 255
benchmarks 41, 42, 76, 137, 289
bias 6, 7, 67, 68, 71, 115, 269
biological development 35
Blink (Gladwell) 220
brain development 35, 80, 221
Brainstorm (Siegel) 221
budgets 171-172

C
Calvin and Hobbes 17
careers. *See* workforce
career services 184, 185
Carey, Benedict 223, 224
change
   books on 218-220
   difficulty of 186-187
   downsides to 187
   drivers of 179
   leading 200, 207
   openness to 178, 179
   resistance 244, 280-281
   risks 149-152
   sense of urgency for 201, 205, 207
   societal 178, 179
   student preparation for 59, 60
change agents 199
charter schools 31, 154, 176, 281
childcare 102, 120, 121
collaboration 92, 99-100
college
   compliance in 63-64
   costs 79-82, 136-137
   diversity at 154, 155
   dual enrollment 158
   entrance qualifications 136-137, 154-155
   qualifying for financial aid 156-159
   readiness 34
   return on investment 80-81
   scholarships 156-159
Collins, Jim 200
commitment 201, 226
Committee of Ten 8-11, 30
communities
   challenges in 241
   defining what constitutes as 277-278, 279
   designing new models for 144-146, 169-171, 278-280
   easing student transitions 108
   history of 202
   homogeneity 36, 56

opinion gathering 246-247
pulse of 201-202
readiness assessment 243-247
resistance 244
resources in 240, 241
school role in 164
self-discovery process 240-242
sense of community 106-108, 127, 161
support from 244
surveys of 202, 246
volunteers from 171
compliance
  for algorithmic tasks 90-91
  behavior with lack of rules 128-129
  versus commitment 46-47
  effect on learning 49-50, 88-90
  versus engagement 50-52
  focus on 45
  and motivation 87, 88
  need for systems of 52-53
  normalizing 63-64
  parent-child dynamic 285, 288
  rewards and punishments 87, 88, 89-90, 90-91
  ritual 51
  strategic 51
  and stress 47-48
  and student potential 28
  token economies 54
compromise 72, 193, 194
Congressional Medal of Honor 197
consensus 193, 262, 269
cooperation 72, 99-100, 280-281
costs
  budgets 171-172
  current model 10, 27, 74, 115, 165, 169
  equipment 168, 169
  facilities 168, 169
  with new model 74, 165-168
  staffing 105, 106
  and technology 166
  of transitioning to new model 168-172
courage 67-68, 72, 197-198
Creating Tomorrow's Schools Today (Gerver) 220
critical thinking 6-7
  and discernment 85
  discouraging 64-66
  history lessons 84
  in leadership team 201
  in military settings 110
  of personal finances 80, 81-82
  practicing 80, 86
  self-reflection on 68
cultural considerations 58
curiosity 89
curriculum

access to academic opportunities 162-163
approved 101
new programs 24
personalized 75, 94
standard 32, 137
time-based 43

D

Daniels, Gilbert 39, 40
democracies 69-72
demographic groups 23-25
Department of Public Instruction (Wisconsin) 175, 236
developmental levels 35, 42, 122
differentiation 36
disabilities 36, 52, 73-75
discernment 85
discrimination 179, 242
diversity
  in colleges 154, 155
  of family situations 121
  on leadership teams 202, 211, 215
  in life experiences 36, 55-57
  and students with disabilities 75
  on student teams 100
Drive (Pink) 89, 218, 222
dual enrollment 158
Dweck, Carol 218, 223, 224

E

early childhood 120-121
economic vitality 108-110
Einstein, Albert 84
Eisenhower, Dwight 257
elementary schools 38, 282
emotional well-being 97-98
emotions 52, 53, 80, 81
employment. *See* workforce
The End of Average (Rose) 39, 40, 42, 218, 221
ends justifying means 192-194
engagement
  versus compliance 50-52
  and information access 85
  levels of 51
  of parents and families 92
English Language Arts (ELA) classes 24
enrollments 105-106
entrepreneurial skills 59, 62, 205
equity
  gender 95-96
  in student potential 22
  in student readiness 31-33
  for students with disabilities 75
ethics 62, 64
evaluation. *See* assessments

expertise 203, 259
exploration 237, 239, 250-256
extracurriculars 131-132, 163

F
facilities 106, 127-128, 168, 169
factory model
  cost-effectiveness 10, 27, 74, 115, 165, 169
  current capacity 21, 26
  design of 10-11, 263-264
  institutionalization 30, 178
  integrity 96
  limitations 36, 38, 56, 57
  need for systematic change 31, 95
  overcoming inertia of 180
  premised on teaching *versus* learning 27, 30, 94
  sustainability 21, 74
  uniformity 115
  validation 42
families
  accommodating 102-103
  diversity of 55, 56, 121
  involvement in learning 92-93
  as resources 93-94
The Fifth Discipline (Senge) 219
finances. *See* costs
financial literacy 79
food service 183
foreign languages 162, 163
Fostering Innovation in Wisconsin Schools 173, 175
frequently asked questions 181-187
funding 105, 171-172
future generations 34, 59, 60, 62

G
gaps
  achievement gaps 21, 22, 23, 26, 41, 74
  between demographic groups 23-25
  individual factors 23, 25
  opportunity gaps 22, 23, 29
  skills gap 26-28, 109
gender equity 95-96
gerrymandering 70
Gerver, Richard 220
gifted and talented programs 32
Gladwell, Malcolm 28, 220, 224
goal-setting 123, 124, 125
Good to Great (Collins) 200
government 64, 66, 69-72, 82
grade levels 35, 42, 122
grades 51, 88
groups. *See also* leadership teams; politics
  allegiance to 64, 66
  generalizations about 23

integrity in 199
power of 64, 67, 72

H
health services 183
Heath, Chip 179, 219
Heath, Dan 179, 219
high school
  academic honors 28, 155-156
  advisors 107
  diplomas 135, 136, 156, 173
  dual enrollment 158
  graduation 135-136
  new model design 282-283
  start times 43
  transcripts 136
history lessons 84
home environments. *See* families; parents
homeschooling 150, 204
How We Learn (Carey) 223, 224

I
ideologies 61, 64, 67, 71, 202-203, 284
immigration 56
implementation stage 238, 239, 273, 274, 275-276
Individualized Education Program (IEP) 73
inequities 3, 22, 31, 53, 95
inertia 178-180
information
  access 83-84
  discernment 85
  sources 85
  use of data 220-221, 289
  web-based 83
instruction. *See* teaching
integrity
  and compromise 193
  and conflict resolution 129
  of consensus 269
  and courage 197-198
  and "elephants in the room" 212, 284
  ends justifying means 192-194
  in factory model 96, 107
  importance of 192
  misalignment of words and actions 195-196
  and trust 196
  and will 198-199
intellectual well-being 97-98
Internet 83, 85
interventions
  and benchmarks 41, 42
  for collective 23-24, 25, 26
  for gifted students 37
  to maintain equal readiness 31-32

"raising the tide" 26

J
job market. *See* workforce
Johnson, Ned 47, 52, 213, 218, 223, 286
journals 225

K
Karklis, Laris 56
Keating, Dan 56
Kidder, Rushworth 67, 193
kindergarten 31, 35, 108, 122
knowledge. *See also* research
    building a base of 216-217
    gaps 22
    long-term retention 30
    memorization 84
    resources 217
Kotter, John 200, 219

L
law-and-order bias 66
laws
    federal 175-176
    state level 173-174
    in Wisconsin 175
leadership
    exploring models of 254-255
    research on 218-220
leadership teams 200
    attributes 201-203
    avoiding negativity 204, 209
    creating 210-211
    discussions 208-209
    diversity 202, 211, 215
    expertise in 203
    formal structure 210, 211
    getting people on board 205-206
    governance 210
    ground rules 211
    growing pool of recruits 207-208
    interpersonal issues 212
    ongoing roles of members 211
    readiness 247-249
    recruiting for 206-207
    representation 203-204, 205, 211
    roles in 201, 202, 210, 211
    skills of 201-203
    student representatives 204, 214-215
Leading Change (Kotter) 200, 219
learning
    assessments 30
    barriers to 253-254
    behaviors 45
    and chronological age 32
    commitment to 45, 46-47
    and compliance systems 49-50, 88-90
    family involvement in process 92-93
    impact of stress 47-48
    individual *versus* group factors in 23
    and motivation 89-90
    and negative self-image 32
    pace of 39, 41, 50
    priorities 183-184
    problem-solving skills 90
    research on 222-224
    and teaching 30, 32, 38, 74
    through failures 49
    during transition to new model 153-154
learning disabilities 36, 52
legislation. *See* laws
literacy 24, 41
local policies 176-177
Love and Logic 288
loyalty 64, 65, 66

M
Marquet, L. David 218, 219
The Marshmallow Test (Mischel) 222
McDonald, Tim 21, 148, 165
mental flexibility 97, 98
mentors 122
middle school 43, 282
military 39, 40, 96, 110-111, 197
Mindset (Dweck) 218, 223-224
Mischel, Walter 222
momentum 178-180, 275
moral courage 67-68, 72
Moral Courage (Kidder) 67, 193
morality 64
More Control Over Their Lives (Stixrud & Johnson) 218, 223
Morrill, Calvin 160
motivation 46, 49, 51, 87-91, 222
Musheno, Michael 160
music instruction 184
My Stroke of Insight (Taylor) 221

N
National Education Association 8
national security 110-111
Navigating Conflict (Morrill & Musheno) 160
networks 201
new school models. *See also* planning; risks; Summitville Learning Community
    administrative functions 254-255
    attendance 182, 253-254
    career and guidance services 185
    content areas 184
    costs 74, 165-172

designing 144-146, 184, 243, 263-265, 267
desired student outcomes 250-252
downsides to 187
exploration stage 237, 239, 250-256
food service 183
frequently asked questions 181-187
health services 183
idea generation 252-253
image of 114-116
implementation 238, 239, 256, 275-276
in large school districts 278-280
learning priorities 184-185
measuring performance of 291-292
ongoing journey with 276
parental adaptation 186, 284-287
readiness assessment 243-249
self-awareness 236, 239, 240-242
for specific age groups only 282-283
structural variables 255-256
student progress tracking 185, 290-291
success of 181-182, 291-292
timeliness 182
transition planning 273-274
vetting process 272
Nominal Group Process 262

O
Olympic athletes 268
opioid epidemic 105
opportunity gaps 22, 23, 29
Outliers (Gladwell) 28, 224

P
paradigm shifts 114, 115, 205, 284-287
parents
 adaptation to new system 186
 approaches to parenting 288
 paradigm-shift of 284-287
 support from 32, 92, 93, 94, 130
Parkland, Florida school shooting 191
Pasupathi, Monisha 224
Pink, Daniel 89, 218, 222
planning
 backward planning 260-262
 capturing ideas 266
 consensus 269
 design methods 270-272
 inspiration 266-269
 model design 263-265, 266-267
 one-pair-team technique 259-260
 overview 239
 research on 218-220
 scope 269
 timeline for 266
 transition planning 273-274
 value of 257-258

vetting process 272
working backward from outcomes 262-263
plutocracies 71
politics 64, 67, 69-72, 284
positivity 283-284
poverty 27
power
 abuse of 62, 63, 64
 of groups 64, 67, 72
 between parents and child 285, 288
 and policy development 61
 in politics 69, 70, 71
 student empowerment 68, 130, 151, 167
prenatal programs 119-120
preschool 31, 120, 121
principles 65, 231, 232-233, 245, 246, 255
private schools 204
punishments. *See* compliance

R
reading levels 41
rebellion 51
reflective questions 244-246, 248, 251
research
 books to read 218, 225
 on brain function 221
 on change 218-220
 journals 225
 on leadership 218-220
 on learning 222-224
 on motivation 222
 on planning 218-220
 resource formats 217-218
 on success 222
 on use of information 220-221
 on willpower 222
resiliency 96-97, 98-99
resources. *See also* research
 for collective *versus* individuals 24, 26
 in communities 240, 241
 families as 93-94
respect 99, 214
retreatism 51
rewards. *See* compliance
Rickabough, James 224
risks
 access to academic opportunities 162-163
 in athletics 161-162
 costs 168-172
 extracurricular opportunities 163
 new *versus* existing systems 149-152
 qualifying for academic honors 155-156
 qualifying for college entrance 154-155

qualifying for financial aid 156-159
safety 160-161
during transition to new system 152-153, 168
risk-taking 62
Rose, Todd 39, 40, 42, 218, 221

S
safety 134-135, 160-161
salutatorians 28, 156
SCANS report 34
Schlecty, Phil 51
school administration 203-204, 254-255
school districts 32, 176, 277, 278-280
schools. *See also* new school models
    adaptability 98-99
    attendance 182, 253-254
    collaboration with families 92-93
    culture in 102
    elementary level 38
    enrollments 105-106
    fitting to students 43-44
    food service 183
    grade-based timelines 35, 42, 122
    local policies 176-177
    private 204
    recognitions 42
    role in the community 164
    security 134-135, 160-161
    start times 43
    structure 102-103, 103-104
    student adapting to 33, 35-37
    as student's job 34
    transitions 108, 119-120, 121, 126, 152-153
Second Amendment paradox 66
security 134-135, 160-161
self-awareness 236, 239
    community readiness 243-249
    community self-discovery 240-242
    organizational readiness 247-249
The Self-Driven Child (Stixrud & Johnson) 47, 52, 213, 218, 223, 286
Senge, Peter 219
Siegel, Daniel 221
The Signal and the Noise (Silver) 221
Silver, Nate 22
Simple Thinking (Gerver) 220
Sinek, Simon 195, 219
skills gap 22, 108-110
social-emotional learning 96-97
societal challenges 103-104, 105
spokespeople 201, 213, 281
staffing 105, 106, 169-171
stakeholders 244
standardized assessments 24, 30, 40, 137-138, 292

standards 39, 137
standards of living 27, 55, 56
Start with Why (Sinek) 219
status quo 60, 61
Stixrud, William 47, 52, 213, 218, 223, 286
stress 47-48, 52, 97
student conduct. *See* compliance
student enrollments 105-106
student loans 79, 80, 81
students
    academic performance 51, 153-154, 185
    achievement gaps 21, 22, 23, 25, 26, 41, 74
    adaptability 33, 35-37
    age cohorts 32, 35, 39, 73, 282
    catering to 185-186
    challenging ideas 61, 65
    curiosity 89
    desired outcomes for 250-252
    developmental levels 35, 42, 122
    with disabilities 36, 52, 73-75
    disadvantaged 28
    empowerment 68, 130, 151, 167, 285, 288
    engagement 50-52
    goal setting 122, 123
    high achievers 28, 32, 37
    keeping pace 39, 41, 50
    life experiences 36, 55
    meeting needs of 36, 253-254
    motivation 49
    personal interests 85, 90, 123
    personal potential 22, 27, 28, 29, 57, 77
    preparation and needs gap 26-28, 34
    progress levels 31, 289
    readiness 31-33, 35, 36, 42, 121
    representation on leadership team 204, 214-215
    responsibility 49, 130, 167, 185-186, 288
    role in change process 213
    safety 134-135
    school as job 34
    self-control 47, 52, 53, 186
    self-image 32, 48
    stick-to-itiveness 65
    stress 47-48, 52
    uniqueness of 23, 24, 25, 26, 56, 75, 264
success
    books about 222
    of new school model 181-182, 291-292
    student tracking 289-290
Summitville 117
Summitville Learning Community 118
    adapting to new system 130

athletics 131-132
beliefs 119
coalitions 126-127
code of conduct 128-129
college acceptance 136-137
courage to establish 139
discipline 128-131
early childhood 120-121
extracurriculars 131-132
goal-setting in 123, 124, 125
graduation 135-136
infrastructure 127-128
learner journey 122-125
prenatal involvement 119-120
principles 118-119
replicating model 144-146
security 134-135
standardized assessments 137-138
standards 137
student case studies 139, 140-143
student support teams 121-122
technology 133-134
transitions 126
transportation 132-133
vision statement 118, 230
world-changing students 138
surveys 202
sustainability 21, 74
Switch (Heath) 179, 219

T

Tapping the Power of Personalized Learning (Rickabaugh) 224
Taylor, Jill 221
teachers
  attrition 100-102
  burn out 77
  classroom management 76, 77
  influence 76
  on leadership team 203-204
  limitations in current model 77-78
  performing to potential 76, 78
  preparation 38, 78
  shortage of 100-102
  staffing costs 105, 106
  staffing in new model 169-171
teaching
  culturally responsive 58
  versus learning emphasis 30, 32, 38, 74, 76
  pace of 39, 41, 50
  personalized 25, 29, 36, 85, 94
  of responsibility 49
  to workforce needs 34
teams. *See* leadership teams
teamwork 100
technical education 184

technology
  access to information 83-84
  advances 27, 59, 60-61
  appropriate use of 85-86, 133-134
  failure to reduce costs 166
  leveraging 61, 62
  policies about 61
  rate of change 59, 60
  and student readiness 34
terminology 237, 262
testing. *See* assessments
token economies 54
transportation 132-133, 169
traumatic events 96-97
trust 130, 131, 194, 196-197, 214
Turn the Ship Around! (Marquet) 218, 219

U

Unsustainable (McDonald) 21, 148, 165
US Air Force 39, 40
US Army 96, 231

V

valedictorians 28, 156
values 65, 67, 193, 245, 246
violence 135, 160-161, 191
vision statements 200
  and commitment 226
  components of 228
  development 228-229, 231
  establishing 227
  internal *versus* external 227
  revisiting 255
  for Summitville Learning Community 118, 230
  using 232-233
volunteers 56, 94, 103, 171

W

Why Don't Students Like School (Willingham) 224
will 198-199
Willingham, Daniel T. 224
willpower 198-199, 222
Wisconsin schools 174, 175, 236
workforce
  needs 32, 34, 108
  readiness 34
  skills gap 26-28, 109

Y

YouTube 83

ABOUT THE AUTHOR

Kevin Miller is founder and director of Know Power, Know Responsibility LLC, an organization dedicated to helping everyone unleash their potential. He is on a mission to help every community design a school model that will unleash the potential of all their children. Kevin is an educator, US Army officer, and combat veteran whose 40-year journey in education included being a student, teacher, principal, charter school developer, and education consultant. A renowned educator and speaker, he is passionate about helping individuals and organizations discover and grow their power so they can take responsibility for unleashing their potential. For more information, visit knowresponsibility.com.

HELP UNLEASHING ANYONE'S POTENTIAL

Kevin Miller is available for speaking engagements, workshops, and consulting to help any organization and its individual members begin to unleash their potential. He will collaborate with your organization to develop a presentation, activities, or plans tailored specifically to meet the organization's unique circumstances and objectives.

Kevin has engaged thousands of people on topics such as organizational culture and change, leadership, critical and creative thinking, vision and mission development, ethics and integrity, developing situational awareness, commitment vs. compliance, and of course, power and responsibility.

Feedback on Kevin Miller from prior participants:

"Created a great learning environment for some challenging subject matter. He created and fostered active learning environments."

"Can tailor any subject to meet the instructional needs of his audience."

"Has the unique ability to weave his soldier and life experience into his instruction."

"Thought provoking, engaging, and a great role model."

To learn more about how Kevin can help unleash the potential of your organization and its members, visit knowresponsibility.com.

www.ingramcontent.com/pod-product-compliance
Lightning Source LLC
Chambersburg PA
CBHW060514080526
44586CB00012B/482